Citizenship: Pu: Boundaries

MW00737792

CONTENTS

Noticeboard   179

Feminist Review is published three times a year. It is edited by a Collective which is supported by a group of Corresponding Editors.

The Collective: Avtar Brah, Ann Phoenix, Annie Whitehead, Catherine Hall, Dot Griffiths, Gail Lewis, Helen Crowley, Merl Storr.

Guest editors this issue: Pnina Werbner and Nira Yuval-Davis

Corresponding Editors: Ailbhe Smyth, Ann Curthoys, Hala Shukrallah, Kum-Kum Bhavnani, Jacqui Alexander, Lidia Curti, Meera Kosambi, Patricia Mohammed, Sue O'Sullivan, Zarina Maharaj.

Correspondence and advertising

Contributions, books for review and editorial correspondence should be sent to: Feminist Review, 52 Featherstone Street, London EC1Y 8RT.
For advertising please write to the publishers:
Journals Advertising, Routledge, 11 New Fetter Lane, London EC4P 4EE, UK.

Subscriptions

Please contact Routledge Subscriptions Department, Cheriton House, North Way, Andover, Hants SP10 5BE, UK. Tel: 44 (0)1264 342755; Fax 44 (0)1264 343005; for sample copy requests, e-mail sample.journals@routledge.com; for subscription and general information, e-mail info.journals@routledge.com. A full listing of Routledge books and journals is available by accessing http://www.routledge.com/routledge.html

Notes for Contributors

Authors should submit four copies of their work to: *Feminist Review*, 52 Featherstone Street, London EC1Y 8RT. We assume that you will keep a copy of your work. Submission of work to *Feminist Review* will be taken to imply that it is original, unpublished work, which is not under consideration for publication elsewhere. All work is subject to a system of anonymous peer review. All work is refereed by at least two external (non-Collective) referees.

Please note that we cannot accept unsolicited book reviews.

Bookshop distribution in the USA

Routledge, 29 West 35th Street, New York, NY 10001, USA.

Typeset by Type Study, Scarborough
Printed in Great Britain by Bell & Bain Ltd, Glasgow

ISSN 0141-7789

The *Feminist Review* office has moved.
Please send all correspondence to:
Feminist Review
52 Featherstone Street
London EC1Y 8RT

Feminist Review was founded in 1979. Since that time it has established itself as one of the UK's leading feminist journals.

• Why not subscribe?
Make sure of your copy

All subscriptions run in calendar years. The issues for 1997 are Nos. 55, 56 and 57.

• Subscription rates, 1997 (3 issues)

Individual Subscriptions

UK/EEC	£29
Overseas	£29
North America	£46

A number of reduced cost (£20 per year: UK only) subscriptions are available for readers experiencing financial hardship, e.g. unemployed, student, low-paid. If you'd like to be considered for a reduced subscription, please write to the Collective, c/o the Feminist Review office, 52 Featherstone Street, London EC1Y 8RT.

Institutional Subscriptions

UK	£80	Single Issues	£9.99
Overseas	£88		
North America	$126		

☐ Please send me one year's subscription to **Feminist Review**

☐ Please send me _____ copies of back issue no. _____

METHOD OF PAYMENT

☐ I enclose a cheque/international money order to the value of _____
   made payable to Routledge Journals

☐ Please charge my Access/Visa/American Express/Diners Club account

Account no. ☐☐☐☐☐☐☐☐☐☐☐☐☐☐☐☐☐

Expiry date _____   Signature _____

If the address below is different from the registered address of your credit card, please give your registered address separately.

PLEASE USE BLOCK CAPITALS

Name _____

Address _____

_____

_____

_____ Postcode_____

☐ Please send me a Routledge Journals Catalogue

☐ Please send me a Routledge Gender and Women's Studies Catalogue

Please return this form with payment to:

Routledge Subscriptions Department, Cheriton House, North Way, Andover, Hants SP10 5BE

Periodicals postage paid at Rahway.

Editorial:

Citizenship: Pushing the Boundaries

FEMINIST REVIEW NO 57, AUTUMN 1997, PP. 1–3

This issue on women and citizenship appears at a moment when questions of citizenship are at the forefront of diverse political agenda. The contributions bring together global perspectives with considerations of issues of citizenship in particular regional and national contexts. 'Citizenship' highlights the complexity of the relationships between individuals and the 'nation-state'; the construction of collectivities within, between and across states and nations; and categories of belonging and the forces of globalization.

Challenging the gender blindness of most hegemonic theories of citizenship, the articles in this issue attempt to draw on and extend the body of feminist scholarship that has developed through a critical interrogation of mainstream political theories. In particular, they examine the limits of active citizenship and reconceptualize the boundary between the public and the private. In so doing the collection traverses and undermines the conceptual boundaries which would separate issues of nation and state from those of family, community, identity and, in this, refigures the analytical terrain of citizenship.

The issue constructs alternative models of citizenship which challenge the closure of the state and conceptualize citizenship as mediated and multi-tiered. Central to these models of citizenship is a rejection of homogeneous notions of 'the citizen', 'the community' and 'women'. In particular, we argue, notions of difference as well as differential access to power are central to the reformulation of these categories. The articles variously make the case that if a more inclusive and democratic notion of citizenship is to be achieved, this differential access to power needs to be analyzed and located within a variety of different areas. Hence, power cannot be understood as solely contained within the public domain just as rights cannot be limited to the individual–state relation.

Nira Yuval-Davis opens the issue with an article which maps the theoretical issues involved in constructing such an alternative understanding of citizenship and develops a notion of transversal politics as a way of linking this understanding to political alliances as a basis for collective action.

The issue of political agency is also of central concern to Ruth Lister who develops a notion of differentiated universalism as a way of bridging the problem of difference and equality. By doing so she reconceptualizes the inclusionary and exclusionary strategies of nation-state citizenship.

One of the central issues Ruth Lister contemplates is the relationship between being a citizen and the enabling institutions which endow persons with the capacity to act as citizens. This is at the heart of the article by Helen Meekosha and Leanne Dowse. In their article, which takes as its setting contemporary Australia, the authors tackle the difficult challenge disability poses for any inclusive theory of citizenship incorporating notions of both rights and duties.

The issue of disability is an excellent example of how the separation of 'the private' and 'the public' can hinder our understanding of the complexities of citizenship as a mediated relationship. Suad Joseph shows that such a distortion can harm not only the analysis of the individual citizen, but also the analysis of communities and their relations with the state. Taking as her example contemporary Lebanon, Suad Joseph demonstrates the limits of westocentric analysis of citizenship and conceptions of private, civil and political societies.

Helma Lutz demonstrates the limits of the Westocentric perspective for analysing issues of women and citizenship within the European community. Looking at the specific constructions of what constitutes immigrant women's citizenships, she shows how both issues of regulation and representation are central to their understanding.

Daiva Stasiulis and Abigail Bakan examine issues of citizenship negotiation by particular groups of immigrant women – Afro-Caribbean and Filipino domestic workers in Canada. Analysing the shifting terms of their inclusion and exclusion, Bakan and Stasiulis emphasize the importance of the international context of both state relations and political economy in shaping these negotiations.

The concluding piece by Zillah Eisenstein extends the consideration of the international setting of citizenship by examining the particular role international feminism plays in responding to global transformations. She signals both the opportunities and the dangers that are contained in the 'post-Beijing' moment.

The papers included in this issue of *Feminist Review* have developed out of some of the presentations given at the conference *Women, Citizenship and Difference*, organized by Nira Yuval-Davis and Pnina Webner, which took place at the University of Greenwich, London, in July 1996.

Helen Crowley
Gail Lewis
Pnina Werbner
Nira Yuval-Davis

Women, Citizenship and Difference

Nira Yuval-Davis

FEMINIST REVIEW NO 57, AUTUMN 1997, PP. 4–27

Abstract

The article discusses some of the major issues which need to be examined in a gendered reading of citizenship. However, its basic claim is that a comparative study of citizenship should consider the issue of women's citizenship not only by contrast to that of men, but also in relation to women's affiliation to dominant or subordinate groups, their ethnicity, origin and urban or rural residence. It should also take into consideration global and transnational positionings of these citizenships. The article challenges the gender-blind and Westocentric character of many of the most hegemonic theorizations of citizenship, focusing in particular on the questions of membership in 'the community', group rights and social difference and the ways binaries of public/private and active/passive have been constructed to differentiate between different kinds of citizenships. The article argues that in order to be able to analyse adequately people's citizenship, especially in this era of ethnicization on the one hand and globalization on the other hand, and with the rapid pace at which relationships between states and their civil societies are changing, citizenship should best be analysed as a multi-tiered construct which applies, at the same time to people's membership in sub-, cross- and supra-national collectivities as well as in states.

Keywords

women; citizenship; difference; nation; state; transversal politics

'Citizenship' has become a very popular subject of debate in the last few years, appropriated nationally and internationally, by both Left and Right, as well as by feminists. The interest in citizenship is not just in the narrow formalistic meaning of having the right to carry a specific passport. It addresses an overall concept encapsulating the relationship between the individual, state and society.

This article discusses some of the major issues which need to be examined in a gendered reading of citizenship. Its basic claim is that a comparative study of citizenship should consider the issue of women's citizenship not only by contrast to that of men, but also in relation to women's affiliation to dominant or subordinate groups, their ethnicity, origin and urban or rural residence. It should also take into consideration global and trans-national positionings of these citizenships.

T.H. Marshall (1950, 1975, 1981), the most influential theorist of citizen-ship in Britain, has defined citizenship as 'a status bestowed on those who are full members of a community' (1950: 14), which includes civil, politi-cal and social rights and obligations. By formally linking citizenship to membership in a community rather than to the state, as liberal definitions of citizenship do, Marshall's definition enables us analytically to discuss citizenship as a multi-tier construct, which applies to people's membership in a variety of collectivities – local, ethnic, national and trans-national. Such a multi-tier construction of citizenship is particularly important these days when neo-liberal states redefine and reprivatize their tasks and obli-gations. It also enables us to raise the question of the relationship between 'the community' and the state and how this affects people's citizenship. The debates in the literature between the 'liberals' and the 'communi-tarians' (see, for example, Avineri and Shalit, 1992; Daly, 1993; Nimni, 1996; Phillips, 1993) and the 'republicans' (Peled, 1992; Roche, 1987; Sandel, 1982; Oldfield, 1990) relate to these issues. The article examines some of the implications of this debate for notions of social rights and social difference.

Bryan Turner (1990) has constructed an influential typology of citizenship based on two dimensions – the public/private and the active/passive. Turner's typology, sadly, is completely Euro- or, rather, Westocentric (Yuval-Davis, 1991a), his 'universal' typology being based on the develop-ment of citizenship in four Western countries – France, the USA, England and Germany. Even more astonishing perhaps, is the fact that Turner's typology is gender blind (Yuval-Davis, 1991a; Walby, 1994), although the two dimensions he considers are ones which have often been used in order to describe gender differences in general and difference in relation to women's citizenship in particular (Pateman, 1988; Grant and Newland, 1991). The article, therefore, explores these two dimensions and how they should be theorized when seeking to construct a comparative non-Westo-centric framework of analysis of gendered citizenship which incorporates notions of difference.

A word of warning, however, is necessary before the exploration of the various issues considered in the paper can start. When dealing with the notion of citizenship it is also important to remember that, as Floya Anthias and myself have commented before (Yuval-Davis and Anthias, 1989: 6), on its own, the notion of citizenship cannot encapsulate adequately all the dimensions of control and negotiations which take place in different areas of social life, nor can it adequately address the ways the state itself forms its political project. Studying citizenship, however, can throw light on some of the major issues which are involved in the complex relationships between individuals, collectivities and the state, and the ways gender relations (as well as other social divisions) affect and are affected by them.

Citizenship, nationalism and 'the community'

As Roche (1987) describes it, in the liberal tradition individual citizens are presumed to have equal status, equal rights and duties, etc., so that principles of inequality deriving from gender, ethnic, class or other contexts are *not* supposed to be of relevance to the status of citizenship as such. The citizens are therefore constructed not as 'members of the community' but as *strangers* to each other, although they are sharing a complex set of assumptions about and expectations of each other which, when not fulfilled, can be enforceable by the state.

This liberal abstraction of self has been criticized, however, by the 'communitarians' who claim that notions of rights and duties, as well as those of equality and privacy, have no meaning outside the context of particular communities (Ackelsberg, 1995). On different grounds, the proponents of republicanism such as Sandel (1982), also find the individualistic construction of citizenship highly unsatisfactory. They argue that such a construction of citizenship denies the possibility of citizenship as constituting a membership in a moral community in which the notion of the common good is antecedent to the individual citizenship choice. Liberal construction of citizenship, according to Sandel, assumes the priority of right over good. Republicanism, on the other hand, constructs citizenship not only as a status but also as a means of active involvement and participation in the determination, practice and promotion of the common good.

However, as Peled comments (Peled, 1992: 433), 'This raises the question of how the republican [moral] community is constituted and what qualities are required for active participation in it'. According to him, two distinct notions of community can be discerned in the current revival of republicanism: a weak community, in which membership is essentially voluntary, and a strong, historical community that is *discovered*, not formed by its members. In a strong community its 'ongoing existence is an important value in and of itself' and becomes one of the, if not the most, important imperatives of the 'moral community' (ibid.).

Membership in such a community involves 'enduring attachment', often a myth of common origin, and is clearly bonded by a myth of common destiny. In other words, this 'strong community' is the national 'imagined community' (Anderson, 1983). There is no difference between republican constructions of the 'moral community' and the *gemeinschaft*-like constructions of the 'national community'.

The question arises, then, what should happen to those members of the civil society who cannot or will not become full members of that 'strong community'. In virtually all contemporary states there are migrants and refugees, 'old' and 'new' minorities and in settler societies there are also indigenous people who are not part of the hegemonic national community (Stasiulis and Yuval-Davis, 1995). In addition, there are many other members of the civil society who, although they might share the myth of common origin of 'the community', do not share important hegemonic value systems with the majority of the population in sexual, religious and other matters.

Peled's solution (following Oldfield, 1990) is a two-tier construction of citizenship: a full membership in the 'strong community' for those who can be included, and for people who cannot:

> a residual, truncated status, similar to the liberal notion of citizenship as a bundle of rights. Bearers of this citizenship do not share in attending to the common good but are secure in their possession of what we consider essential human and civil rights.

> (Peled, 1992)

In other words, Peled is suggesting the institutionalization of an exclusionary two-tier system of citizenship as a way of solving the discrepancy between the boundaries of the civil society and the boundaries of the national collectivity. This solution is far from being satisfactory. Politically it openly condones discrimination and racialization of citizens on national grounds (Peled brings Israel and its treatment of the Palestinians who have been citizens of the state since 1948 as the ideal case of a state which successfully managed to do so). Theoretically, this model dichotomizes the population into two homogenous collectivities – those who are in and those who are out of the national collectivity, without paying attention to other dimensions of social divisions and social positionings, such as gender, intra-national ethnicity, class, sexuality, ability, stage in the life cycle, etc., which are crucial to constructions of citizenship.

Yet, with all these reservations, the above position at least recognizes the potential inherently contradictory nature of citizenship as individual and communal, inclusionary and exclusionary. In Marshall's works, these issues were not problematized at all and there has been an automatic assumption of an overlap between the boundaries of civil society and those of the national community. Not incidentally, as Theodor Shanin (1986) has commented, in English, unlike other languages (such as Russian or Hebrew), there is a missing term which expresses the notion of ethnic nationality, to differentiate it from nationality which is equivalent to formal citizenship in the state. In different states and societies the relationship between the two differs hugely and can be structured formally or informally, in ways which prioritize one hegemonic ethnic/national collectivity or several; in which such a membership would be primarily important for one's identity or not; which could provide members easier or more difficult access to a whole range of social, economic and political facilities; and which may or may not actually ground legally that members in different collectivities would be entitled to a differential range of civil, political and social citizenship rights. A common status in Europe, for instance, is that of the 'denizen': someone who is entitled to most social and civil rights but is deprived of the political rights of national voting.

Paradoxically, although Marshall's theory of citizenship does not relate to any of these issues, his conceptual definition of citizenship as a membership of the community rather than of the state can provide us with the framework to study specific cases of the differential multi-tier citizenship. A word of caution is necessary here, however. As elaborated elsewhere (Cain and Yuval-Davis, 1990; Yuval-Davis, 1991a) it is important not to view 'the community' as a given natural unit. Collectivities and 'communities' are ideological and material constructions, whose boundaries, structures and norms are a result of constant processes of struggles and negotiations, or more general social developments (Anthias and Yuval-Davis, 1992). The moral imperative which interprets the 'good of the community' as a support for its continuous existence as a separate collectivity can become an extremely conservative ideology which would see any internal or external change in the community as a threat.

Social rights and social difference

The liberal definition of citizenship constructs all citizens as basically the same and considers the differences of class, ethnicity, gender, etc., as irrelevant to their status as citizens.[1] On the other hand, the welfare state assumes a notion of difference, as determined by *social needs*. In the words of Edwards 'Those with similar needs ought to get similar resources and those with different needs, different resources, or – more succinctly – treatment as equals rather than equal treatment' (1988: 135). These differences were initially conceived exclusively as class differences. As originally envisaged by Beveridge (1942), social welfare rights were aimed at improving the quality of life of the working classes (as well as the smooth working of capitalism). As Harris (1987) put it, welfare was conceived as the institutionalized recognition of social solidarity within the political community of the citizens.

This social solidarity is being threatened by a variety of groupings, ethnic, racial, religious and sexual sub-collectivities which exist within the marginal matrix of society and 'which experience informal and formal discrimination consonant with their credited lower social worth' (Evans, 1993: 6). A primary concern of many relevant struggles and debates (Gordon, 1989; Hall and Held, 1989) has been around the right to enter or to remain in a specific country. The 'freedom of movement within the European community', the Israeli Law of Return and the Patriality clause in British immigration legislation are all instances of ideological, often racist, constructions of boundaries which allow unrestricted immigration to some and block it completely to others.

Even when questions of entry and settlement have been resolved, the concerns of groupings constituted as ethnic minorities might be different from those of other members of the society. For example, their right to formal citizenship might depend upon the rules and regulations of their country of origin in addition to those of the country where they live, as well as the relationship between the two. Thus, people from some Caribbean Islands who have been settled in Britain for years were told that they could not have a British passport because their country does not recognize dual citizenship and because they had not declared on time their intent to renounce the citizenship of their country of origin after it received independence. Concern over relatives and fear of not being allowed to visit their country of origin prevent others (such as Iranians and Turks) from giving up their original citizenship. Women workers who have children in other countries are often ineligible to receive child benefits like other mothers. Countries like Israel and Britain confer citizenship on those whose parents are citizens rather than on those born in the country. Further, the right of entry to a country is often conditional on a commitment by the immigrant that neither s/he or any other member of their family will claim any welfare benefits. Citizenship needs to be examined, therefore, not just in terms of state, but often in relation to multiple formal and informal citizenships in more than one country, and most importantly, to view them from a perspective which would include the different positioning of different states as well as the different positionings of individuals and groupings within states (Bakan and Stasiulis, 1994).

A whole different set of citizenship issues relates to indigenous minorities in settler societies (Stasiulis and Yuval-Davis, 1995; Dickanson, 1992). It is not just that in many societies indigenous populations have been very late, if at all, entrants to the formal citizenship body of the state. It is that if their claim on the country – in the form of land rights – were to be taken seriously and in full, this would totally conflict with the claim of the settler national collectivity for legitimacy. Attempts to solve the problem by transforming the indigenous population into another 'ethnic minority' have usually met with a strong and understandable resistance (de Lepervanche, 1980). Formal treaties, which would institutionalize and anchor in law the relations between what Australian Aboriginals have been calling 'the imposing society' and the indigenous people, often create a complex situation in which there exist two national sovereign entities over the same territory – one which owns the state and one which attempts to establish a sovereign stateless society within it. Somewhat similar, if less racialized, struggles are present in the many regionalist secessionist movements which claim the right of national self-determination *vis-à-vis* their states which themselves have been constructed as nations.

The most problematic aspects of citizenship rights for racial and ethnic minorities relate to their social rights and to the notion of multi-culturalism (Parekh,1990; Jayasuriya, 1990; Yuval-Davis, 1992, 1997). For some (e.g. Harris, 1987; Lister, 1990), the problem remains within the realm of individual, though different, citizens. The homogenous community of Marshall is being transformed into a pluralist one by the reinterpretation of his emphasis on equality of status into mutual respect (Lister, 1990: 48). However, such a model does not take into account potential conflicts of interest among the different groupings of citizens, nor does it consider the collective, rather than the individual, character of the special provisions given to members of groupings defined as ethnic minorities (Jayasuriya, 1990: 23).

The question of a collective provision to meet the needs of 'ethnic minorities' relates to policies of positive action aimed at group rather than individual rights. Multiculturalist policies construct these populations, or rather, effectively, the poor and working classes within them, in terms of ethnic and racial collectivities. These collectivities are attributed with collective needs, based on their different cultures as well as on their structural disadvantages. Resistance to these policies has been expressed by claims that constructing employment and welfare policies in terms of group rights can conflict with individual rights and are therefore discriminatory. However, at least in countries which officially adopted multiculturalist policies, such as Canada, Britain and the USA, it has been widely accepted, at least until recently, that in order to overcome the practical effects of racism rather than just its ideology, collective provisions and positive action, based on group membership, are the only effective measures to be taken (see Burney, 1988; Young, 1989; Cain and Yuval-Davis, 1990). Similar policies have been constructed in other pluralist states, such as India and South Africa.

The question becomes more problematic when positive provisions relate to the different 'cultural needs' of different ethnicities. These can vary from the provision of interpreters to the provision of funds to religious organizations. In the most extreme cases, as in the debates around Aboriginals, on the one hand, and Muslim minorities around the Rushdie affair, on the other hand, there have been calls to enable the minorities to operate according to their own customary and religious legal systems. While the counter-arguments have ranged from the fact that this would imply a *de facto* apartheid system to arguments about social unity and political hegemony, those who support these claims have seen it as a natural extrapolation of the minorities' social and political rights.

This raises the question of how one defines the boundaries of citizens' rights. Kymlicka (1995) suggests a differentiation between 'two kinds of group rights': one which involves the claim of a group against its own members and one which involves the group's claim against the larger society (or the state). Kymlicka opposes the use of state powers in the support of claims of the first kind, because he suspects that very often individuals within the group would be oppressed in the name of culture and tradition. In the second case, however, the issue often involves protection of a disadvantaged group by others and so, in this case, state intervention should be welcome. While the general line of argument of Kymlicka can be supported, he reifies and naturalizes the groups' boundaries and does not differentiate between people with specific power positionings within the groups (which are not homogenous and can be with differing and conflicting interests) and 'the group'.

Jayasuriya (1990), in a somewhat different terminology when grappling with the same question, suggests a distinction between needs, which are essential and which therefore require satisfaction by the state, and wants, which fall outside the public sector and are to be satisfied within the private domain in a voluntary way. This conceptualization of 'wants' and 'needs' as objective differences between essential and non-essential cultural demands of specific sub-collectivities within the civil society is, of course, highly suspect. Cultural needs are not fixed a-historical essentialist characteristics of collectivities. Cultures are highly heterogeneous resources which are used selectively, and often in contradictory ways, in different ethnic projects which are promoted by members of specific collectivities, often in a way which disadvantages women. Women often suffer from the acceptance by the state of the definition of what constitutes 'the cultural needs of the community' in matters of education, marriage and divorce and other provisions such as women's refuges (Sahgal and Yuval-Davis, 1992; for testimonies on these issues from women activists from various post-colonial countries in a South African mobilization conference on this issue, see Amy Biehl, 1994).

FEMINIST REVIEW NO 57, AUTUMN 1997

The private and the public

Jayasuriya establishes the boundary line of provision by the state in between the public and private domains, as if this boundary is natural and static. This boundary is, however, highly problematic and is both gender and culture specific.

There is a high degree of inconsistency in the ways that different authors discuss the public/private boundary and its relationship to other concepts such as political and civil society, the family, the economy, the voluntary sector, etc. Feminists like Carol Pateman (1988, 1989) and Ursula Vogel (1989) identify the public sphere as identical with the political, while the private sphere relates primarily to the family domain. Pateman examined the writings of social contract theorists as 'the most famous influential political story of modern times'. 'Fraternity' (one of the three slogans of the French revolution which also called for liberty and equality) signalled, she argued, the transformation of the hegemonic power relations in the society from a patriarchy – in which the father (or the king as a father figure) ruled over both other men and the women, to a fraternity – in which the men get the right to rule over their women in the private domestic sphere, but agree on a contract of a social order of equality among them-selves within the public, political sphere. Women, therefore, were not excluded from the public sphere incidentally but as part of the bargain between the new regime and its member citizens. In a similar way Vogel has shown that women were not simply latecomers to citizenship rights, as in Marshall's evolutionary model. Their exclusion was part and parcel of the construction of the entitlement of men, not only as individuals but also as 'representatives of a family (i.e. a group of non-citizens)' (1989: 2). Indeed, in Britain women lost their citizenship during Victorian times, when they got married; they continued to lose it if they got married to 'for-eigners' until 1948, and it was not until 1981 that they got the indepen-dent right to transfer their citizenship to their children (WING, 1985; Bhabha and Shutter, 1994).

In contrast to Pateman and Vogel's construction of the private as the domain of the family, Jayasuriya (1990) regards the private domain as that which is not financed and/or controlled by the state, including religious institutions. Bryan Turner (1990) includes in the private domain self enhancement and other leisure, as well as spiritual activities. Sylvia Walby (1994: 383) criticizes him for adopting 'the male viewpoint' in this by con-flating two meanings of 'private' – one which relates to the autonomy of the individual, and one which relates to freedom from the interventions of the state. She argues that, while the family may or may not be free from the intervention of the state, it is not an autonomous and free space for women, nor has it a unitary set of interests. Different members of the family – nuclear and extended – have different social positionings, powers and interests within it.

If we accept the meaning of 'private' as that in which the individual is autonomous, then this can be exercised to a lesser or greater extent in all social spheres, where people – and not just women – can act both as part of social structures and collectivities with all the constraints these provide, and as autonomous individual agents, whether it is in the family, in the civil or in the political domain. Similarly, depending on people's preferences and hobbies, leisure and self-enhancement activities can be spent with the family or other personal friends, with the trade union, church or ethnic sports associations, or as a councillor in the local government in the political domain. At the same time, political power relations with their own dynamics exist in each social sphere. The most important contribution of feminism to social theory has been the recognition that power relations operate within primary social relations as well as within the more impersonal secondary social relations of the civil and political domains.

The recognition that power lines operate horizontally as well as vertically has given rise to the Foucauldian perspective that there is no need to theorize the state as a separate unitary sphere. However, as elaborated elsewhere (Anthias and Yuval-Davis, 1989: 6), while the state is not unitary in its practices, its intentions or its effects, there is a need to retain the state as a separate sphere, 'a body of institutions which are centrally organized around the intentionality of control with a given apparatus of enforcement at its command or basis'. While ideological production, like education and the media, can lie both inside and outside the state, the exercise of individual and collective rights continues to be tied to the state (Soysal, 1994). Thus control over the state continues to be the primary political target. Especially in the modern welfare state, there is no social sphere which is protected from state intervention. Even in cases where there is no direct intervention, it is the state which has usually established, actively or passively, its own boundaries of non-intervention. In other words, the construction of the boundary between the public and the private is a political act in itself.

Given all these inconsistencies and confusions in the determination of the 'private' domain, I suggest that we abandon the public/private distinction. Rather, we should differentiate between three distinct spheres of the state, civil society and the domain of the family, kinship and other primary relationships. Feminists, such as Ann Orloff (1993) and Julia O'Connor (1993), have already pointed out that there is a need to add the family domain to that of the state and the market when examining the ways societies organize the provision of welfare. However, the family domain has also to be added when we discuss different locations for political organization and power.

It is misleading to see in the rise of the 'modern nation-state' a completely different form of social organization from the 'pre-modern' ones. In many states, especially post-colonial states, one's extended family and kinship relationships have continued to be used as foci of loyalty and organization. Political, social and probably even civil rights might depend on the familial positioning of the particular citizen (Saudi Arabia or Jordan are probably good examples of such a state but in more diluted forms this phenomenon is spread much more widely, especially when looking at ruling parties' élites). Traditional social, and especially familial, relations continue to operate and often women have few or no formal citizenship rights. Paradoxically, where familial relations are important in the politics of a country, women who are widows or daughters of political leaders have the highest chance of becoming political leaders, as has been the case in the Indian sub-continent, for instance.

At the other end of the continuum, we have the states of the former Soviet Bloc, where an attempt was made to incorporate into the state all facets of the civil – and to some extent also familial – domains. All political, economic and cultural activities were aimed to be controlled by the state; all forms of organization or expression which did not follow the state (and the CP) line tended to be repressed and controlled; and membership in the party brought with it higher civil, political and social rights. There was a virtually complete recruitment of women into the labour force and the collectivization of certain aspects of domestic labour, such as child-care facilities and public canteens – although women tended to occupy lower labour and political positions to men and be responsible for all remaining domestic responsibilities (Voronina, 1994: 733).

In Western welfare states, such as the Scandinavian countries, the state has also supplied public facilities to help with women's domestic responsibilities and child care, so as to enable women to go out into the labour market. Women work more than men in the public sector and, unlike in the former Soviet bloc, have had high rates of political representation. However, as Helga Hernes (1987) argues, in countries like Norway the corporations in civil society are those which carry the most significant economic and social powers, and they have tended to be controlled by men.

Welfare states are considered to be those where the influence of civil society is the greatest in terms of the location of political, as well as economic power. Marshall (1981) described the capitalist society as the hyphenated society in which there are inevitable tensions between a capitalist economy and the welfare state. Esping Andersen (1990) described the variations between different welfare state regimes as dependent on the extent to which the market forces or the state have the upper hand in the struggle for domination. It is important to remember, however, that the civil domain is not just the market. It is not only economic, but political and social relations which operate there, in collusion and/or resistance to the market forces. Political parties, social movements and trade unions are not part of the state even if they are often organized and focus their activities on the state. Education and media can be owned or not by the state and can have ideological projects which are autonomous to a larger or lesser extent from the state. Of particular importance to our concern here are formal and informal organizations, associations and institutions in civil society which are organized by/for members of a particular ethnic/racial/national collectivity. Such collectivities play a larger or smaller role in the construction of state policies and social and political relations. The formal ethnicization of the different regions in Yugoslavia in the revised constitution approved by Tito during the last years in his life has been a major stepping stone in its history and a partial explanation of later developments.

In general terms the above examples demonstrate the differential relative importance of the familial, the civil and state agencies domains in the determination of the social, political and civil rights of citizens. Any comparative theory of citizenship, therefore, must include an examination of the individual autonomy allowed to citizens (of different gender, ethnicity, region, class, stage in the life cycle, etc.) *vis-à-vis* their families, civil society organizations and state agencies.

Active/passive citizenship

The other axis of Bryan Turner's comparative typology of citizenship is that of active–passive which he defines as 'whether the citizen is conceptualized as merely a subject of an absolute authority or as an active political agent' (1990: 209). The conventional differentiation, then, between 'citizen' and 'subject' is removed in Turner's definition, and instead becomes a continuum of passivity and activity.

The history of citizenship is different in different countries. In some countries, like in France and the USA, it has been the result of a popular revolutionary struggle, while in others, like Britain and Germany, it has been more of a 'top to bottom' process. Similarly, in some post-colonial countries, like in India or Kenya, national independence was achieved after a long period of popular struggle, while in others, like in certain islands of the Caribbean, that transition was much more peaceful and political rule was passed smoothly from the colonial élite to the local one. Today, virtually all the world's population live in countries in which some form of citizenship exists, at least in the Marshallian sense of being a member of a community.

As to participating in some form in ruling as well as being ruled, the Aristotelian definition of citizenship (Allen and Macey, 1990), the picture is, of course, very different. Only a minority of people, in probably the minority of world states, can be said to have this kind of active citizenship status. This is not just a question of formal rights. Even in the most democratically active societies there are strata of the population which are passive, too disempowered and/or alienated to participate even in the formal act of voting. Among them can be not only children, migrants, ethnic minorities and indigenous people in settler societies, but also what has come to be labelled as the 'underclass', which in the USA is to a large extent black, but which in Britain and other countries can also be largely white, and in which lone mothers loom large (Lister, 1990; Morris, 1994). Gender, sexuality, age and ability as well as ethnicity and class are important factors in determining the relationship of people to their communities and states.

The notion of the 'active citizen' has been a focus of debates and policies in recent years within both the 'Left' and the 'Right', especially in Britain. The recent growth in interest in citizenship among the Left has coincided with signs that many of the social rights which have come to be taken for granted in the welfare state have come under threat, in the areas of health care, education, retirement, child benefits, etc. Rather than concentrating on social rights, however, the Left (and Centre) has used citizenship as a call for political mobilization and participation and in Britain it also became part of a campaign for a written constitution (Charter 88) in which social citizenship entitlement would be enshrined so that a radical Rightist government would not again be able to transform the relationship between people and state so easily.

The language of citizenship has also been a major discourse of the Right. In Britain 'the active citizen' has been put forward as an alternative to the welfare state, in which 'the citizen', constructed as an economically successful middle-class male head of a family, would fulfil his citizenship duties by giving his spare money and time 'to the community' (Lister, 1990; Evans, 1993). In this discourse, therefore, citizenship stops being a political discourse and becomes a voluntary involvement within civil society, in which the social rights of the poor are transferred, at least partly, from entitlements into charities. Lister (1990: 14) quotes the Conservative Minister Douglas Hurd defining active citizenship: 'Public service may once have been the duty of an élite, but today it is the responsibility of all who have time or money to spare'. Obligations are shifted from the public sphere of tax-financed benefits and services to the private sphere of charity and voluntary service. Rights become gifts and active citizenship assumes a top-down notion of citizenship. Typically, quangos, which are appointed rather than elected, have come to be the means by which various public services, like health and welfare, are being managed.

This depoliticization of the notion of citizenship has been enhanced with the publication of the government's Citizen's Charter in 1992 which constructs citizens as consumers whose prime rights are to have the freedom to make well- informed choices of high-quality commodities and services in public and private sectors and to be treated with due regard for their 'privacy, dignity, religious and cultural beliefs' (Evans, 1993: 10). The balance of citizenship rights has shifted away from social rights of welfare towards civil rights of an economic kind. Its aim is to promote individual persona and autonomy rather than the relationship between the individual and community and would clearly fall within the liberal mode of citizenship described above.

The Thatcherite notion of citizenship as consumerism is not based on a completely free market model, in spite of its universalist rhetoric. There are legal and moral constraints which prevent a variety of marginal or minority groups from pursuing their religious and cultural beliefs or economic needs in equal measure (Evans, 1993: 6). The state's management of these 'moral aliens', who are to be found in the marginal matrix of citizenship, is exercised in social, political and economic arenas. This is the twilight zone between the liberal and republican constructions of citizenship, where religious, ethnic and sexual minorities are located outside the national 'moral community' but inside the civic nation.

To those who can afford it, this is not a completely closed-off system. Evans describes how sexual minority groups have developed socio-economic 'community' infrastructures around their identities, organized to obtain further housing, insurance, medical, parenting, marital rights, etc., and spend a significant proportion of their income on distinguishable lifestyles in segregated or specifically gay social and sexual territories (1993: 8). Multiculturalism which is aimed at ethnic minorities can be described in similar terms. Multiculturalist policies are aimed at simultaneously including and excluding the minorities, locating them in marginal spaces and secondary markets, while reifying their boundaries.

The question of citizenship rights and social difference has been a difficult one in feminist political theory. Iris Young (1989) has suggested that representative democracy should treat people not as individuals but as members of groups. She argues that a discourse of universal citizenship which would ignore these differences would just enhance the domination of groups which are already dominant, and would silence the marginal and oppressed groups. She suggests, therefore, that special mechanisms have to be established to represent these groups as groups. Such an approach, however, can easily fall into politics, in which the groups are constructed as homogenous and with fixed boundaries, the interests of specific individuals within groups constructed as representing the interests of the whole group and the advancement of the specific group becomes primary.

An alternative approach is suggested by Anne Phillips (1993). While recognizing that notions of difference cannot just be ignored, she suggests (following Mary Dietz, 1987) that the participation in the public arena of politics should be based on what she calls 'transformation', getting beyond one's immediate sphere, rather than transcendence: the first, she sees, as rightly stressing the limits of localized and specific identities, while the latter involves pursuing this to the point of jettisoning all group differences and concerns. John Lechte (1994), inspired by Kristeva's theory of the relationship between the semiotic and the symbolic, argues that the private, which is the domain of difference, and the public political domain, can be posited not as a dyad of opposites, but as the first being the materiality of the latter, which gives it its particular meaning. In other words, every discussion of individual differences already involves the public domain. Young's construction of 'oppressed groups' is no more 'natural' than any other political discourses, and the transformation/transcendence process is inherent to the act of naming.

Suggestions of other feminists and activists who attempted to deal with the question of citizenship rights and social difference focus differentially on the social and on the political. Correa and Petchesky (1994) argue that, rather than abandoning rights discourse, we should reconstruct it so that it both specifies differences, such as gender, class, cultural and other differences and recognizes social needs. Sexual and reproductive (or any other) rights, understood as private 'liberties' or 'choices', are meaningless, especially for the poorest and most disenfranchised, without enabling conditions through which they can be realized. In the post-GLC era in London with the massive backlash against the identity politics which was practised there, some black and other radical activists came to the conclusion that the alternative to group politics should be a politics of confronting these disabling conditions. The argument has been that, if black people suffer disproportionally from unemployment, for instance, political discourse which focuses on unemployment will particularly benefit black people. However, this approach would not exclude, nor create a construction of otherness for other unemployed (Wilson, 1987).

Zillah Eisenstein's approach to questions of difference is to ask whether we can construct an 'understanding of human rights which is both universal and specific' (1993: 6). Her solution is to construct a woman of colour as an alternative, inclusive standard norm to that of the white male. It might be more difficult, but I much prefer her earlier position that, while we cannot do without some notion of what human beings have in common, we can and must do without a unitary standard against which they are all judged (Eisenstein, 1989).

Instead of a given unitary standard, there has to be a process of constructing a standard norm for each specific political project. Black feminists like Patricia Hill Collins (1990) and Italian feminists like Raphaela Lambertini and Elizabetta Dominini (see Yuval-Davis, 1994, 1997) have focused on the transversal politics of coalition building, in which the specific positioning of political actors is recognized and considered. This approach is based on the epistemological recognition that each positioning produces specific situated knowledge which cannot be but an unfinished knowledge, and therefore dialogue among those differentially positioned should take place in order to reach a common perspective. Transversal dialogue should be based on the principle of remaining centred in one's own experiences while being empathetic to the differential positionings of the partners in the dialogue, thus enabling the participants to arrive at a different perspective from that of hegemonic tunnel vision. The boundaries of the dialogue would be determined, as Hill Collins has argued (1990), by the message rather than its messengers. The result of the dialogue might still be differential projects for people and groupings positioned differently, but their solidarity would be based on a common knowledge sustained by a compatible value system. The dialogue, therefore, is never boundless.

Of course, in 'real politics', unlike in grass-roots social movements, there is often no time for extensive continuous dialogue. When the Women's Unit in the GLC in the early 1980s tried to work in this manner, it ended up being largely ignored by the daily hierarchical structures of decision making which were working at a much faster pace. Transversal politics should not be seen as necessarily opposing the principle of delegation, so long as the political delegates are seen as advocates, rather than representatives, of specific social categories and groupings and so long as their message is a result of transversal dialogues.

Citizenship's rights and duties

The various definitions of citizenship emphasize that citizenship is a two-way process and involves obligations as well as rights. Sometimes the two can get confused. For example, voting is considered a primary citizenship right. However, there are quite a few states – often not the most democratic ones but those in need of legitimation of their powers – in which voting has become the duty of the citizens (in some of them – as in Egypt where this is the duty only of the men – women have had to ask for this right specifically and in writing, proving that they are literate), and if they do not comply with that duty they can be heavily fined.[2]

Defending one's own community and country has been seen as an ultimate citizen's duty – to die (as well as to kill) for the sake of the homeland or the nation (Yuval-Davis, 1985, 1997). This duty has given rise to Kathleen Jones's claim (1990) that the body is a significant dimension in the definition of citizenship. Traditionally, she claims, citizenship has been linked with the ability to take part in armed struggle for national defence, this ability has been equated with maleness, while femaleness has been equated with weakness and the need for male protection. Some feminist organizations (as NOW in the USA, ANMLAE in Nicaragua and others) have fought for the inclusion of women on an equal footing to that of men in the military, arguing that once women share with men the ultimate citizens' duty – to die for one's country, they would also be able to gain equal citizenship rights to those of men. In the Gulf War women fought together with the men in the American army, in almost indistinguishable tasks as well as uniforms – uniforms designed for ABC (atomic, biological and chemical) warfare which seem to be quite indifferent to the 'type' of human 'bodies' underneath them.

This experience raises several sobering thoughts in relation to this kind of argument. First, the experience of some of the women who had to leave small babies behind (mostly in the care of their own mothers, as often the husbands of these women serve in the army as well), shows that feminist equal opportunity slogans can be used to create further pressures on women, rather than to promote their rights. Second, their experience shows that the differential relations of power between men and women, including sexual harassment, continue also within the military domain and therefore it cannot automatically be considered as empowering women. Third, this argument ignores the general social and political context of the military and its use.

Probably even more importantly for our concern here is the fact that virtually none of the soldiers who fought in the Gulf War on the side of the Western Allies did it as part of national service. Women and men were professional soldiers who see the military as their professional career. I have elaborated on this elsewhere (Yuval-Davis, 1991b, 1997: ch. 5), but the clear implication is that, in modern warfare, fighting is often no longer a citizen's duty.

Originally, citizenship has been conditioned by owning property and therefore the universal duty was to pay taxes. With the expansion of citizenship over the different classes, this duty is now conditioned by the amount of earnings a person has, and therefore, again, cannot be seen as a universal duty. For propertyless people, earnings are based on employment. Carol Pateman (1989) points to the fact that Marshall mentions 'the right to employment' as one of the citizenship rights, just at a time when the architects of the welfare state were constructing men as breadwinner-worker and women as dependant-wife. A major fight of the feminist movement has been for equal pay and equal opportunities in employment. In spite of certain achievements in this field, the gender gap and the segregated labour market have largely remained and women continue to be primarily constructed as wives and mothers. Similarly, often less successful results have been achieved in fights against discrimination on the labour market for racial and ethnic groupings.

Moreover, it became clear that equal opportunities policies can be effective only in relation to those who have actually entered the labour market. Meekosha and Dowse (in this volume) point out the even more fundamental point that disability sometimes excludes people from being incorporated into the citizenship body in any way whatever (whether in terms of entering a country, the right to vote, for employment, etc). As mentioned above in the discussion on 'active citizenship', citizenship duties can become a marker of the privileged. This, of course, tallies historically with the emergence of citizenship in the Greek polis, in which citizenship rights and duties were the privilege of the few, on the back of women, slaves and denizens who were excluded from it.

Recent discussions on 'workfare' as a substitute for 'welfare' have used the discourse of citizenship duties as a condition for citizenship rights, and 'community service' is constructed as the way the 'have-nots' can fulfil their duties. Many of the people who call for this shift express a sincere desire to break the perpetual cycle of dependency, deprivation and alienation of welfarism. However, 'workfare', in addition to its inherently selective nature and the side effects that its execution can bring to other sections in the labour market, shifts the primary ground of the debate on citizenship from political to social, from personal and collective empowerment into coerced, that is, unfree labour.

Citizenship rights are anchored in both the social and the political domains. Without 'enabling' social conditions, political rights are vacuous. At the same time, citizenship rights without obligations also construct people as passive and dependent. The most important duty of citizens is, therefore, to exercise their political rights and to participate in the determination of their collectivities', states' and societies' trajectories.

Concluding remark

The article discusses some of the issues which are relevant to the development of a theory of citizenship which will not only be non-sexist, non-racist and non-Westocentric, but would also be flexible enough to deal with the far-reaching changes in the global (dis)order and reconstructions of state and society. Such a theory needs to dismantle the identification of the private with the family domain and the political with the public domain; it needs to construct citizenship as a multi-tier concept and to sever it from an exclusive relation to the state. The various sub-, cross- and supra-national and state collectivities of which people are formally and informally citizens can exist in a variety of co-operative and conflicting relationships which would differentially determine the positionings and the access to resources of different people at different times.

Considering these complexities and separating the notion of citizenship from the notion of the 'nation-state' is probably more prevalent than ever in these days of 'glocalization' (as Zygmund Bauman entitled his closing plenary address at the 1997 BSA annual conference). Similarly, such an analytical separation is necessary given the growing number of states which privatize a growing number of their institutions. Many feminists – most notably the Latin American ones (Vargas, 1996) – have found the notion of 'citizenship' to be the most appropriate political mobilization tool in the post-Beijing era. It could be used to integrate separate feminist struggles, such as those about reproductive rights, political participation, poverty, etc. Moreover, once the notion of citizenship is understood as a concept wider than just a relationship between the individual and the state, it could also integrate the struggles of women against oppression and exploitation in the name of culture and tradition within their own ethnic and local communities and transcend the politically dangerous but intellectually sterile debate which took place in the UN conference on human rights in Vienna in 1993 about whether the struggle for human rights should be on an individual or a 'group' level. Power relations and conflict of interests apply within 'groups' as well as between them. At the same time, individuals cannot be considered as abstracted from their specific social positionings.

As I discuss elsewhere (Yuval-Davis, 1997: ch.6), there is no 'end of history', nor is there an 'end goal' for political struggles. Transversal politics might offer us a way for mutual support and probably greater effectiveness in the continuous struggle towards a less sexist, less racist and more democratic society, a way of agency within the political, economic and environmental continuously changing contexts in which we live and act. The struggle for citizenship should engage us in our homes, our local, ethnic and national collectivities as well as in our struggles with states and international agencies. It is quite an agenda!

Notes

Nira Yuval-Davis is a Professor and Post-Graduate Course Director in Gender and Ethnic Studies at the University of Greenwich, London. Among her books are *Racialized Boundaries*, Routledge, 1992 (with F. Anthias); *Refusing Holy Orders: Women and Fundamentalism in Britain* (ed. with G. Sahgal), Virago, 1992; *Un-settling Settler Societies: Articulations of Gender, Ethnicity, Race & Class* (ed. with D. Stasiulis), Sage, 1995; and *Gender and Nation*, Sage, 1997.

A version of this paper was circulated as a background paper among the partici-pants of the conference *Women, Citizenship and Difference* organized by Nira Yuval-Davies and Pnina Werbner at the University of Greenwich, July 1996. The conference was funded by the Equal Opportunity Unit of the EU and by the Wenner-Gren Foundation for Anthropological Research.

1 This view, incidentally, was also shared by Marx, as has been developed in his article 'On the Jewish Question' (1975).

2 For a contrasting example, in Australia, one of the world's oldest democracies in terms of voting rights for both (non-Aboriginal) men (1850s) and women (1890s–1901), voting is also compulsory (thanks to Ann Curthoys for that point of information).

References

ACKELSBERG, Martha (1995) 'Liberalism' and 'Community Politics', unpub-lished papers written as draft entries for the forthcoming *Encyclopedia of Women's Studies* London: Simon and Schuster.

ALLEN, Sheila and MACEY, Marie (1990) 'At the cutting edge of citizenship: race & ethnicity in Europe 1992', a paper presented at the conference on New Issues in Black Politics, University of Warwick, May.

ANDERSON, Ben (1983) *Imagined Communities* London: Verso.

ANTHIAS, Floya and YUVAL-DAVIS, Nira (1989) 'Introduction' in Yuval-Davis and Anthias (1989).

—— and —— (1992) *Racialized Boundaries: Race, Nation, Gender, Colour and Class and the Anti-Racist Struggle* London: Routledge.

ARENDT, Hannah, (1951) *The Origins of Totalitarianism* New York: Harcourt, Brace.

AVINERI, S. and SHALIT, A. (1992) editors *Communitarianism & Individualism* Oxford: Oxford University Press.

BAKAN, Abigail B. and STASIULIS, Daiva (1994) 'Foreign domestic worker policy in Canada and the social boundaries of modern citizenship', *Science & Society* Vol.58, No.1: 7–33.

BARBALET, J.M. (1988) *Citizenship*, Milton Keynes: Open University Press.

BEVERIDGE, William, (1942) *Report on Social Insurance and Allied Services* London: HMSO.

BHABHA, Jacqueline and SHUTTER, Sue (1994) *Women's Movement: Women under Immigration, Nationality and Refugee Law* Stoke-on-Trent: Trentham Books.

BIEHL, Amy (1994) 'Custom and religion in a non-racial, non-sexist South Africa', *Women Against Fundamentalism Journal*, No. 5: 51–4.

BURNEY Elizabeth (1988) *Steps to Social Equality: Positive Action in a Negative Climate* London: Runnymede Trust.

CAIN, Harriet and YUVAL-DAVIS, Nira (1990) '"The Equal Opportunities Community" and the anti-racist struggle', *Critical Social Policy* No. 29: 5–26.

CHHACHHI, Amrita (1991) 'Forced Identities: the State, Communalism, Fundamentalism and Women in India' in D. Kandiyoti editor, *Women, Islam & the State* London: Macmilan, pp. 144–75.

CORREA, Sonia and PETCHESKY, Rosalind (1994) 'Reproductive and social rights: a feminist perspective' in G. Sen, A. Germain and L.C. Cohen editors, *Population Policies Considered*, HCPD & IWHC, pp. 107–26.

DALY, M. (1993) editor, *Communitarianism: Belonging & Commitment in a Pluralist Democracy* New York: Wadworth Publishing Company.

DEAN, Mitchel (1992) 'Review essay: Pateman's dilemma: women and citizenship', *Theory and Society* No. 21: 121–30.

de LEPERVANCHE, Marie (1980) 'From race to ethnicity', *Australian & New Zealand Journal of Sociology* Vol. 16, No. 1.

DICKANSON, Olive P. (1992) *Canada's First Nations* Toronto: McClelland & Stanley.

DIETZ, Mary G. (1987) 'Context is all: feminism and theories of citizenship', *Daedalus* 116: 4.

EDWARDS, J. (1988) 'Justice and the bounds of welfare', *Journal of Social Policy* No. 18.

EISENSTEIN, Zillah R. (1989) *The Female Body and the Law* Berkeley: University of California Press.

—— (1993) *The Color of Gender – Reimaging Democracy* Berkeley: University of California Press.

ESPING-ANDERSON, Gosta (1990) *The Three Worlds of Welfare Capitalism* Cambridge: Polity Press.

EVANS, David T. (1993) *Sexual Citizenship: The Material Construction of Sexualities* London: Routledge.

EVANS, Mary (1994) editor, *The Woman Question* London: Sage.

GORDON, Paul (1989) *Citizenship for Some? Race and Government Policy 1979–1989* London: Runnymede Trust.

GRANT, Rebecca and NEWLAND, Kathleen (1991) editors, *Gender and International Relations* Bloomington: Indiana University Press.

HALL, Catherine (1994) 'Rethinking imperial histories: the Reform Act of 1867' *New Left Review* No. 208: 3–29.

HALL, Stuart and HELD, David (1989) 'Citizens and citizenship', in Stuart Hall and Martin Jacques editors, *New Times* London: Lawrence & Wishart.

HARRIS, D. (1987) *Justifying State Welfare: The New Right v The Old Left* Oxford: Blackwell.

HERNES, Helga Maria (1987) 'Women and the welfare state: the transition from private to public dependence' in Anne Showstack Sassoon (1987).

HILL COLLINS, Patricia (1990) *Black Feminist Thought* Boston: Unwin Hyman.

IGNATIEFF, Michael (1993) *Blood and Belonging: Journeys into the New Nationalisms* London: BBC and Chatto & Windus.

JAYASURIYA, Laksiri (1990) 'Multiculturalism, citizenship and welfare: new directions for the 1990s', a paper presented at the 50th Anniversary Lecture Series, Dept. of Social Work and Social Policy, University of Sydney.

JONES, Kathleen B. (1990) 'Citizenship in a woman-friendly polity', *signs* Vol. 15, No.4.

JOSEPH, Suad (1993) 'Gender and civil society', *Middle East Report* No. 183: 22–6.

KANDIYOTI, Deniz (1991) 'Identity and its discontents: women and the nation', *Millennium*, Vol. 20, No. 3: 429–44.

KOSMARSKAYA, Natalya (1995) 'Women and ethnicity in former day Russia – thoughts on a given theme' in H. Lutz, A. Phoenix and N. Yuval-Davis editors, *Crossfires: Nationalism, Racism and Gender in Europe* London: Pluto Press.

KYMLICKA, Will (1995) *Multicultural Citizenship: A Liberal Theory of Minority Rights* Oxford: Clarendon Press.

LECHTE, John (1994) 'Freedom, community and cultural frontiers', paper presented to the Citizenship and Cultural Frontiers conference at Staffordshire University, Stoke-on-Trent, 16 September.

LISTER, Ruth (1990) *The Exclusive Society: Citizenship and the Poor* London: Child Poverty Action Group.

MANN, Michael (1987) 'Ruling class strategies and Citizenship', *Sociology* No.21: 339–54.

MARSHALL, T.H. (1950) *Citizenship and Social Class* Cambridge: Cambridge University Press.

—— (1975) (original edition 1965) *Social Policy in the Twentieth Century* London: Hutchinson.

—— (1981) *The Right To Welfare and Other Essays* London: Heinemann Educational.

MARX, Karl (1975) 'On the Jewish question', *Early Writings* Harmondsworth: Penguin, pp. 211–42.

MOLYNEUX, Maxine (1994) 'Women's rights and international context: some reflections on the post communist states', *Millennium: Journal of International Studies* Vol. 23, No. 2.

MORRIS, Lydia (1994) *Dangerous Classes: The Underclass and Social Citizenship* London: Routledge.

MOUFFE, Chantal (1993) 'Liberal socialism and pluralism: which citizenship' in J. Squires editor *Principled Positions* London: Lawrence & Wishart.

NIMNI, Ephraim (1996) 'The limits of Liberal Democracy', unpublished paper given at the departmental seminar for the Sociology Subject Groups at the University of Greenwich, London.

O'CONNOR, Julia S. (1993) 'Gender, class & citizenship in the comparative analysis of welfare state regimes: theoretical & methodological issues', *British Journal of Sociology* Vol. 44, No. 3: 501–18.

OLDFIELD, Adrian (1990) *Citizenship and Community: Civic Republicanism and the Modern World* London: Routledge.

OLIVER, Michael (1995) *Understanding Disability: From Theory to Practice* Basingstoke: Macmillan.

ORLOFF, Ann Shola (1993) 'Gender & the social rights of citizenship: the comparative analysis of gender relations and welfare states', *American Sociological Review* Vol. 58: pp. 303–28.

PAREKH, Bhiku (1990) 'The Rushdie affair and the British press: some salutary lessons', in *Free Speech*, a report of a seminar by the CRE, London.

PATEMAN, Carole (1988) *The Sexual Contract* Cambridge: Polity Press.

—— (1989) *The Disorder of Women* Cambridge: Polity Press.

PELED, Yoav (1992) 'Ethnic democracy and the legal construction of citizenship: Arab citizens of the Jewish state' *American Political Science Review*, Vol. 86, No. 2: 432–42.

PETTMAN, Jan (1992) *Living in the Margins: Racism, Sexism & Feminism in Australia* Sydney: Allen & Unwin.

PHILLIPS, Anne (1993) *Democracy & Difference*, Cambridge: Polity Press.

PHILLIPS, Melanie (1990) 'Citizenship sham in our secret society', *Guardian*, 14 September.

ROCHE, Maurice (1987) 'Citizenship, social theory and social change', *Theory and Society* No. 16: 363–99.

SAHGAL, Gita and YUVAL-DAVIS, Nira (1992) editors, *Refusing Holy Orders: Women and Fundamentalism in Britain* London: Virago.

SANDEL, Michael J. (1982) *Liberalism and the Limits of Justice* Cambridge: Cambridge University Press.

SHANIN, Theodore (1986) 'Soviet concepts of ethnicity: the case of a missing term', *New Left Review* No. 158: 113–22.

SHOWSTACK SASSOON, Anne (1987) editor, *Women and the State: The Shifting Boundaries of Public and Private* London: Hutchinson.

SMITH, Anthony D. (1986) *The Ethnic Origins of Nations* Oxford: Blackwell.

SOYSAL, Yasemin (1994) *Limits of Citizenship: Migrants and Postnational Membership in Europe* Chicago: University of Chicago Press.

STASIULIS, Daiva and YUVAL-DAVIS, Nira (1995) editors, *Unsettling Settler Societies: Articulations of Gender, Ethnicity, Race & Class* London: Sage.

TURNER, Bryan (1990) 'Outline of a theory on citizenship', *Sociology* Vol. 24, No. 2: 189–218.

VARGAS, Virginia (1996) presentation in panel 3: 'Unity, equality and difference: women's citizenship in contemporary Europe and beyond' at the Greenwich conference on Women, Citizenship and Difference, London.

VOGEL, Ursula (1989) 'Is citizenship gender specific?', paper presented at PSA Annual Conference, April.

VORONINA, Olga A. (1994) 'Soviet women and politics: on the brink of change' in B.J. Nelson and N. Chowdhury editors, *Women and Politics Worldwide* New Haven, Conn.: Yale University Press pp., 722–36.

WALBY, Sylvia (1994) 'Is citizenship gendered?', *Sociology* Vol. 28, No. 2: 379–95.

WILSON, William J. (1987) *The Truly Disadvantaged* Chicago: University of Chicago Press.

WING (Women, Immigration & Nationality Group) (1985) *Worlds Apart: Women under Immigration and Nationality Laws* London: Pluto Press.

YOUNG, Iris Marion (1989) 'Polity and group difference: a critique of the ideal of universal citizenship', *Ethics* No. 99.

YUVAL-DAVIS, Nira (1985) 'Front & rear: sexual divisions of labour in the Israeli military', *Feminist Studies* Vol. 11, No. 3.

—— (1991a) 'The citizenship debate: women, ethnic processes and the state', *Feminist Review* No. 39: 58–68.

—— (1991b) 'The gendered Gulf War: women's citizenship and modern warfare', in **Haim Bresheeth** and **Nira Yuval-Davis** *The Gulf War and the New World Order* London: Zed Books.

—— (1992) 'Multi-culturalism, fundamentalism and women' in **J. Donald** and **A. Rattansi** editors, *Race, Culture & Difference* London: Sage.

—— (1993) 'Gender and nation', *Ethnic and Racial Studies* Vol. 16, No. 4: 621–32.

—— (1994) 'Women, ethnicity & empowerment', *Feminism and Psychology* Vol. 4, No. 1: 179–97.

—— (1997) 'Colour, culture and anti-racism' in **C. Lloyds, F. Anthias** and **N. Yuval-Davis** editors, *Rethinking Racism & Anti-Racism in Europe* London: Macmillan, forthcoming.

YUVAL-DAVIS, Nira and ANTHIAS, Floya (1989) *Woman-Nation-State* London: Macmillan.

Citizenship:
Towards a feminist synthesis

Ruth Lister

FEMINIST REVIEW NO 57, AUTUMN 1997, PP. 28–48

Abstract

A synthesis of rights and participatory approaches to citizenship, linked through the notion of human agency, is proposed as the basis for a feminist theory of citizenship. Such a theory has to address citizenship's exclusionary power in relation to both nation-state 'outsiders' and 'insiders'. With regard to the former, the article argues that a feminist theory and politics of citizenship must embrace an internationalist agenda. With regard to the latter, it offers the concept of a 'differentiated universalism' as an attempt to reconcile the universalism which lies at the heart of citizenship with the demands of a politics of difference. Embracing also the reconstruction of the public–private dichotomy, citizenship, reconceptualized in this way, can, it is argued, provide us with an important theoretical and political tool.

Keywords

agency; citizenship; difference; exclusion; obligations; political participation; rights; synthesis

This paper[1] is divided into two main parts. The first reviews the different meanings of citizenship in order to argue for a synthesis of the rights and participatory traditions, linked through the notion of human agency. The second considers citizenship's exclusionary tensions which have served to exclude women and minority groups from full citizenship, both from within and from without the nation state. In doing so, it addresses the challenge of diversity and difference for citizenship to argue the case for a 'differentiated universalism' with regard to both participation and rights-based conceptions of citizenship.

What is citizenship?

A contested concept

The impossibility of arriving at an exhaustive and comprehensive definition of citizenship, commented on even by Aristotle, is a common refrain running through the literature. Rather than attempt such a definition of this 'slippery concept' (Riley, 1992: 180), many today fall back on that provided by T. H. Marshall: 'Citizenship is a status bestowed on those who are full members of a community. All who possess the status are equal with respect to the rights and duties with which the status is endowed' (1950: 28–9).

The key elements here are membership of a community (itself an increasingly contested concept); the rights and obligations which flow from that membership and equality. In each case, we are talking about not simply a set of legal rules governing the relationship between individuals and the state in which they live but also a set of social relationships between individuals and the state and between individual citizens (the latter receiving particular emphasis in the Scandinavian literature). The Scandinavian literature also attaches especial importance to the participatory meaning of membership in a community. This provides a bridge between Marshallian rights and more republican approaches to citizenship which stand in two competing traditions: the liberal rights and the civic republican, conceptualized by Adrian Oldfield (1990) as citizenship as a status vs citizenship as a practice.

Rights or obligations?

Rights

Marshall's tripartite formulation of the civil, political and social is usually taken as the starting point for any discussion of citizenship rights. However, the legitimacy of social rights has been subject to renewed challenge with the renaissance of classical liberalism in the form of the New Right. Two key arguments *for* social rights are, first, that they help to promote the effective exercise of civil and political rights by groups who are disadvantaged in terms of power and resources (Lister, 1990a, 1993); and, second, that they are essential to the promotion of individual autonomy. This, according to Doyal and Gough's theory of human needs, constitutes one of the preconditions for action in any culture and as such one of the 'most basic human needs – those which must be satisfied to some degree before actors can effectively participate in their form of life to achieve any other valued goals' (Doyal and Gough, 1991: 54). Doyal and Gough maintain that their theory of human needs provides a justification not only for civil and political rights but also for social rights of citizenship as critical to autonomy, recognizing that autonomy cannot be understood in purely individualistic terms, since it has a social dimension also. The issue of autonomy has especial significance for many women in the light of the economic dependency which has traditionally undermined their citizenship (though this is less true in the case of Black women).[2]

FEMINIST REVIEW NO 57, AUTUMN 1997

The work of Doyal and Gough exemplifies a growing willingness on the British Left to engage in a rights discourse in contrast with the traditional Marxist approach which tended to dismiss the idea of citizenship rights as an individualistic bourgeois charade, designed to obscure fundamental economic and social class divisions behind a veneer of equality. Doyal and Gough (1991: 224) reject such an approach as 'counterproductive and dangerous' for it ignores the ways in which rights can help protect human needs, thereby (although they do not finish the argument) mitigating economic and social inequalities.

Feminist attitudes towards rights stretch from their embrace by liberal feminists as central to any reform programme to their dismissal by radical feminists as merely the expression of male values and power (for a discussion, see Bryson, 1992). Those writing in a socialist tradition are wary of the individualistic nature of rights; a number of feminist theorists have counterpoised an ethic of care against an ethic of justice or rights and feminist legal theorists tend to caution against placing too much faith in rights, while also counselling against outright rejection. Feminist scepticism about citizenship rights overlaps with that of the radical Left who have highlighted 'the failure of citizenship rights vested in liberal democratic institutions to meet the needs of women and racialised groups and the socially and economically marginalised' (Taylor, 1989: 29).

In part, this reflects citizenship's exclusionary tensions, which I will discuss in the next section. At the same time, it also suggests another avenue which is the 'radical extension' (Doyal and Gough, 1991) of Marshall's triad to embrace other categories of rights which have been demanded by social movements, in particular reproductive rights. To the extent that the latter *are* now recognized, it represents a triumph for feminist 'needs discourses' in the 'politics of needs interpretation' (Fraser, 1987). David Held (1995), who has made the case for such a 'radical extension', identifies seven clusters of rights corresponding to key sites of power – health, social, cultural, civil, economic, pacific and political – which, he contends, are key to the entrenchment of the principle of autonomy and to the facilitation of free and equal political participation.

In similar vein, Carol Gould (1988: 212) argues that 'the right of participation in decision-making in social, economic, cultural and political life' should be included in the nexus of basic rights. Her approach is echoed in attempts on the left to develop a more dynamic and active form of social citizenship rights than those traditionally associated with the post-war welfare state. Dissatisfaction with the passive nature of the latter has prompted explorations of the potential for user involvement and greater democratic accountability of welfare institutions (see, for instance,

Beresford and Croft, 1993). This is not to be confused with the recasting of the citizen as consumer of welfare services under the Citizen's Charter introduced by the Conservatives.

Obligations

The market-oriented conceptualization of social citizenship rights exemplified by the Citizen's Charter is nicely complemented by the political Right's growing emphasis on citizenship obligation and in particular the obligation to undertake paid employment. This reflects what Maurice Roche (1992) has dubbed a 'duties discourse', which is becoming increasingly influential in Western European and US social policy. Roche points to the influence of new social movements (in particular greens and feminists) in the development of this duties discourse. A key issue for feminists is how care fits into any configuration of citizenship obligations (Bubeck, 1995; Lister, 1997). However, it is, as Roche points out, the Right (in particular neo-conservatives) who have deliberately challenged the existing 'rights discourse' and who have done most to shift the fulcrum of the citizenship paradigm which dominates contemporary politics in countries such as the UK and US.

Most of the key texts contributing to this shift originate in the US, including influential works by Mead (1986) and Novak *et al.* (1987) which identify engagement in paid work by welfare recipients to support their families as the prime obligation. The key policy issue – of whether this obligation should apply to those caring for children, and in particular lone parents – underlines its gendered nature.[3] More generally, a number of British politicians across the political spectrum, together with influential commentators, have embraced the communitarian message of Amitai Etzioni's *The Spirit of Community*. Etzioni calls for 'a moratorium on the minting of most, if not all, new rights', together with the re-establishment of the link between rights and responsibilities and recognition that the latter do not necessarily entail the former. His goal is correction of 'the current imbalance between rights and responsibilities' (1993: 4).

Few would dispute that responsibilities as well as rights enter into the citizenship equation. The question is: what is the appropriate balance and relationship between the two and how does that balance reflect gender and other power relations (an aspect of the question which is particularly pertinent when considering the obligation to take paid work)? One helpful formulation, which attempts to encapsulate a reciprocal relationship between rights and obligations, is that put forward by Geraint Parry of a 'mutual society' based on the principle of 'from each according to his or her ability, to each according to his or her need for the conditions of agency' (1991: 186).

As I shall argue below, the notion of agency helps knit together the different approaches to citizenship. It can also be found implicitly in notions of 'active citizenship' which have been promoted in the British context, from very different standpoints. The term was first coined by government ministers as an exhortation to discharge the responsibilities of neighbourliness, voluntary action and charity, largely discredited because of the context of the rundown of public sector services and the privatization programme within which it was advanced. Nevertheless, in both the UK and the US ideas for citizens' or community service have been put forward and some have argued that community service should equate with paid work as a means of discharging the general obligations of citizenship (Leisink and Coenen, 1993).

There is, too, a more radical conception of active citizenship on offer, reflected in an alternative definition provided by Ray Pahl as 'local people working together to improve their own quality of life and to provide conditions for others to enjoy the fruits of a more affluent society' (1990). This is a form of active citizenship which disadvantaged people, often women, do for themselves, through for example, community groups, rather than have done for them by the more privileged; one which creates them as subjects rather than objects. A vivid example of this kind of active citizenship can be found among the myriad of women's groups in Northern Ireland (Lister, 1994a; WCRG, 1995: Fearon, 1996). The notion of active citizenship duty has also been broadened out to encompass ideas of ecological citizenship obligations which stretch beyond the geographical and temporal boundaries of the citizen's community (Weale, 1991; Twine, 1994; van Steenbergen, 1994).

Citizenship as political obligation

It is in the civic republican tradition that we find the source of today's duties discourse. Originating in the classical Graeco-Roman world, it appeals to the values of civic duty, the submission of individual interest to that of the common good and the elevation of the public sphere in which the citizen is constituted as political actor. The renaissance of civic republicanism, particularly in the US, the appeal of which is not confined to any one point in the political spectrum, represents a reaction against the individualism of the previously dominant liberal citizenship paradigm. This, it is argued, represents an impoverished version of citizenship in which individual citizens are reduced to atomized, passive bearers of rights whose freedom consists in being able to pursue their individual interests.

The reclaiming of active, collective politics as the essence of citizenship is pivotal to contemporary civic republicanism and in particular to its appropriation, suitably modified, by some feminist writers, most notably Mary

Dietz. For Dietz, it is only 'through active engagement as citizens in the public world' and the recognition of the activity of citizenship as itself a value that feminists will 'be able to claim a truly liberatory politics as their own' (1987: 15). Others have been attracted by the portrayal of citizenship as active political participation, while remaining critical of some of its other key tenets (see, for instance, Young, 1989, 1990; Phillips, 1991, 1993). Potentially problematic for feminists are: the demanding nature of republican citizenship which has particular implications for women, disadvantaged by the sexual division of time; its narrow conception of the 'political' built on a, generally, rigid separation of public and private spheres; and its uncritical appeal to notions of universalism, impartiality and the common good. Without pursuing all the arguments here (see Lister, 1995, 1997), it is possible, I would argue, to develop a modified model which draws on the civic republican tradition but in a way which promotes the interests of women's citizenship.

In particular, an important element of any feminist citizenship project is to query establishment understandings of the 'common good' and to define both citizenship and the 'political' in broad terms so as to encompass the kind of informal politics in which women often take the lead and the struggles of oppressed groups generally. Under such a definition (which differs from that espoused by traditional civic republicanism), citizenship politics can be oppositional and disruptive. Thus, for instance, non-violent direct action of the kind being taken by anti-road protesters in the UK, even though sometimes crossing the boundaries of what is deemed lawful, represents a form of citizenship which is implicitly appealing to an alternative version of the common good. Likewise, traditional civic republicanism's dictum that citizenship requires impartiality and the transcendence of group differences is rejected on the grounds that it serves to reinforce the very exclusion against which disadvantaged groups are fighting, in the name of a common good which has subordinated their interests to those of more powerful groups (Young, 1989, 1990; Phillips, 1991, 1993).[4]

It is the local rather than the national which provides the arena for many citizenship struggles of this kind. As a process, community action can both strengthen deprived communities and, through collective action, promote the citizenship of individuals within those communities. Such action can boost individual and collective self-confidence, as individuals and groups come together to see themselves as political actors and effective citizens. This is especially true for women for whom involvement in community organizations can be more personally fruitful than engagement in formal politics which are often experienced as more alienating than empowering (Coote and Pattullo, 1990; Lovenduski and Randall, 1993; Ferree and Martin, 1995). The process has been described by an American anthropologist, Sue Hyatt, who worked with women on a Bradford council estate, as 'accidental activism', through which 'women who previously did not see themselves as in any way political are becoming advocates for social change' (1992: 6). Similarly, a Northern Ireland study by the Women and Citizenship Research Group (1995) underlines the sense of personal power or effectiveness that women, previously inexperienced in political action, have gained as a result of such activism. This contrasts with their exclusion from the formal political system. Placing value on informal politics as an expression of citizenship does not, however, mean ignoring the continuing need both to open up formal political arenas to women and also to make formal politics more accountable to informal.

Synthesis

Recognizing the limitations of both the main citizenship traditions, we need, as Chantal Mouffe argues, 'to go beyond the conceptions of citizenship of both the liberal and the civic republican traditions while building on their respective strengths'(1992: 4). This conception would, she suggests, draw on both the liberal formulation of free and equal rights-bearing citizens and the richer republican conceptualization of active political participation and civic engagement (but based on a radical, pluralist reframing of the 'common good'). A reading of the literature suggests that, while the rights and participatory approaches to citizenship remain conceptually different, they do not necessarily have to conflict; instead, they can be seen as mutually supportive, even if tensions between them remain.

An example of how the two coalesce is provided by the process of negotiation with welfare state institutions, by individuals as well as groups, the main responsibility for which tends to fall to women (Nelson, 1984; Jones, 1990). This perspective on citizenship is exemplified by the work of Scandinavian feminist scholars such as Helga Hernes and Birte Siim. Hernes, for example, writes:

> The welfare state literature, to the extent that it deals with individual citizens, deals with those aspects of citizenship that are related to social policy entitlements. Democratic theories and empirical studies of democratic politics emphasise the participatory aspects of citizenship. Any adequate account of contemporary citizenship in Scandinavia must include all these dimensions if the interplay between material rights, multi-level participation, and political identities is to be grasped.
>
> (Hernes, 1987: 138)

The interaction between social and political citizenship has also been key in the development of women's position as citizens in the twentieth century (Dale and Foster, 1986; Gordon, 1990; Bock and Thane, 1991; Sarvasy,

1992; Koven and Michel, 1993; Lewis, 1994). The nature of the social rights that have emerged has, in part, been a reflection of the extent to which women have been involved in their construction. Conversely, the extent of women's political involvement has, in part, been a reflection of the nature of the social and reproductive rights they have achieved and their mobilization has been, in part, a function of their relationship with the welfare state.

This helps to underline the importance for a feminist theory of citizenship of a 'synthetic' approach, which embraces elements of the two main historical citizenship traditions. A rounded and fruitful theorization of citizenship, which can be of potential value to women, has to embrace both individual rights (and, in particular, social and reproductive rights) and political participation and also has to analyse the relationship between the two (Sarvasy and Siim, 1994). At the core of this conceptualization lies the idea of human agency.[5] Citizenship as participation represents an expression of human agency in the political arena, broadly defined; citizenship as rights enables people to act as agents. Moreover, citizenship rights are not fixed. They remain the object of political struggles to defend, reinterpret and extend them. Who is involved in these struggles, where they are placed in the political hierarchy and the political power and influence they can yield will help to determine the outcomes. Citizenship thus emerges as a dynamic concept in which process and outcome stand in a dialectical relationship to each other. Such a conceptualization of citizenship is particularly important in challenging the construction of women (and especially minority group women) as passive victims, while keeping sight of the discriminatory and oppressive male-dominated political, economic and social institutions which still deny them full citizenship. People can be, at the same time, both the subordinate objects of hierarchical power relations *and* subjects who are agents in their own lives, capable of exercising power in the 'generative' sense of self-actualization (Giddens, 1991).

Finally, to tie up this discussion with the earlier one on obligation, I draw a distinction between, on the one hand, an emphasis on the importance for citizenship of political participation, broadly defined, and, on the other, a construction of active political participation as a citizenship obligation. Given the constraints on women's lives and the obstacles they face, there is a real danger of creating a measuring rod of citizenship against which many women might, yet again, fall short. Moreover, it is one which could deny the citizenship of those constrained by severe disability, chronic illness or frailty (Meekosha and Dowse, this issue). I therefore draw a distinction between two formulations: to *be* a citizen and to *act* as a citizen, thereby bringing together Oldfield's bifurcation of citizenship as a status and a practice. To be a citizen, in the sociological sense, means to enjoy the rights necessary for agency and social and political participation. To act as a citizen involves fulfilling the full potential of the status. Those who do not fulfil that potential do not cease to be citizens. Moreover, in practice, political participation tends to be more of a continuum than an all or nothing affair; it can fluctuate during the individual's life-course, reflecting, in part, the demands of caring obligations which can also be interpreted as the exercise of citizenship obligations.

Citizenship's exclusionary tensions

The greater or lesser ability of certain groups to act as citizens and the degree to which they enjoy both formal and substantive rights as citizens depends on where they stand on a continuum of inclusion and exclusion which, at the extremes, represent the two sides of citizenship's coin. Whereas much of the citizenship literature has traditionally focused on its *in*clusionary face, more radical contemporary writings tend to portray citizenship as a force for *ex*clusion which creates non or partial citizens. These can be characterized as 'those who are excluded from without' and 'those who are excluded from within' specific citizenship communities or nation states (Yeatman, 1994: 80).

Exclusion from without

The exclusionary force of nation-state-bound citizenship has been thrown into relief in the West and North with the growth in the number of migrants and asylum-seekers in recent decades. Although generally not reflected in the mainstream migration literature, women form a significant proportion of migrants and of asylum-seekers and for them the exclusionary force is compounded by laws which construct them as economic dependants (Morokvasic, 1984, 1991, 1993; Kofman & Sales, 1992; Bhabha and Shutter, 1994; Knocke, 1995). In Europe, this force is now being strengthened as members of the EU become European citizens behind the racialized ramparts of Fortress Europe.

The status of large numbers of peoples resident in states of which they are not legally citizens raises a number of question marks over the meaning of citizenship in a world where migratory pressures are likely to intensify (Hammar, 1990; Castles and Miller, 1993). William Rogers Brubaker (1992) and Joseph Carens (1989) underline the symbolic importance of the stance taken by a state towards access to formal citizenship as a signifier of an inclusive or exclusive understanding of membership and national belonging. The latter thus argues forcefully that to require cultural assimilation as a precondition of citizenship is a violation of the liberal-democratic 'principles of toleration and diversity' (Carens 1989: 38) and calls into question the equal status of existing minority groups. This, it has been suggested, points to a 'multicultural' model of citizenship (Castles and Miller, 1993).

The exact nature of such a model is, however, contested. In particular, it runs the risk of treating cultural groups as homogeneous, ignoring differences such as gender, sexuality, age and class (Yuval-Davis, 1991; Ali, 1993; Bhavnani, 1993). In his treatise on multicultural citizenship, Will Kymlicka (1995) makes a helpful distinction between minority rights which promote the interests of minority groups in relation to the majority and those which allow minority groups to impose restrictions on their own members in the name of traditional authorities and practices. Support for the former but not the latter, he argues, helps to ensure not just equality between groups but freedom and equality within groups. As he acknowledges, maintaining such a distinction may be difficult in practice. Moreover, it still leaves open the question of whose interpretation of minority rights is listened to. Nevertheless, Kymlicka does offer a possible framework for addressing claims for minority group rights while recognizing different interests *within* groups.

There is also a danger that the multi-cultural model essentializes and freezes cultural differences (Ali, 1993). Conversely, it can represent mere liberal toleration of diversity, confined to the 'private' sphere, rather than genuine acceptance and recognition of such diversity in the 'public' (Parekh, 1991; Galeotti, 1993). The notion of 'trans-culturalism', which neither reduces people to cultural groups nor ignores cultural identities, has been put forward as a possible way of avoiding some of these pitfalls. Its implications, both theoretically and politically, would need further exploration.[6]

From an international perspective, widening economic inequalities between North and South fuel migration, on the one hand, and exclusionary responses, on the other. Paradoxically, there is an impetus to heighten the barriers around nation-states (or groups of nation-states as in the EU) at the very time when the nation-state is itself becoming less pivotal economically and politically. The image of a weakened nation-state caught in a pincer movement between globalizing and localizing forces is a common refrain in the contemporary citizenship literature, although one should not exaggerate the demise of its power, not least its power still to exercise control over membership and citizenship.

Rather than jettison the concept of citizenship in the face of the pressures on the nation-state, citizenship theorists have tended to seek a more multi-layered conception, operating on several frontiers (Heater, 1990; Parry,

1991) and to argue for the development of an analysis of citizenship at a global level (Turner, 1990; Held, 1995; Falk, 1994). This can incorporate notions of rights and responsibilities as well as democratic accountability and political action, through both formal and informal channels. Arguably, we are today witnessing the emergence of a global civil society, in which women are playing a central role, witness the participation of thousands of women from all over the world in the Non-Governmental Organisation Forum at Beijing and the wider electronic networks which linked up with it (*Journal of International Communication*, 1996).

Developments such as these have led to some recognition that a feminist theory and politics of citizenship must embrace an internationalist agenda (see, in particular, Jones, 1994). Conversely, it is crucial that the theorization of global citizenship is informed by feminist perspectives and does not recreate the exclusionary tendencies which have typified much of the mainstream citizenship literature.

Exclusion from within

These exclusionary tendencies are inherently gendered, reflecting the fact that women's long-standing expulsion from the theory and practice of citizenship, in both its liberal and republican clothes, is far from accidental and only partially rectified by their formal incorporation in virtually all societies in the twentieth century. Gendered patterns of exclusion interact with other axes of social division such as class, 'race', disability, sexuality and age in ways which can be either multiplicative or contradictory, and which shift over time (Brewer, 1993; Brah, 1996).

The de-construction of the unitary woman

Thanks to feminist scholarship, the veil of universalism which enshrouds 'malestream' political theory has been lifted to make visible the female non-citizen who stood outside it and to reveal the male citizen lurking beneath it. This challenge to political theory's 'false universalism' (Williams, 1989: 118) has now been matched by a similar challenge to the false universalism of the category 'woman'. This has come from both the theoretical advance of post-structuralism and from Black and other groups of women whose identities and interests have been ignored, marginalized or subsumed. They have underlined how the category 'woman' has, in fact, been representative of dominant groups of women in the same way that the abstract individual of traditional political theory has been representative of dominant groups of men (Fraser and Nicholson, 1990). This also helps to illuminate how women's exile from the community of impartial, disembodied citizens has been paralleled in some ways by that of other groups, which, of course, also include women.

Acknowledgement of the need to problematize the category 'woman' in recognition of the differences between women and the ways in which these differences shape the economic, social and political relationships between women as well as between women and men and women and the state does, though, run into the danger that, if 'woman' is simply deconstructed and left in fragments, there is no woman left to be a citizen. The fact that the category 'woman' is not unitary does not render it meaningless (Maynard, 1994). Black feminists, such as bell hooks (1984), Audre Lorde (1984) and Patricia Hill Collins (1991) have argued that, provided the differences between women are fully acknowledged, they do not preclude solidarity on the basis of those interests still shared as women. Central to these interests is women's exclusion from full citizenship, as the patterns of entry to the gateways to the various sectors of the public sphere remain profoundly gendered. Thus, the project of engendering citizenship is not invalidated, but it has to be conceived of as part of a wider project of differentiating citizenship.

The challenge of diversity and difference for citizenship

Feminist theory's dual challenge to the false universalism of citizenship and the category 'woman' has underlined the need for 'a conception of citizenship which would accommodate all social cleavages simultaneously' (Leca, 1992: 30). While attempts to elaborate such a conception demonstrate the difficulties,[7] it is my view that this is the direction which citizenship theory has to take, if it is to match up to its inclusionary and universalist claims. It is not a case, therefore, of abandoning citizenship as a universalist project, for to do so is also to abandon the 'emancipatory potential' which strikes such a political resonance for many people (Vogel, 1988; Riley, 1992). Instead, our goal should be a universalism which stands in creative tension to diversity and difference and which challenges the divisions and exclusionary inequalities which can stem from diversity.[8] We might call this a 'differentiated universalism', drawing on contemporary radical political theory which is attempting to 'particularize' the universal in the search for 'a new kind of articulation between the universal and the particular' (Mouffe, 1993: 13; Yeatman, 1993: 229).[9] Universalism is understood here not as false impartiality but as a 'universality of moral commitment' to the equal worth and participation of all (Young, 1990).

We can apply this theoretical stance to the question of both citizenship rights and participation. Nira Yuval-Davis (1994, this issue) has explored the implications of these tensions for citizenship participation through the notion of a politics of 'transversal dialogue'. This involves a process of 'rooting' and 'shifting' in which participants remain rooted in their own identities and values but at the same time are willing to shift views in dialogue with others. A similar stance is taken by Anna Yeatman, using the vocabulary of a 'politics of difference' which involves 'a commitment to a universalistic orientation to the positive value of difference within a democratic political process' (1994: 89). Such a politics of difference requires, she argues, both 'an inclusive politics of voice and representation' and 'a readiness on the part of any one emancipatory movement to show how its particular interest in contesting oppression links into and supports the interests of other movements in contesting different kinds of oppression' (1993: 231).

It is, as is so often the case, easier to envisage such a process in theory than in practice. As Yuval-Davis warns, there are some situations in which conflicting positions are not reconcilable and, by and large, political systems do not provide the time and space for such dialogue. Moreover, there is a tendency to underestimate the difficulties some groups, in particular those in poverty, would have in entering the dialogue in the first place. Nevertheless, there are examples which indicate that such a transversal politics is possible. To take just two from conflict areas: first, during the period of transition to the new South Africa, a Women's National Coalition was formed which represented an 'extraordinary convergence of women across geographical, racial, class, religious, and political lines' and 'a forum through which women who harbored deep animosities could also identify common concerns' (Kemp *et al.*, 1995: 150–1). Through a process of dialogue and negotiation and despite fissures and disagreements, the Coalition drafted a Women's Charter for Effective Equality which gave women in their diversity a voice in the writing of the new constitution. Second, in a photo-essay called 'different together', Cynthia Cockburn describes how a form of transversal politics is being pursued by women's centres in Belfast:

> Individually women hold on to their political identities – some long for a united Ireland, others feel deeply threatened by the idea. But they have identified a commonality in being women, being community based and being angry at injustice and inequality, that allows them to affirm and even welcome this and other kinds of difference.

(Cockburn, 1996: 4)

Yeatman relates a politics of difference to questions of rights. It would, she suggests, involve 'a new kind of rights talk' in which 'rights are understood as dialectical and relational in respect of opening debate and discussion about how to positively alter relationships of oppression. They are dialogical rights, predicated fundamentally on a right to give voice and be listened to within the dialogical process of decision-making' (Yeatman, 1994: 90). With regard to the content of citizenship rights, on the face of it they do not appear very amenable to a politics of difference, given their representation as essentially abstract and universal. Nevertheless, it is possible to distinguish two, complementary, approaches to the accommodation of diversity and difference in the conceptualization of citizenship rights.

The first is to recognize that rights can be particularized to take account of the situation of specific groups both in the 'reactive' sense of counteracting past and present disadvantages which may undermine their position as citizens and in the 'proactive' sense of affirming diversity, particularly with regard to cultural and linguistic rights. Examples of the former are affirmative action programmes and the kind of wide-ranging disability discrimination legislation enacted in the US. Examples of the latter are, first, multicultural language policies, which give official recognition to the languages of significant minority ethnic groups, as in Sweden and Australia (Castles, 1994), and, second, the specific political, legal and collective rights enjoyed by indigenous American Indians in parallel with their rights as US citizens (Young, 1989, 1990, 1993). Such attempts to rearticulate the relationship between the universal and the particular are, however, politically charged as can be seen in the US where the growth of the Hispanic community has led to pressures for English to be declared the official language and where there is a growing backlash against affirmative action programmes (see also Bacchi, 1996).

The second approach, advocated by David Taylor (1989), is to anchor citizenship rights in a notion of need on the basis that need can be seen as dynamic and differentiated, as against the universal and abstract basis of rights. This formulation is useful in opening up the political dynamics of the relationship between needs and rights in citizenship struggles, or 'the politics of needs interpretation' (Fraser, 1987).[10] However, Taylor's distinction between needs as differentiated and rights as abstract and universal is, arguably, something of an oversimplification. As I have just suggested, rights can be differentiated on a group basis and Doyal and Gough's theory of needs (1991), upon which Taylor draws is, as he himself notes, rooted in a universalistic understanding of basic human needs which are then subject to different cultural and historical interpretations (Hewitt, 1994). Likewise, from a feminist perspective, Zillah Eisenstein contends that 'a radicalised feminist rights discourse recognizes particularity and individuality of need even as it calls upon the similarity (rather than identity) of women' (1991: 122). What this discussion suggests is that both needs and rights need to be understood as tiered, embracing both the universal and the differentiated, and standing in a dynamic relationship to each other through a 'politics of needs interpretation'.

Realigning the public and private

The first step in this politics, as outlined by Nancy Fraser (1987: 117–18), is the legitimization of 'women's needs as genuine political issues as

FEMINIST REVIEW NO 57, AUTUMN 1997

opposed to "private" domestic or market matters', recognizing that needs and priorities will vary for different groups of women. The feminist struggles which this has entailed have involved the deconstruction of the 'patriarchal separation' (Pateman, 1989: 183) between the 'public' and the domestic 'private' which underpins the very (gendered) meaning of citizenship as traditionally understood.

As a result, the public–private divide can be understood as a shifting political construction, under constant renegotiation, which reflects both historical and cultural contexts as well as the relative power of different social groups. The public and private define each other and take meaning from each other. We cannot, for instance, understand the gendered patterns of entry to citizenship in the public sphere without taking into account the sexual division of labour within the private. Similarly, women's treatment under asylum laws, which tend to deny refugee status to women fleeing sexual persecution, is governed by the public-private divide. The struggle to control the meaning and positioning of the divide is central to the project of engendering citizenship. It is one of feminism's achievements that it has successfully challenged the positioning of the divide in relation to a number of issues. Yet, its implications still tend to be ignored or discounted by male citizenship theorists, despite the fact that the link was made between women's exclusion from citizenship and their position in the private sphere by Mary Wollstonecraft and John Stuart Mill back in the eighteenth and nineteenth centuries.

Conclusion

The starting point of this paper has been the attempt to synthesize through the notion of human agency the two different historical traditions of citizenship in which citizenship is constructed both as a status and a practice. This provides a framework for thinking about women's citizenship which both recognizes the structural constraints which still diminish and undermine that citizenship while not reducing women to passive victims.

In examining the exclusionary tensions which serve to perpetuate women's exile as a group from full citizenship, emphasis has been placed on the need to locate a gendered analysis within the wider framework of difference and the divisions and exclusionary inequalities which flow from it. This points to a conception of citizenship grounded in a notion of 'differentiated universalism' which represents an attempt to reconcile the universalism which lies at the heart of citizenship with the demands of a politics of difference. Together with the reconstruction of the public–private dichotomy, these ideas are offered as possible building blocks in the elaboration of a feminist theory of citizenship, which draws on principles of synthesis rather than dichotomy. Thus, recast on feminist lines, citizenship offers us both a valuable perspective on the position of women in their diversity and an important political tool for women and other oppressed groups.

Notes

Ruth Lister is Professor of Social Policy in the Department of Social Sciences, Loughborough University.

1 This is a revised version of the paper given at the Women and Citizenship Conference, Greenwich, and of an earlier paper given at the DIOTIMA Gender of Rights conference, Athens, February 1996. It is based on a forthcoming book (Lister, 1997). I am grateful to the Nuffield Foundation for a personal fellowship which enabled me to write the bulk of the book.

2 The issue of autonomy and economic independence in the context of notions of interdependence is key to the construction of women's citizenship (see Lister 1990b, 1994b, 1995).

3 The policy trend in both the US and Europe is to include lone parents in the obligation to undertake paid work. The clearest example in Europe is the Netherlands where the presumption that lone mothers are exempt from the obligation to undertake paid work is progressively being abandoned. In contrast, the UK is one of very few countries which still permit lone parents to claim social assistance until their youngest child is of school-leaving age without being required to register for paid work.

4 This does, though, as Phillips (1993) warns, raise difficult questions as to where the dividing line is drawn between such a definition of citizenship politics and sectional interest group politics.

5 My conceptualization of human agency is influenced by the work of Carol Gould and her articulation of the actions and choices of autonomous actors as a process of self-development: 'of concretely becoming the person one chooses to be through carrying out those actions that express one's purposes and needs' (1988: 47). In developing her self, the individual is also acting upon, and thereby potentially changing the world, a world which at the same time structures the choices available (see also Twine, 1994). Moreover, individuals are understood to be 'social from the start, both in the fact that social relations are an essential mode of their individual self-development and that they characteristically engage in common activities, oriented to common and not merely individual ends' (Gould, 1988: 71).

6 The notion of 'transculturalism' was suggested by Philomena Essed at a seminar on citizenship and peace held in Cork, the Republic of Ireland, November 1995.

7 See, for instance, the criticisms of Iris Marion Young's 'politics of difference and group assertion' (1990) which attempts to incorporate difference into the

theory and politics of political citizenship (e.g. Mouffe, 1992; Phillips,1993; Wilson, 1993).

8 I am here following Fiona Williams (1996) who distinguishes between diversity, difference and division, making clear that they are not fixed categories. Diversity is used to refer to a shared collective experience which does not necessarily imply relations of subordination, for example based on age, nationality, sexual identity. Division occurs where diversity *is* translated into relations of subordination. Difference signifies a situation where diversity becomes the basis for resistance against such subordination.

9 See also Benhabib (1992); Gunew and Yeatman (1993) and Judith Squires' edited collection, *Principled Positions* (1993), which attempts to resurrect a notion of social justice by means of bridge-building 'between the supposed universalism of modernism and the fragmented particularities left behind by post-structuralist deconstructions' (Harvey, 1993: 102).

10 The disability rights movement provides a good example of a political challenge to orthodox needs interpretations. It has also underlined the dangers of disconnecting a needs from a rights discourse; in the UK, disability rights activists have argued that a shift of emphasis from the rights to the needs of disabled people has opened the way for the professional domination of welfare provision and 'a retreat from active to passive citizenship' (Oliver and Barnes, 1991: 8).

References

ALI, Yasmin (1993) ' "Race", ethnicity and constitutional rights' in **Anthony Barnett, Caroline Ellis** and **Paul Hirst** editors, *Debating the Constitution* Cambridge: Polity Press.

BACCHI, Carol (1996) *The Politics of Affirmative Action* London: Sage.

BENHABIB, Seyla (1992) *Situating the Self* Cambridge: Polity.

BERESFORD, Peter and CROFT, Suzy (1993) *Citizen Involvement* Basingstoke: Macmillan.

BHABHA, Jacqueline and SHUTTER, Sue (1994) *Women's Movement: Women Under Immigration, Nationality and Refugee Law* Stoke: Trentham Books.

BHAVNANI, Kum-Kum (1993) 'Towards a multi-cultural Europe? "Race", nation and identity in 1992 and beyond', *Feminist Review* No. 45, 30–45.

BOCK, Gisela and THANE, Pat (1991) editors, *Maternity and Gender Policies* London: Routledge.

BRAH, Avtar (1996) *Cartographies of Diaspora* London and New York: Routledge.

BREWER, Rose (1993) 'Theorizing race, class and gender: the new scholarship of Black feminist intellectuals and Black women's labor', in **Stanlie James** and **Abena Busia** editors, *Theorizing Black Feminisms: The Visionary Pragmatism of Black Women* London and New York: Routledge.

BRUBAKER, William Rogers (1992) *Citizenship and Nationhood in France and Germany* Cambridge, Mass.: Harvard University Press.

BRYSON, Valerie (1992) *Feminist Political Theory* Basingstoke: Macmillan.

BUBECK, Diemut (1995) *A Feminist Approach to Citizenship* Florence: European University Institute.

CARENS, Joseph (1989) 'Membership and morality: admission to citizenship in liberal democratic states' in **William Rogers Brubaker** editor, *Immigration and the Politics of Citizenship in Europe and North America* Lanham: German Marshall Fund of the United States/University Press of America.

CASTLES, Stephen (1994) 'Democracy and multi-cultural citizenship. Australian debates and their relevance for Western Europe' in **Rainer Bauböck** editor, *From Aliens to Citizens: Redefining the Status of Immigrants in Europe* Aldershot: Avebury.

CASTLES, Stephen and MILLER, Mark J. (1993) *The Age of Migration* Basingstoke: Macmillan.

COCKBURN, Cynthia (1996) 'Different together: women in Belfast', *Soundings* No. 2: 32–47.

COOTE, Anna and PATTULLO, Polly (1990) *Power and Prejudice* London: Weidenfeld & Nicolson.

DALE, Jennifer and FOSTER, Peggy (1986) *Feminists and State Welfare* London: Routledge & Kegan Paul.

DIETZ, Mary (1987) 'Context is all: feminism and theories of citizenship', *Daedalus* Vol. 116, No. 4: 1–24.

DOYAL, Len and GOUGH, Ian (1991) *A Theory of Human Need* Basingstoke: Macmillan.

EISENSTEIN, Zillah (1991) 'Privatising the state: reproductive rights, affirmative action and the problem of democracy', *Frontiers* Vol. 12, No. 1: 98–125.

ETZIONI, Amitai (1993) *The Spirit of Community* New York: Simon & Schuster.

FALK, Richard (1994) 'The making of global citizenship' in **Bart van Steenbergen** editor, *The Condition of Citizenship* London: Sage.

FEARON, Kate (1996) editor, *Power, Politics, Positionings: Women in Northern Ireland* Belfast: Democratic Dialogue.

FERREE, Myra Marx and MARTIN, Patricia Yancey (1995) editors, *Feminist Organisations: Harvest of the New Women's Movement,* Philadelphia: Temple University Press.

FRASER, Nancy (1987) 'Women, welfare and the politics of need interpretation', *Hypatia* Vol. 2, No. 1: 103–21.

FRASER, Nancy and NICHOLSON, Linda J. (1990) 'Social criticism without philosophy; an encounter between feminism and postmodernism' in **Linda J. Nicholson** editor, *Feminism/Postmodernism* London: Routledge.

GALEOTTI, Anna Elisabetta (1993) 'Citizenship and equality: the place for toleration', *Political Theory* Vol. 21, No. 4: 585–605.

GIDDENS, Anthony (1991) *Modernity and Self-Identity* Cambridge: Polity Press.

GORDON, Linda (1990) editor, *Women, the State and Welfare* Madison: University of Wisconsin Press.

GOULD, Carol (1988) *Rethinking Democracy* Cambridge: Cambridge University Press.

GUNEW, Sneja and YEATMAN, Anna (1993) *Feminism and the Politics of Difference* Australia: Allen & Unwin.

HAMMAR, Tomas (1990) *Democracy and the Welfare State* Aldershot: Avebury.

HARVEY, David (1993) 'Class relations, social justice and the politics of difference' in Squires (1993).

HEATER, Derek (1990) *Citizenship* London: Longman.

HELD, David (1995) *Democracy and the Global Order* Cambridge: Polity.

HERNES, Helga (1987) *Welfare State and Woman Power* Oslo: Norwegian University Press.

HEWITT, Martin (1994) 'Social policy and the question of postmodernism' in Robert Page and John Baldock editors, *Social Policy Review 6* Canterbury: Social Policy Association.

hooks, bell (1984) *Feminist Theory from Margin to Center* Boston, Mass.: South End Press.

HILL COLLINS, Patricia (1990) *Black Feminist Thought* London: Routledge.

HYATT, Susan (1992) *'Putting Bread on the Table' The Women's Work of Community Activism* Bradford: Work & Gender Research Unit.

JONES, Kathleen B. (1990) 'Citizenship in a woman-friendly polity', *Signs* Vol. 15, No. 4: 781–812.

—— (1994) 'Identity, action and locale: thinking about citizenship, civic action and feminism', *Social Politics* Vol. 1, No. 3: 256–70.

JOURNAL OF INTERNATIONAL COMMUNICATION (1996) 3(1) special issue on international feminism(s).

KEMP, Amanda, MADLALA, Nozizwe, MOODLEY, Madlala and SALO, Elaine (1995) 'The dawn of a new day: redefining South African feminism' in Amrita Basu editor, *The Challenge of Local Feminisms* Boulder, Colo., and Oxford: Westview Press.

KNOCKE, Wuokko (1995) 'Migrant and ethnic minority women: the effects of gender-neutral legislation in the European Community', *Social Politics*, Vol. 2, No. 2: 225–38.

KOFMAN, Eleonore and SALES, Rosemary (1992) 'Towards fortress Europe?', *Women's Studies International Forum* Vol. 15, No. 1: 29–39.

KOVEN, Seth and MICHEL, Sonya (1993) *Mothers of a New World* London: Routledge.

KYMLICKA, Will (1995) *Multicultural Citizenship: A Liberal Theory of Minority Rights* Oxford: Clarendon Press.

LECA, Jean (1992) 'Questions on citizenship' in Mouffe (1992).

LEISINK, Peter and COENEN, Harry (1993) 'Work and citizenship in the New Europe' in Harry Coenen and Peter Leisink (1993) editors, *Work and Citizenship in the New Europe* Aldershot: Edward Elgar.

LEWIS, Jane (1994) 'Gender, the family and women's agency in the building of "welfare states": the British case', *Social History* Vol. 19, No. 1: 37–55.

LISTER, Ruth (1990a) *The Exclusive Society. Citizenship and the Poor* London: Child Poverty Action Group.

—— (1990b) 'Women's economic dependency and citizenship', *Journal of Social Policy* Vol. 19, No. 4: 445–67.

—— (1993) 'Welfare rights and the constitution' in Anthony Barnett, Caroline Ellis and Paul Hirst editors, *Debating the Constitution* Cambridge: Polity.

—— (1994a) 'Social policy in a divided community: reflections on the Opsahl Report on the Future of Northern Ireland' *Irish Journal of Sociology* Vol 4: 27–50.

—— (1994b) ' "She has other duties" – women, citizenship and social security' in **Sally Baldwin** and **Jane Falkingham** editors, *Social Security and Social Change: New Challenges to the Beveridge Model* Hemel Hempstead: Harvester Wheatsheaf.

—— (1995) 'Dilemmas in engendering citizenship', *Economy and Society* Vol. 24, No. 1: 1–40.

—— (1997) *Citizenship: Feminist Perspectives* Basingstoke: Macmillan.

LORDE, Audre (1984) 'Age, race, class and sex: women redefining difference' reproduced in **Helen Crowley** and **Susan Himmelweit** (1992) editors, *Knowing Women* Cambridge: Polity/Open University Press.

LOVENDUSKI, Joni and RANDALL, Vicky (1993*) Contemporary Feminist Politics* Oxford: Oxford University Press.

MARQUAND, David (1991) 'Civic republicans and liberal individualists: the case of Britain', *Archive Européenne de Sociologie* Vol. 32: 329–44.

MARSHALL, T.H. (1950) *Citizenship and Social Class* Cambridge: Cambridge University Press.

MAYNARD, Mary (1994) ' "Race", gender and the concept of "difference" in feminist thought' in **Haleh Afshar** and **Mary Maynard**, *The Dynamics of 'Race' and Gender: Some Feminist Interpretations* London: Taylor & Francis.

MEAD, Lawrence (1986) *Beyond Entitlement: The Social Obligations of Citizenship* New York: The Free Press.

MOROKVASIC, Mirjana (1984) 'Birds of passage are also women', *International Migration Review* Vol. 18, No. 4: 886–907.

—— (1991) 'Fortress Europe and migrant women', *Feminist Review* No. 39: 69–84.

—— (1993) 'In and out of the labour market: immigration and minority women in Europe', *New Community* Vol. 19, No. 3: 459–83.

MOUFFE, Chantal (1992) editor, *Dimensions of Democracy* London: Verso.

—— (1993) *The Return of the Political* London: Verso.

NELSON, Barbara (1984) 'Women's poverty and women's citizenship: some political consequences of economic marginality', *Signs* Vol. 10, No. 21: 209–31.

NOVAK, Michael *et al.* (1987) *A Community of Self-Reliance: The New Consensus on Family and Welfare* Milwaukee: American Enterprise Institute for Public Policy Research.

OLDFIELD, Adrian (1990) *Citizenship and Community: Civic Republicanism and the Modern World* London: Routledge.

OLIVER, Mike and BARNES, Colin (1991) 'Discrimination, disability and welfare: from needs to rights' in **Ian Bynoe, Mike Oliver** and **Colin Barnes** *Equal Rights for Disabled People* London: Institute for Public Policy Research.

PAHL, Ray (1990) 'Prophets, ethnographers and social glue: civil society and social order' (mimeo: paper presented at the ESRC/CNRS Workshop on Citizenship, Social Order and Civilising Processes, Cumberland Lodge, September).

PAREKH, Bhikhu (1991) 'British citizenship and cultural difference' in **Geoff Andrews** editor, *Citizenship* London: Lawrence & Wishart.

PARRY, Geraint (1991) 'Conclusion: paths to citizenship' in **Ursula Vogel** and **Michael Moran** editors, *The Frontiers of Citizenship* Basingstoke: Macmillan.

PATEMAN, Carol (1989) *The Disorder of Women* Cambridge: Polity Press.

PHILLIPS, Anne (1991) *Engendering Democracy* Cambridge: Polity Press.

—— (1993) *Democracy and Difference* Cambridge: Polity Press.

RILEY, Denise (1992) 'Citizenship and the welfare state', in **John Allen, Peter Braham** and **Paul Lewis** editors, *Political and Economic Forms of Modernity* Cambridge: Polity Press.

ROCHE, Maurice (1992) *Rethinking Citizenship* Cambridge: Polity Press.

SARVASY, Wendy (1992) 'Beyond the difference versus equality policy debate: postsuffrage feminism, citizenship and the quest for a feminist welfare state', *Signs* Vol. 17, No. 2: 329–62.

SARVASY, Wendy and SIIM, Birte (1994) 'Gender, transition to democracy and citizenship', *Social Politics* Vol. 1, No. 3: 249–55.

SQUIRES, Judith (1993) editor, *Principled Positions* London: Lawrence & Wishart.

TAYLOR, David (1989) 'Citizenship and social policy', *Critical Social Policy* No. 26: 19–31.

TURNER, Bryan (1990) 'Outline of a theory of citizenship', *Sociology* Vol. 24, No. 2: 189–218.

TWINE, Fred (1994) *Citizenship and Social Rights* London: Sage.

VAN STEENBERGEN, Bart (1994) 'Towards a global ecological citizen' in **Bart van Steenbergen** editor, *The Condition of Citizenship* London: Sage.

VOGEL, Ursula (1988) 'Under permanent guardianship; women's condition under modern civil law' in **Kathleen B. Jones** and **Anna G. Jónasdóttir** editors, *The Political Interests of Gender* London: Sage.

WEALE, Albert (1991) 'Citizenship beyond borders' in **Ursula Vogel** and **Michael Moran** editors, *The Frontiers of Citizenship* Basingstoke: Macmillan.

WILLIAMS, Fiona (1989) *Social Policy: A Critical Introduction* Cambridge: Polity Press.

—— (1996) 'Postmodernism, feminism and the question of difference' in **Nigel Parton** editor, *Sociological Theory, Social Change and Social Work* London: Routledge.

WILSON, Angelia R. (1993) 'Which equality? Toleration, difference or respect' in **Joseph Bristow** and **Angelia Wilson** editors, *Activating Theory: Lesbian, Gay, Bisexual Politics* London: Lawrence & Wishart.

WOMEN AND CITIZENSHIP RESEARCH GROUP (1995) *Women and Citizenship: Power, Participation and Choice* Belfast: WCRG.

YEATMAN, Anna (1993) 'Voice and representation in the politics of difference' in **Gunew** and **Yeatman** (1993).

—— (1994) *Post-modern Revisionings of the Political* London: Routledge.

YOUNG, Iris Marion (1989) 'Polity and group difference: a critique of the ideal of universal citizenship', *Ethics* No. 99: 250–74.

—— (1990) *Justice and the Politics of Difference* Oxford: Princeton University Press.

—— (1993) 'Together in difference: transforming the logic of group political conflict' in **Squires** (1993).

YUVAL-DAVIS, Nira (1991) 'The citizenship debate: women, ethnic processes and the state', *Feminist Review* No. 39: 58–68.

—— (1994) 'Women, ethnicity and empowerment', *Feminism and Psychology* Vol. 4, No. 1: 179–97.

Enabling Citizenship:
Gender, disability and citizenship in Australia

Helen Meekosha and Leanne Dowse

FEMINIST REVIEW NO 57, AUTUMN 1997, PP. 49–72

Abstract

This paper queries the absence of disabled voices in contemporary citizenship literature. It argues that the language and imagery of the citizen is imbued with hegemonic normalcy and as such excludes disability. Feminist perspectives, such as those which argue for a form of maternal citizenship, largely fail to acknowledge disability experiences. Exclusionary practices are charted and links are made between gender, race and disability in this process. A citizenship which acknowledges disability is fundamental to re-imaging local, national and international collectivities.

Keywords

disability; citizenship; gender; Australia; international relations; racism

> Tomorrow I am going to rewrite the English Language.
> I will discard all those striving ambulist metaphors of power and success
> And construct new ways to describe my strength.
> My new different strength.
>
> (Lois Keith, 1994: 57)

The last decade has seen renewed academic interest in citizenship and the construction of an Australian identity, a growth which parallels increased public debate and government interest. Former Labor Prime Minister Paul Keating made a major commitment in June 1995 to a renewed and refined idea of citizenship in his attempts to lead Australia towards being a republic, while the Liberal/National Federal Coalition Government elected in March 1996, committed to a return to conservative values, pledged to create a nation in which people could feel 'secure'. The new Minister for Immigration was soon to describe the act of citizenship as 'the ultimate expression of a person's commitment to the nation' (Millett, 1996).

Mindful of the history of a nation built on the colonization of indigenous peoples and immigration, some sections of the Australian community are

FEMINIST REVIEW NO 57, AUTUMN 1997

now focused on the development of an inclusive identity and creation of a republic. At the same time contemporary feminist and progressive thinking has highlighted issues of race and gender[1] as crucial in contesting a white male space, raising simultaneously issues about inclusion, exclusion and co-option of those at the margins of civil society (Hunter, 1996: 60).

Disability is a feminist issue, but is largely ignored in citizenship debates. Disability is gendered, affecting men and women differentially. A process of exclusion, disability diminishes the well-being of both those affected and those, who consciously or unconsciously, participate in such a process. Women with disabilities/disabled women,[2] largely inhabiting these margins, may experience the illusion of inclusion. The public imagination conceives of most people with disabilities, especially women, as passive citizens. They represent a source of increasing demand for services in an environment of ever-diminishing state and public finances. Dominant ideologies within the disability arena are changing from welfare to rights, yet people with disabilities still do not appear as active members of the community. Forced to claim 'special rights', their status as citizens with existing rights (albeit unacknowledged/inaccessible) is negated. Paradoxically, the active citizenry that the current economic rationalist ideology in Australia calls into being requires the continuing existence in a state of dependency of recipients of charitable largesse who constitute a significant component of the group 'the cared for'.

Race, ethnicity, class or gender identity influence some of the major citizenship debates in Australia, such as the proposed rewriting of the Constitution, the formulation of a republic and the unequal representation of women in Parliament. These debates neglect disability and people with disabilities, yet hegemonic normalcy invests the very language and imagery of citizenship. We speak of upright and upstanding citizens, we stand to attention to the playing of the national anthem. The good citizen is embodied as male, white, active, fit and able, in complete contrast to the unvalued 'inactive' disabled Other.

Disability is a marginalized status in contemporary society, one that is nearly always described in negative and offensive language (Barnes, 1992: 42). The concept of a disabled citizen could be described as a contradiction in terms. The incarceration of some people with disabilities, particularly those with intellectual and/or psychiatric disabilities, has been and continues to be an act of denial of citizenship, through the loss of freedom without proof of guilt for the breach of any law; their bodies or minds constitute their crime. Ironically, the responsible citizen (male) who performs the supreme act of citizenship in fighting for his country may return disabled by war, transformed into a non-citizen and a burden on the state.

Figure 1 Citizenship campaign poster, Department of Immigration and Ethnic Affairs, Canberra 1995.

The struggle by the Vietnam veterans for recognition and inclusion in public life inspired the beginnings of the contemporary disability movement in the United States.

Yet disability is an essential element in understanding state and market agendas as well as political struggles around citizenship. Power and power relations are fundamental to the comprehension of the position of people with disabilities. To become disabled in contemporary Western society ensures a fundamental loss of political and economic power and status; people with disabilities are not players in the main game.[3] Individuals born with disabilities, particularly developmental disabilities, have usually had very limited access to any form of effective participation within civil society and are regarded as having little/no role in any of the public, private,

FEMINIST REVIEW NO 57, AUTUMN 1997

domestic or familial spheres. Disability challenges fundamental notions of normalcy and, thus, ironically may have great potency for widening citizenship debates. Simple binaries such as rights/duties, active/passive citizenship and exclusion/inclusion are inappropriate when viewed from a disability perspective because they contain within them unspoken assumptions that social relations are carried out by able-bodied individuals free to contest or follow civil mores.

People who experience disability find themselves propelled from the 'normal' range of taken-for-granted 'rights', into the realm of passivity and lack of agency. Downward social mobility and social status often converge with acquired disability status.[4] Since Athenian times, men with disabilities, along with women, slaves and so on, have been either excluded by law from citizenship status, physically prevented from taking any active role in democratic societies or indirectly constrained by discriminatory and oppressive institutions and ideologies. At one extreme they have been viewed as sub-human – 'freaks' – and, like some indigenous peoples, the objects of extermination policies, justified through 'scientific' discourses. Recently a more benevolent and enlightened approach has seen the construction of people with disabilities as fully human and 'capable' of some assimilation into mainstream society. This new approach remains problematic, especially in Australia under a conservative/radical right-wing government as the mainstream rapidly becomes the space inhabited, not by a plurality of diverse groups, but by those aligned to dominant male, white conservative and economic rationalist ideologies and interests.

Contemporary citizenship debates – are they relevant?

Contemporary debates around citizenship emerge from a number of different perspectives. First, a revival of interest in the Marshallian conception of rights within a liberal pluralist framework is coupled with a call for a renewed commitment to public and civic life from both Left and Right of the political spectrum. Second, critiques from feminists, progressive groups and social movements organizing around identity issues in the wake of the demise of class-based/trade-union political organizing have raised concerns about exclusive universalistic concepts. Third, these debates have occurred during the rise of fundamentalist groupings with ultra 'traditionalist' political agendas – from the Gun Lobby and Anti-Abortion Lobby in Australia and the USA to the emergent nationalisms in the former Eastern Bloc. Thus, the intensification/re-emergence of racism, religious fundamentalisms and outbreaks of violence/war globally have also prompted a reconceptualization of the meanings and multiple dimensions of democracy and civil society.

Rights and responsibilities . . .

A crisis of public confidence in the state has precipitated a revival of interest in civil society and communal responsibility. This parallels a fracturing of the body politic and a rise of self-centred individualism (Eisenstein, 1996). Marshall's conception of social, civil and political rights is being re-examined by the progressive groupings and feminists at a time of the demise of trade-union rights and the erosion of the welfare state. Meanwhile the conservative side of the political spectrum is keen to use the rights/duties debate to introduce notions of active and responsible citizens who are less dependent on the state, and less able, therefore, to make claims against the common weal.

Active citizenship calls on members of a collectivity to take seriously their responsibilities in addition to making claims regarding their rights. Calls abound for loyalty to a local, regional or national collectivity. Such calls raise difficult issues for those having competing or different communities or those having no obvious community of interests – this is often the case for people with disabilities living in relative isolation, including those who have been de-institutionalized. People with disabilities who have been taken into care by the state or removed from their parents do not have access to the resources associated with ties to kin and family. Moreover, many people with disabilities resist the pressure to return to the care of family; women may experience oppressive protection – an illusion of care. Tensions exist between the needs and rights of people with disabilities and the interests of those who care for them, often women kin. Yet, paradoxically, the family may sometimes provide a safe haven and support base for people with disabilities shunned by social institutions and locked out by discriminatory processes.

Those who are cared for by the state experience a different set of constraints dictated by changing trends in policy and service delivery. Opportunities to form communities of interest and support are often mediated by and dependent on paid carers and professionals whose role is primarily informed by the duty of care rather than an interest in promoting improved citizenship rights and democratic participation for the 'client'. Policies of de-institutionalization have contradictory and multiple intentions, ostensibly focusing on integration of people with disabilities into the wider society and away from enclaves or closed communities. Here, policies of normalization can operate to weaken communities of interest.

The concept of active citizenship poses further paradoxes for people with disabilities as they struggle for access in wider society and to ensure an implementation of their rights; for instance, they are not usually in a

FEMINIST REVIEW NO 57, AUTUMN 1997

position to undertake voluntary and community service which is seen as a defining indication of the active citizen. 'It's very hard for an oppressed group to take care of another oppressed group. I remember the bitterness of not being embraced by my sisters in the women's movement in the 1970s. . . . That's fair enough because you can only carry so much' (Interview Disability Activist, 17 July 1995).

Challenging exclusionary practices . . .

The foundation of the Australian nation state has been based on exclusionary practices imbued with eugenic ideologies. The philosophy of eugenics argues that polluted, dangerous and transgressive groups should not be allowed to reproduce. The most extreme form of this philosophy calls for the extermination of certain groups for fear of contaminating those deemed morally and physically superior. The primordial and savage image of the Aboriginal population under colonization justified policies of extermination. This genocide of the indigenous population in Australia and removal of children from their families to hasten the process is well documented (McGrath, 1995). The Australian Constitution written in 1901 excluded Aborigines from citizenship. Strategies to keep Australia a white European settlement included repatriation of indentured Kanak labour and the instigation of a White Australia policy at the beginning of the twentieth century (Markus, 1994). This racist policy, while arguably based originally on a commitment to equalitarianism among the white population and which continued to the mid-1960s, was designed to select those perceived as most fit for reproducing the population, those who could fulfil the needs of the labour market and would be most likely to adapt to British culture and norms. While these discriminatory policies have been formally abandoned, the Australian Migration Act (1958) continues to exclude other categories of people deemed unfit, namely those with 'physical' or 'mental' disabilities.

This is not a phenomenon unique to Australia. In the US in the early part of the century feebleminded migrants were excluded. Henry Goddard, an influential eugenicist visiting Ellis Island claimed that 79 per cent of Italian immigrants, 80 per cent of Hungarian immigrants, 83 per cent of Jewish immigrants and 87 per cent of Russian immigrants qualified under this category. Following this finding strict immigration legislation was introduced (Pfeiffer, 1994: 494). Discourses of race, ability/disability come together at this point in the exclusionary process. Women have historically migrated as partners to males and are seen as potential breeders of the nation; thus their capacities for these duties mean that they fall under an intensified scrutiny of the authorities.

After the ground-breaking referendum in 1967 which effectively resulted in the granting of citizenship to indigenous peoples in all of Australia, progressive groups have largely addressed issues of citizenship rights (as distinct from human rights) within the context of immigration. Australia has always been a country of high immigration yet only in the 1970s was there any recognition by governments of the serious disadvantage and discrimination experienced by ethnic groups. The ethnic rights movement opposed formal and informal areas of discrimination. Vigorous campaigning by ethnic and community groups regarding entry criteria (such as competence in English) and family reunions and access for same sex partners have resulted in a limited range of victories. However, services for newly arrived migrants – such as English classes, eligibility for social security benefits are constantly under threat by New Right governments, even though the organized ethnic lobby is committed to their defence. Many of these benefits were withdrawn from immigrants less than two years in the country in August 1996. In the same context, the concern of the state has been with ensuring that newly arrived groups and individuals learn to demonstrate loyalty to the Australian nation and assume an Australian identity that is not in conflict with their ethnic, religious or racial origins.

In the 1990s campaigning by feminist activists and academics together with the unearthing of the role of women in the establishment of the Australian nation state have brought forth a wider set of concerns relating to the absence of women's voices and women's issues (Lake, 1994; Bulbeck, 1996). Liberal notions of citizenship have been criticized for failing to include a diverse population differentiated by race, class, gender, age and other categories of difference (Pettman, 1996). Equally, discriminatory structures and systems have prevented many from gaining access to basic rights such as education, employment, housing, health and so on.

The debate over equal access to existing structures or the establishment of specific/different rights and responsibilities has been reflected in the broad church of feminist thought and political strategy. Feminist critiques have argued that, while the state overtly maintains a universality of values, they are derived from a masculine model which denies women's experiences (Young, 1989; Phillips, 1993). From a gendered perspective questions are raised about who is being asked/allowed to participate. Processes for participation are constantly being interrogated, although usually by women from the dominant collectivity. A fundamental flaw in the concept of citizen argued strongly by Pateman and others is the separation of the public from the private so that men's role in the workplace determines their citizenship while women have either been excluded or their contribution has not been counted (Pateman, 1989). In the Australian context, the citizenship role of white women has been described as being breeders of the nation (de Lepervanche, 1989). Women as mothers at certain times are included in what constitutes the nation and at other times are excluded (Pettman, 1996).

This separation of these spheres has not encompassed an examination of the situation of people/women with disabilities. Yet they often inhabit a unique space that hovers stateless, somewhere between the private and public sphere, while they remain a 'burden' in both. Conceived as having neither domestic nor familial responsibility nor public presence, the disabled person can be neither constituted in traditional masculinist terms nor embraced by feminist critiques which equate care-giving with responsibility as a form of citizenship. Maternal citizenship as an alternative to masculinist conceptions is given legitimacy within feminist discourse and politics by those arguing that women's experience of care could introduce a more humane dimension (Elshtain, 1981). Only when caring work is supported by men can we fully claim democratic citizenship (Cass, 1994). Yet maternal citizenship fails to comprehend the unequal power relationships inherent in care (Voet, 1994). In this context, arguing for special/particular rights for women, as a universal category, can conflict with the lived experiences of some women with disabilities, who have been subject to abuse in the hands of carers and parents (Mulder, 1996; Chenoweth, 1993). In the United States, despite the passage of the Americans with Disabilities Act – one of the more progressive pieces of legislation in the world, many states still retain legislation promulgating sterilization and segregation of disabled persons (Pfeiffer 1994: 495).

Gender, disability and denial of citizenship rights come together most starkly in the area of sexuality, reproductive and marriage rights. People with disabilities have been seen in some cultures as potentially disruptive of the race and nation – they constituted a threat to the gene pool. From the turn of the century until the present day medical experts, parliamentarians and academics have supported sterilization of certain groups (Goldhar, 1991). Despite normalization policies, women with disabilities, like, and sometimes as indigenous women, continue to be sterilized often as an alternative to education and contraception or as a form of menstrual management. The proposed cutbacks in health and welfare funding by the Federal government could mean that care in community group homes comes under more pressure and sterilization may become an easy option to regulate the behaviour of women with disabilities. This notion of sexual rights rewrites rights discourse. It redefines the relationship between public and private life because sexual rights break through the borders of patriarchal citizenry. A woman's control over her body becomes a fundamental human right (Eisenstein, 1996: 44).

While cases involving sterilization are in theory to be decided by the courts, in practice many operations are done covertly under the cover of other medical intervention. Men, particularly those with intellectual disabilities, are often portrayed as having an aggressive sexuality, preying on innocent non-disabled women, whereas women with disabilities may be seen as dangerously fertile – potential breeders of freaks and monsters. Not seen as having sexual desire or even being the objects of (male) desire – especially true for women who are positioned furthest away from the 'ideal' such as those with spasticity, women with disabilities have their bodies policed and are denied their reproductive rights. Policing the boundaries of citizenship and the nation incorporates the policing of disabled women's sexual freedom. The proposal by some feminists for a type of maternal citizenship is as problematic for women with disabilities as it is for Aboriginal women in Australia (McGrath, 1993: 104).

Yet, like women, and sometimes as women, people with disabilities contribute substantially to the public sphere. A massive industry has developed which sustains medical, human service, engineering, educational and training sectors. These industries have focused on the regulating of people with disabilities who provide the raison d'etre, but who often themselves have no status or access to their power. Recently the discourse of citizenship has expanded to encompass a wider range of rights and responsibilities. It has become more than a legal concept; it is a desirable activity within the context of generating new nationalist identities. A Civics Expert Group, established by the Federal Australian government examined opportunities for public education on civic issues (Civics Expert Group, 1994). These new public debates are troubling for many who are positioned on the margins, who, because of their gender, race, ethnicity class or disability, do not feel attachment to the notion of an Australian identity (Rowse, 1993; Curthoys, 1993; McGrath, 1993). Furthermore, globalization of economies, permeabilities of state boundaries and the universalizing of the market demand that we consider fundamental issues of inclusion and exclusion within both a national and international context (Pettman, 1996).

Race, community and nationalism . . .

With state boundaries simultaneously threatened by increasing globalization and the intensification of nationalistic projects, we are witnessing an acceleration and revival of the citizenship debate. Nationalism and disability interpenetrate in a variety of ways with a complex array of outcomes. Nationalist struggles can produce disabled citizens, and nationalism can seek deliberately to exclude disabled citizens from the newly

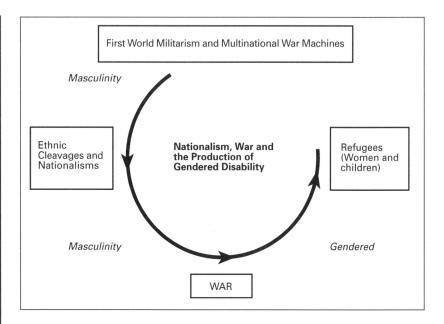

emerging state. On the other hand, people with disabilities can make claims for inclusion in a restructured collective life (Tollifson, 1985). People with disabilities have also actively constructed identities which parallel ethnicities and the making of separate cultures.

The rise of religious and ethnic fundamentalisms has been a major element in the production of war and violent conflict. Here gender differences have been noted; women are being accorded different rights from men at the same time as being vital to and symbolic of the reproduction of the collectivity (Anthias and Yuval-Davis, 1992; Pettman, 1996). But women in this context are assumed to be able bodied. Injured women and women with disabilities do not have these roles to play in the construction and reproduction of nationalist ideologies. They cannot symbolically signify the nation if they are not embodied as 'perfect' women. A gendered politics of nationalism needs to understand the interests of the dominant collectivity in disabling and destroy 'enemy' women who represent potential breeders of the inferior group. In many developing countries, as in the West, few men consider marrying a disabled woman. Afghanistan, Angola and Mozambique are examples of countries where recent conflict has left large numbers of the population with amputations, blindness and spinal cord injuries. Yet women and children are reported to receive less than 10 or 20 per cent of available rehabilitation services (UNICEF 1990, quoted in Heumann, 1991).

While war remains a major cause of disability on a global scale, links between revanchist nationalisms of the late twentieth century and production of disability remain unexplored. Yet a series of consequences flow from the hegemonic militarism exemplified by the US New World Order. First, war technologies and industries supported by countries such as the US and the UK are responsible for maiming and disabling millions of citizens world-wide. Second, first world imperialism, in a post-colonial world, stimulates ethnic cleavages in its own economic and political interests and supports insurgent nationalisms which lead to war (Moghadam, 1994). Third, war results in the dislocation of hundreds of thousands of peoples who become refugees, the majority of whom are women and children (estimated as 85 per cent) and many of whom are injured and disabled. Similar passive imagery is used to portray both refugees and/or women with disabilities. Both groups need to take control over their lives in terms of positive self-identity and social action, yet both groups are frequently rendered passive victims (Coleridge, 1993: 170).

Disabling women and children renders families economically disadvantaged. Land-mines injure women and children who are responsible for collecting firewood and food. The disability experience in developing countries makes travel and work exceptionally difficult and, once injured, these disabled war victims enter the category of persons deemed too expensive to be given refuge by the Western/rich countries which profited from their injuries. Most women refugees enter host nations as spouses, a process which places disabled women in extreme jeopardy. They are seen as neither productive nor potential citizens by the refugee-sponsoring nations. The 'illusion of inclusion' of people with disabilities needs to be set in a transnational context that identifies processes and ideologies beyond local and national boundaries.

The process of building/imagining ethnic and nationalist communities often actively seeks to exclude certain groups which threaten a sense of cohesiveness. A national community may encompass ideas of shared race, history, culture and language, as well as mythologies of blood lines, gene pools and kin. People with disabilities, often without a voice, are rarely included in these discourses. In the most extreme case, Nazi Germany, the first 'purification' was directed at people with disabilities – at first sterilization, then extermination. The nationalist project and disability are linked not only in the process of exclusion but also in the claiming of a political and social space. Davis (1995) traces the development of deaf communities who at the beginning of the nineteenth century were 'transnational' and were later forced into the status of an ethnic minority – a process of assimilation involving the destruction of their language and culture. At certain periods in history, the deaf sought to establish their own state, a strategy similar to that of other ethnic minorities suffering persecution (Davis, 1995: 84–5).

FEMINIST REVIEW NO 57, AUTUMN 1997

A disability perspective

De-institutionalization: care and control . . .

Developments in disability policy of the last decade have begun to address the marginalized status of people with disabilities. Beginning in the 1960s, initially in Scandinavia and then in the United States, a form of paternalistic reform emerged. Normalization particularly focused around people with intellectual disabilities. Albeit clothed in the language of a liberation movement, this philosophy, strongly influenced by emerging notions of individual rights, reconceptualized people with disabilities as subjects in their own lives rather than as objects of medical and social regimes of control. This new discourse paralleled other innovations in the human services areas (for example, in rehabilitative strategies in penology) and argued for 'de-institutionalization', directly attacking the large factory model of containment. It proposed a 'training' model, in which people with disabilities would as far as possible be 'socially educated' to adopt patterns of behaviour which would allow them to be accepted in the wider community.

These shifts have reconstituted people with disabilities as consumers of services, resulting in demands for changing practice around participation, choice and decision making. Yet, despite the pervasiveness of the new discourse, practice lags behind policy and people with disabilities continue to be locked into roles of recipients of services of questionable quality with inferior outcome measurements. The policy change has filtered down to the level of middle management in disability services but the experience of people with disabilities at the hands of direct service workers/carers has changed little (Shaddock et al., 1993).

While, at the level of official discourse, de-institutionalization has occurred on a major scale, we are now witnessing a different form of 'institutionalization' in community-based 'enclaves'. Citizenship as a right received lip service through the normalizing processes whereby restrictions on such activities as freedom of association and movement are supposedly removed by abolishing the spectre of the institution. But new controlling processes are now evident at lower levels in the power structure of the caring industry. Poorly supported and resourced direct-service workers often use questionable discretionary powers to determine rights and responsibilities of people with disabilities. Sexual and physical violence and abuse are a constant concern for both women workers and women residents in group homes and segregated living units. Researchers' estimates vary but it has been argued that between 68 and 99 per cent of women with intellectual disabilities will experience sexual exploitation by the age of 18 (cited in Mulder, 1996).

There is little evidence of democratic structures in group homes; the fundamental philosophy is grounded in a discourse of 'duty of care' rather than human and citizen rights. Residents remain dependent on workers to mediate social relationships either within the group home or within the public domain of shops and cafés. Here power/professional relationships still operate to limit full citizenship rights. These difficult and complex relations, with real potential for abuse as well as support, are not being addressed by that part of the feminist agenda which calls for women's caring work to be incorporated into reformulations of citizenship.

Rights and responsibilities

People with disabilities have been deprived either formally or informally in both historical and contemporary environments of most of the social, political and civil rights formulated by T.H. Marshall (see also Walmsley, 1993; Oliver, 1996). Despite the strength of the disability movement and the introduction of anti-discrimination legislation, most Western societies still formally prohibit/limit many people with disabilities from participation in a range of activities through legislation and administrative rulings. Examples of areas of formal exclusion cover the right to reproduce, parent or marry, immigrate, gain employment in the armed forces, access to superannuation and insurance and to the right to bequeath property and assets. These prohibitions differentially affect the person with a disability depending on their stage in the life-cycle, gender, race, ethnicity and type of disability.

The perversity of the situation is revealed in the requirement to demonstrate extreme 'incapacity' when seeking access to social rights, benefits and service provision, such as Child Disability Allowance. These rights are enshrined in a deficit model which directly contradicts the press towards 'independent' living which highlights 'capacity', thus revealing another contradictory facet of ideologies and practices of integration (Chenoweth, 1996).

Even where anti-discrimination legislation exists, as in Australia, people with a disability still have no legal rights to disability services. The provisions of the Disability Services Act 1986 (Commonwealth) focus instead on funding services and do not advance the representation of people with a disability, despite Australia being a signatory to the UN Declarations (Australian Law Reform Commission, 1996). Access to services is often dependent on receipt of income support – a process which severely disadvantages women who are often ineligible because of their husband's income (Meekosha, 1986; Australian Law Reform Commission, 1996).

FEMINIST REVIEW NO 57, AUTUMN 1997

Fundamental responsibilities and privileges (*sic*) of a citizen as outlined in the Australian Government's official application form for naturalization can be summarized as:

- political participation; realized through the ballot box (voting is mandatory in Australia) and standing for public office,
- defending the nation/state,
- and jury duty (Commonwealth of Australia, 1995: 6).

While these rights and responsibilities do not encompass the broader commonly understood social and civil rights and responsibilities, they provide a useful starting point for critiques of what constitutes normalcy in the citizenship debate.

The Australian Government's Disability Strategy (Commonwealth of Australia, 1994), a ten-year planning framework for Commonwealth agencies to ensure access to all programmes, services and functions for people with a disability, identified citizenship as a target area. Issues identified are constructed around the right of access to formal mechanisms of democratic governance, which include standing (sic) for election, serving in public office and voting. Physical access and preparation of materials in alternative formats were identified as areas for action, but no consideration was given to the more complex concerns of other barriers, in particular those for people with intellectual and psychiatric disabilities.

> It gets down to almost the lowest common denominator factor . . . the words that are in the strategy are words that are going to be acceptable to a wide range of [government] departments. [Words] that weren't going to arouse so much opposition. . . . It's a compromise.'
>
> (Interview Roger Barston – Head, Commonwealth Office of Disability 16 November 1995)

Our preliminary investigations concerning the mechanisms and educational opportunities that may exist for people with disabilities, to exercise and understand their right to elect representatives in the Australian context, met with a host of unknowns. No formal exclusion of people with intellectual and/or psychiatric disabilities from the voting process (other than apparent issues of physical access) exists, yet 'capacity' is used as the determining yardstick. In practice, if there is some doubt about a person's capacity, then the onus to prove the incapacity is on the electoral officer. Yet the issue is clearly more complex. How does a person with a disability demonstrate 'capacity' to vote if they are not encouraged to learn about the issues and offered appropriate political and civic education? Arguments about 'capacity' and 'deficiency' echo turn of the century struggles for suffrage by women in the West. Disability is not only gendered, but feminized.

Thus a person with an intellectual disability can execute their right to vote only with extreme difficulty. The act of voting is perhaps not the most pressing problem; rather, it is education for participation in the political process which is woefully absent. Unlike Britain, there is no visible representation of people with disabilities in the Australian parliament and, while major political parties address issues of female representation in pre-selection, and calls for equal representation of men and women in Parliament are at the forefront of feminist claims, there is no evidence to suggest any effort will be made to recruit women with disabilities to the cause of equity.

Being on the electoral roll leads to a series of other responsibilities such as jury duty. In New South Wales, juries are chosen by the Sheriff's Office which creates a pool of possible members from the electoral roll. Thus, most people with intellectual disabilities are excluded from the outset because they generally do not register to vote. Furthermore people with disabilities can be disqualified due to illness or infirmity. Ostensibly there is nothing preventing a person with a disability from serving so long as they are 'prepared to undergo hardship; no facilities are currently available for people with sensory disabilities, most courts are old and inaccessible'. Therefore it remains 'too hard' for such people to serve on a jury (Personal Communication, NSW Sheriff's Office, 16 May 1996).

Lists of potential jurors are then subjected to the challenge of the legal representatives as to whether they are deemed acceptable to serve. People with intellectual disabilities are over-represented both in the criminal justice system and in the prison population in Australia. Female prisoners with intellectual disability appear more likely than males to also have a further disability such as a psychiatric diagnosis (New South Wales Law Reform Commission, 1993). Following massive de-institutionalization prisons now provide some of the only long-term supervised care. People with disabilities are also systematically being denied the right to be tried by a jury of their peers. These trends are comparable with the situation for Aboriginal people in Australia; one particular study demonstrates that issues of race compound issues of disability. In two rural courts in New South Wales with a high Aboriginal populations, it was found that more than one third of those appearing were intellectually disabled and a further 20 per cent were borderline, indicating that over half would have difficulty in understanding the court processes (New South Wales Law Reform Commission, 1996).

While the Australian Disability Discrimination Act 1992 (Commonwealth) has been welcomed by disability activists and hailed as one of the most important initiatives by government, discriminatory provisions exempting migration met with little resistance at the time of passage. Neither ethnic groups nor disability groups mounted significant opposition. According to the Disability Commissioner the exemptions were conceded as a strategy for ensuring the passage of the legislation. Interviewed in 1993 about whether the issue was on the agenda for imminent scrutiny she agreed: 'Yes, I don't know what impact I can have on it. It will be on my personal agenda, but on the backburner' (Slee, 1993: 10). In 1996, she described the exemption as 'repellent', but admitted she had never spoken to the Minister for Immigration and Ethnic Affairs about the matter.[5]

Under the Migration Act 1958, entry can be denied on the basis that the person would require significant care or treatment or require the use of community resources in short supply or would be unable to pursue an intended occupation or result in being a *significant* (our italics) charge on public funds. Clearly the intent is to restrict many persons with disabilities from settlement in Australia. The meaning of significant is contentious, leaving assessment of the person and their capacities open to subjective interpretation. Most community resources are in short supply, given continuing fiscal crises, making exclusion a *fait accompli* in most cases.

More importantly, there is an implicit assumption that disability is an individual attribute, adhering to the strictly medical model of disability, rather that seeing disability as largely socially constructed – a form of oppression. Thus the potential of people with disabilities to participate and contribute to civil society remains unrecognized, marginalized and under-utilized. Costs (medical and/or health) legitimate the exclusion of people with disabilities. Yet all immigrants bring with them potential social infrastructure costs, as well as contributions to civil society. While the White Australia policy which sought to preserve racial homogeneity had disappeared into history, the remaining prescribed requirements of the Migration Act constitute a seemingly immoral and insupportable continuation of a very similar philosophy.

Other exemptions listed in the DDA, such as employment in the armed forces, rights to superannuation and insurance policies and the provision of some telecommunication services such as pay phones, suggest a lack of real commitment to full citizenship and a continuation of a paternalistic/protective approach. Citizenship as yet encompasses an imagining of neither a fully participating disabled citizen nor a fully representative political sphere. This parallels much contemporary social policy and government-funded research which still focuses on the needs and costs of the provision of services for people with disabilities, not on their political and social rights and contributions (for example, Fine, 1995).

Another dimension of neglect includes failure to make reasonable accommodation to the disabled person's experience of the world. These issues are barely canvassed in debates around political, social and civil rights. The report into Civics and Citizenship Education (Civics Expert Group, 1994) while addressing groups with 'special needs' reduces people with disabilities to simple access needs – the development of materials for visually and hearing impaired people. People with disabilities might, given the opportunity, articulate a different conception of/or relationship to citizenship from that of the dominant groups. Their only relationship to citizenship is that problematized by sensory capacities. An indication of the group's level of commitment to an exploration of these issues is reflected in the lack of any submissions (180 received in total) from either community-based or government disability organizations. The concept of 'capacity' for citizenship, influenced by medical discourse, remains a major hurdle in the liberation of people with disabilities.

Challenging exclusionary practices . . .

People with disabilities experience a sense of community most widely when taking action against oppression. But shared stigmatization as disabled can be a limited basis for the development of community, despite attempts by some people with disabilities and some specific groups to articulate a culture of disability. Most notably, the deaf community in Australia have sought to constitute themselves as an ethnic group – qualifying for the same rights as other non-English speaking and culturally and linguistically diverse communities under a National Language Policy. Here, demands for inclusion into a mainstream multicultural society can leave others excluded in the process – for example, those with hearing impairments who do not sign and those deemed to be without cultural capital and/or potential for integration into economic relations/exploitation, such as those who have severe communication disabilities.

Disability movements have provided a sense of community as well as a focal organizing point for some people with disabilities. People with disabilities in Western countries have successfully organized for basic human rights – such as the right to an income and the right to an education – and form an increasingly important and vocal minority. Social movements emerge from a common need to raise a voice against hegemonic power structures, but at the same time are characterized by a heterogeneous group of individuals with a variety of experiences and differential needs. Power struggles within the disability movement result in some groups with less voice – such as those with intellectual disabilities and/or women – being marginalized. Not only do class, race, ethnicity and gender hierarchies

FEMINIST REVIEW NO 57, AUTUMN 1997

operate, but levels of pain, mobility and energy can militate against the involvement of women who are more likely to have chronic illnesses than men (Meekosha, 1986, 1990; Crow, 1996).

The Australian DDA, introduced following the success of the Americans with Disabilities Act, has been an important advance for people with disabilities in securing rights, such as access to public places, services and facilities. Using the DDA and against much opposition from the major telecommunications company, the deaf and the disability movements were successful in getting the Commonwealth Government to fund a tele-type-writer (TTY) relay system. This provides a telephone operator link between TTY users and other telephone users (Australian Association of the Deaf, Disabled People's International (Australia) Ltd. (1995) v. Telstra Corporation Ltd. H94/34). This ruling constitutes an important milestone in realizing the citizenship rights of disabled and/or deaf women, given the well-documented links between gender and telephone usage. Women are greater users of public transport than men. The action by the South Australian disability movement to require TransAdelaide to purchase accessible buses will have significant benefits in ensuring mobility rights for women.

However, the legislation is complaints-driven, ultimately putting the onus on those who experience discrimination to take action. Until such action is taken many employers and public institutions will not voluntarily undertake measures such as the construction of buildings and the design of work practices to accommodate people with disabilities. A crucial number of provisions in the legislation restrict the citizenship rights of people with disabilities. A fundamental provision allowing 'unjustifiable hardship' – a vague concept at best – as a reason for non-compliance with the objectives of the Act is problematic. Here again people with disabilities become reduced to the category of individual burdens on society and its institutions.

For women, the DDA raises a number of issues. There is the inevitable danger of complainants falling between the Sex Discrimination Act (SDA) and the DDA. Informal mechanisms of discrimination are far more likely to affect women than men. While women with disabilities struggle against stereotypes, community attitudes suggest traditional roles for women are seen as the most appropriate (Meekosha and Dowse, 1997). Entry into the world of education or paid work is still discouraged by many parents, rehabilitation workers and charities in their portrayal of achievement for women as limited to managing a domestic role. A letter seeking public financial assistance from the Multiple Sclerosis Society of New South Wales during the traditional Christmas giving season of 1995 described the situation of 'Anne', a sole parent thus: 'With a little help from the MS Society Anne is able to chain herself to the kitchen sink and still count her blessings.'

Conclusions

What price might have to be paid by people with disabilities if they engage with the increasing demands by marginalized groups to be included in what may effectively constitute token negotiations around citizenship? How do we begin to rewrite the story of what it might mean to be a disabled citizen, where the language of activity, productivity and capacity become transformed? The discourse of rights driven by disability activists rarely ventures into the difficult waters of responsibilities and contributions to civil society by all people with disabilities – a society that may well be structured very differently with the benefit of a disability perspective. Western political thought may be incapable of adapting to the existence of groups of citizens outside the economic rationalist agenda, people who may never sell their labour power in a competitive market place in the 'national economic interest'. Women, often constituted as outside the public sphere, remain even more so if disabled. We need a redefinition/re-negotiation of the public that incorporates groups of disabled citizens granted social and welfare rights and benefits, but not classified as passive recipients. The significant contribution of people with disabilities, in particular women, to the well being and diversity of the human experience are rarely documented and resist quantification in the language and practices of managerialism, 'core' family values and economics.

A citizenship that acknowledges people with disabilities is fundamental to a re-imagining of local, national and international collectivities. It is clear that the introduction of rights legislation is a necessary but not sufficient step to the achievement of this goal. Equally, current critiques from the margins which attempt to encompass difference are limited by their failure to examine the concept of a 'normal functioning' citizen and the institutions that assume such a citizen as the norm. Here, the concept of normalcy has to be challenged or the marginalization of people with disabilities will continue to be justified.

Women with disabilities cannot be part of a wider citizenry when they are subject to charitable works which require their continuing subordination. Until the unearthing of the histories, cultures and contributions of women/people with disabilities throughout history occurs, the narratives of disability will tend to be dominated by the perspectives of the able-bodied majority. Feminist critiques need to carefully examine concepts of citizenship which similarly may either exclude women with disabilities, as

FEMINIST REVIEW NO 57, AUTUMN 1997

in maternal citizenship, or necessitate their categorization as objects of others' caring work. The issue then, is to develop strategies which clearly articulate the range of experiences of women/people with disabilities and allow for a detailing of the measures necessary for their effective participation and empowerment.

Notes

This paper is part of a larger project on Disability, Representation and Participation and we are grateful for the ideas of many people with disabilities and workers in disability rights. Specifically, we are grateful to Shaun Keays Byrne of the NSW Intellectual Disability Rights Service, Sydney, for advice on some aspects of this paper.

Helen Meekosha teaches in the School of Social work at the University of New South Wales in Sydney and is currently working on a book for Sage, *Body Battles: Disability, Representation and Participation*.

Leanne Dowse is researching the social relations of severe communication impairments for a PhD at the School of Social Work at the University of New South Wales.

1 While this paper uses a feminist perspective, the paucity of research in the area of citizenship, rights and disability often makes it impossible to disaggregate research data by gender.

2 The terminology used in this paper is that preferred by the majority of people active in the disability movement in Australia. Language is never neutral and is an issue of much debate within the disability movement (see, for example, Pfeiffer, 1993). The description of the category of people who are the subject of this paper varies within and between societies. In the UK many disability activists use 'disabled people' as the preferred term, seeing in it a reference to social oppression of disablement, and thus an escape from the language of medicalization or rehabilitation. In Australia, the movement uses 'people with disabilities' both to place the emphasis on the individual as a person and to acknowledge the multiple identities that individuals can have – gender, race, ethnicity, etc. – rather than privileging disability status.

3 Disability is a culturally and historically determined phenomenon. For example, among the Native American Navajo people, disabled people are apparently accorded citizenship rights, that is, their disability is seen as part of the self, not as a deficiency. There is a tolerance of potentially disruptive behaviour and there is respect for individuality and autonomy. This is changing with the introduction of western diseases and western notions of aetiology (Connors and Donnellan, 1993). On the other hand, Franklin D. Roosevelt engaged in sustained subterfuge to hide his level of disability and thus retain the status and power of the premier citizen of the United States.

4 Jenkins (1991) points out that disability is a factor related to class and occupation, but also independent of labour market processes and class relations. Thus disability is a factor in stratification sui generis (575). Enforced dependency is a critical element in disability status.

5 Interview with Commissioner Hastings 28 Feb. 1996.

References

ANTHIAS, F. and YUVAL DAVIS, N. (1992) *Racialized Boundaries: Race, Nation, Gender, Colour and Class and the Anti-racist Struggle* London: Routledge.

AUSTRALIAN FEMINIST STUDIES (1994) Special issue on Women and Citizenship, Autumn.

BARBALET, J. (1988) *Citizenship: Rights, Struggle and Class Inequality* Milton Keynes: Open University Press.

BARNES, C. (1992) *Disabling Imagery and the Media: An Exploration of the Principles for Media Representations of Disabled People* Halifax: British Council of Organisations of Disabled People.

BARNES, C. and MERCER, G. (1996) *Exploring the Divide: Illness and Disability* Leeds: The Disability Press.

BARTON, L. 'The struggle for citizenship: the case of disabled people', *Disability, Handicap and Society* Vol. 8, No. 3: 235–48.

BOCK, G. and JAMES, S. (1992) *Beyond Equality and Difference: Citizenship, Feminist Politics and Female Subjectivity* London: Routledge.

BROWNE, S., CONNORS and STERN (1985) editors, *With the Power of Each Breath: A Disabled Women's Anthology*, Pittsburgh: Cleis Press.

BULBECK, C. (1996) '"His and hers Australias": national genders' in Hoorn and Goodman (1996).

CANBERRA: AUSTRALIAN GOVERNMENT PUBLISHING SERVICE *Making Rights Count, Services for people with a disability*, Report No. 79, Australian Government Publishing Service, Canberra.

CASS, B. (1994) 'Citizenship, work and welfare: the dilemma for Australian women', *Social Politics* Vol. 1, No. 1.

CHAPPELL, A. (1992) 'Towards a sociological critique of the normalization principle', *Disability, Handicap and Society* Vol. 7, No. 1: 35–51.

CHENOWETH, L. (1993) 'Invisible acts: violence against women with disabilities', *Australian Disability Review* Vol. 2: 22–8.

—— (1996) 'Re parents and professionals', posting to listserve: disability-research@mailbase.ac.uk, 29 August.

CIVICS EXPERT GROUP (Australia) (1994) *Whereas the People: Civics and Citizenship Education* Canberra: Australian Government Publishing Service.

COLERIDGE, P. (1993) *Disability, Liberation and Development* Oxford: Oxfam.

COMMONWEALTH OF AUSTRALIA (1994) *Disability Strategy: A Ten Year Framework for Commonwealth Departments and Agencies* Canberra: Office of Disability.

—— (1995) 'Application for grant of Australian citizenship' Department of Immigration and Ethnic Affairs.

CONNORS, J. and DONNELLAN, A. (1993) 'Citizenship and culture: people with disabilities in Navajo Society', *Disability, Handicap and Society* Vol. 8, No. 3: 265–80.

CROW, L. (1996) 'Including all of our lives: renewing the social model of disability' in **Barnes** and **Mercer** (1996).

CURTHOYS, A. (1993) 'Feminism, citizenship and national identity', *Feminist Review* Vol. 44: 19–38.

DE LEPERVANCHE, M. (1984) 'Breeders for Australia: a national identity for women?', *Australian Journal of Social Issues* Vol. 24, No. 3: 163–81.

DIETZ, M. (1985) 'Citizenship and maternal thinking' *Political Theory* Vol. 13, No. 1: 19–37.

—— (1992)'Context is all: feminism and theories of citizenship', in **Mouffe** (1992).

EISENSTEIN, Z. (1996) 'Women's publics and the search for new democracies' paper delivered at the Women and Citizenship Conference, London, July.

ELSHTAIN, J. (1981) *Public Man, Private Woman* Princeton, NJ: Princeton University Press.

FINE, M. (1995) 'Community-based services and the fragmentation of provision: a case study of home and community care services in a suburban community', *Australian Journal of Social Issues* Vol. 30, No. 2: 143–61.

GOLDHAR, J. (1991) 'The sterilization of women with an intellectual disability', *University of Tasmania Law Review* Vol. 10: 157–96.

HEUMANN J. (1991) 'How women with disabilities can advance into the mainstream of society', *Australian Disability Review* Vol. 3: 65–90.

HOORN, J and GOODMAN, D. (1996) editors, *Vox Republicae: Feminism and the Republic* a special edition of the *Journal of Australian Studies*.

HUNTER, R. (1996) 'Working the Republic: some feminist reflections', in **Hoorn** and **Goodman** (1996).

JENKINS, R. (1991) 'Disability and social stratification', *British Journal of Sociology* Vol. 42, No. 4: 557–80.

KEITH, L. (1994) editor, *Mustn't Grumble* London: The Women's Press.

KYMLICKA, W and NORMAN, W. (1994) 'Return of the citizen: a survey of recent work on citizenship theory', *Ethics* Vol. 104, No. 2: 352–81.

LAKE, M. (1994) 'A republic for women', *Arena Magazine* Vol. 9: 32–3.

LARRABEE, M. (1993) editor, *An Ethic of Care* London: Routledge.

LISTER, R. (1991) 'Citizenship engendered', *Critical Social Policy* Vol. 11, No. 2: 65–71.

—— (1995) 'Dilemmas in engendering citizenship', *Economy and Society* Vol. 24, No. 1: 1–40.

McGRATH, A. (1993) 'Beneath the skin: Australian citizenship, rights and Aboriginal women', *Journal of Australian Studies* Vol. 27: 99–114.

—— (1995) *Contested Ground: Australian Aborigines under the British Crown* Sydney: Allen & Unwin.

MARKUS, A. (1994) *Australian Race Relations 1788–1993* Sydney: Allen & Unwin.

MEEKOSHA, H. (1986) *Breaking In and Breaking Out: A Study of Women, Disability and Rehabilitation* Canberra: Dept. of Community Services.

—— (1990) 'Is feminism able-bodied? Reflections from between the trenches' *Refractory Girl* August.

MEEKOSHA, H. and DOWSE, L. (1997) 'Distorting images, invisible images: gender, disability and the media' *Media International Australia*, forthcoming.

MILLETT, M. (1996) 'Plans to change citizenship oath' *Sydney Morning Herald* 25 January.

MOGHADAM, V. (1994) *Gender and National Identity: Women and Politics in Muslim Societies* London: Zed.

MOUFFE, C. (1992) *Dimensions of Radical Democracy: Pluralism, Citizenship, Community* London: Verso.

MULDER, L. (1996) *Reclaiming Our Rights* Sydney: NSW Department for Women.

NEW SOUTH WALES LAW REFORM COMMISSION (1993) *People with an Intellectual Disability and the Criminal Justice System: Appearances Before Local Courts* New South Wales Law Reform Commission Research Report 4.

—— (1996) *People with An Intellectual Disability and the Criminal Justice System: Two Rural Courts* Sydney: New South Wales Law Reform Commission Research Report 5.

OLIVER, M. (1996) *Understanding Disability: From Theory to Practice* London: Macmillan.

PATEMAN, C. (1989) *The Disorder of Women: Democracy, Feminism and Political Theory* Cambridge: Polity.

—— (1988) *The Sexual Contract* Stanford, Calif.: Stanford University Press.

PETTMAN, J. (1992) *Living in the Margins* Sydney: Allen & Unwin.

—— (1996) *Worlding Women: A Feminist International Politics* Sydney: Allen & Unwin.

PFEIFFER, D. (1993) 'The problem of disability definition', *Journal of Disability Policy Studies* Vol. 4, No. 2: 77–82.

PHILLIPS, A. (1991) *Engendering Democracy* Cambridge: Polity.

—— (1993) *Democracy and Difference* Cambridge: Polity.

RILEY, D. (1992) 'Citizenship and the welfare state' in J. Allen *et al.* (eds.) *Political and Economic Forms of Modernity* Cambridge: Polity, pp. 179–228.

ROWSE, T. (1993) 'Diversity in indigenous citizenship' in G. Hage and L. Johnson editors, *Republicanism/Citizenship/Community, (Communal/Plural 2)* Kingswood, NSW: Research Centre in Intercommunal Studies, pp. 47–64.

SHADDOCK, A., RAWLINGS, M. and GUGGENHIEMER, S. (1993) 'To soy or not to soy? An exploratory study of choice making in a community group home', *Australian Disability Review* Vol. 4: 59–66.

SILVERS, A. (1995) 'Reconciling equality to difference: caring (f)or justice for people with disabilities', *Hypathia* Vol. 10, No. 1: 30–55.

SLEE, R. (1993) 'Interview with Commissioner Elizabeth Hastings', *Australian Disability Review* Vol. 1: 4–13.

SWAIN, J., OLIVER, M., FRENCH, S. and FINKELSTEIN, V. (1993) editors, *Disabling Barriers, Enabling Environments* London: Sage.

TOLLIFSON, J. (1985) 'Nicaragua: a victory for disabled women' in **Browne** *et al.* (1985).

TUCKER, B. (1994) 'Overview of the Disability Discrimination Act and comparison with the Americans with Disabilities Act', *Australian Disability Review* Vol. 3: 23–37.

VOET, R. (1994) 'Women as citizens – a feminist debate', *Australian Feminist Studies* 61–77.

WALMSLEY, J. (1993) ' "Talking to top people': some issues relating to the citizenship of people with learning difficulties', in **Swain** *et al.* (1993).

WATSON, S. *et al.* (1993) 'Symposium on disability policy part one: disability issues in public policy', *Policy Studies Journal* Vol. 21, No. 4: 720–800.

YOUNG, I. (1989) 'Polity and group difference: a critique of the idea of universal citizenship', *Ethics*.

—— (1990) *Justice and the Politics of Difference* Princeton, NJ: Princeton University Press.

The Public/Private – The Imagined Boundary in the Imagined Nation/State/Community:

The Lebanese case

Suad Joseph

FEMINIST REVIEW NO 57, AUTUMN 1997, PP. 73–92

Abstract

The nation/state as an imaginative enterprise encompasses multiple imagined sub-national boundaries. The 'public/private', I suggest, is a 'purposeful fiction' constitutive of the will to statehood. As such, its configurations are impacted upon by the institutions and forces competing with and within state-building enterprises. Proposing the terms government, non-government and domestic as analytical tools to demarcate discursive and material domains, I argue that, in Lebanon, the fluidity of boundaries among these spheres is constitutive of patriarchal connectivity, a form of patriarchal kinship linked to the state-building enterprise.

Keywords

public/private; gender; citizenship, patriarchy; selfhood; Lebanon

Imagine all the people

The nation/state, as an imaginative enterprise, encompasses multiple imagined subnational boundaries.[1] A number of feminist theorists have argued that the 'public/private' boundary and its gendering are products of state-level societies (Reiter, 1975; Joseph, 1975, 1983; Gailey, 1987). I argue in this paper that the public/private divide, central to classical Western constructs of citizenship and nation/statehood, is also constructed as an imaginative enterprise. Adapting Gauri Viswanathan's (1995: 31) phrase, I suggest that it is a 'purposeful fiction' constitutive of the will to statehood. Thus, not only does the site, porousness and shape of the public/private divide vary from state to state and time to time, but these configurations are impacted upon by institutions and forces competing with and within state-building projects.

I use Lebanon as a case study of the culturally and historically specific dynamics at play in the imaginative state-building enterprise that leads to different

constructions of the public/private under different sociopolitical circumstances. I argue that in Lebanon the boundaries have been porous and fluid,
in part, because of the centrality of patriarchal kinship structures, modes of
operation and idioms in all spheres of social life. The continuity of patriarchal kinship structures, modes and idioms with other spheres, is constitutive
of the Lebanese state-building project. Patriarchal kinship is valorized in
social, cultural, religious, economic and political practices. It is encoded in the
constitution. The elevation of religious family law to public law, which constructs a legal pluralism constitutive of the sectarian pluralism authorizing
élite rule, further codifies patriarchal kinship. While many of the dynamics I
describe are not unique to Lebanon, their confluence with each other and with
a culturally specific form of patriarchy that I call patriarchal connnectivity,
linked to a particular construct of selfhood, produces culturally and historically specific dynamics linked to the Lebanese state-building enterprise.

In Western political discourses, the purposeful fiction of the public/private
divide has served as an enabling metaphor in conjunction with other state-
elaborated notions of boundary such as the individualized citizen (Joseph,
1994a), the social and sexual contract (Pateman, 1988), citizen rights
(Nedelsky, 1990, 1993; Sullivan, 1995), civil society (Keane, 1988a; Seligman, 1992; Sadowski, 1993; Joseph, 1993a, in press; Young, 1987) and
democracy (Keane, 1988b; Phillips, 1991). The public/private divide has
been instrumental also in the gendering, as well as racialization (Williams,
1991; Eisenstein, 1994), of state and nation (Yuval-Davis and Anthias,
1989; Joseph, 1996). Western classical liberalism has presumed the universal necessity of differentiated public/private spheres for the development of citizenship, civil society and democratic nation statehood. It has
so abnormalized and dysfunctionalized continuities of structures, modes
of operation and idioms of discourse between the spheres (Benn and Gaus,
1983; Keane, 1988a, 1988b; Seligman, 1992) that many Western political
theorists have faulted the 'inadequacies' of boundaries between public and
private for the limitations on democratic citizenship (Sadowski, 1993).

Western feminist preoccupation with the public/private divide developed
in part because of its gendering in the formative period of the second wave
of feminism (Rosaldo and Lamphere, 1974; Elshtain, 1981). Feminist
activists as well as academics have found the notion of the public/private
divide useful. The public/private has been the bedrock for critiques of
domestic patriarchy and liberal feminists' strategic efforts to mobilize the
legislative and judicial powers of the state to intervene on behalf of women
in private spheres and to create equitable public spaces.

That the valorization of a boundary between public and private is not as
prominent in the discourses and practices of citizenship and nation/

state-making in many Southern societies, however, suggests a need for closer examination of the diverse histories of the public/private divide. My examination of the historical and cultural specificity of these divides, though, should not be read as a willingness to compromise on the advances in civil rights achieved through a differentiation of spheres. Nor is my purpose to create yet another binary – Western versus Southern discourses or practices concerning the public/private, citizenship, kinship or personhood. Neither the 'West' nor the 'South' are homogeneous categories. Many of my observations about Southern states are relevant to parts of 'the West' or do not apply to all the 'South.' I use 'West' to refer to the historical origins of the classical liberal discourses of citizenship and the relatively modern construction and gendering of the public/private divide. I use 'South' to refer to postcolonial states whose state boundaries, institutions and constitutions have been impacted by the colonial experience. While both categories may disintegrate on close interrogation, they are useful to refer to the genealogies of contemporary political discourses.

Similarly, the categories of public/private, citizen, family and individual – important abstractions in political theory and law – do not translate directly to the lived experiences of women or men in the 'West' or 'South'. The public/private are not as separate in reality in the West as Western classical liberal discourse would imagine. The citizen may be an abstracted, contractual, self-possessive, autonomous male in political discourse, yet real men in the West may not approximate this abstraction. The Western state and civil society may be distinct not only from each other, but from religion and patriarchal kinship in legal theory, yet state and civil society may be shot through with religious and patriarchal idioms, moralities and practices; while religion and patriarchal kinship may be shot through with state and political regulations and procedures. Nevertheless, as analytical tools, concepts such as state, kinship, citizenship, personhood are useful for discerning differences in the ways in which culturally specific constructs are understood, valued and played out.

All boundaries and categories are sites of struggle. Rarely is there consensus on the meanings of boundaries and categories. Rarely is there homogeneity on any side of a divide. Boundary making is about difference making for purposes of empowering or disempowering. As Sullivan (1995:128) observes, 'The demarcation of public and private life within society is an inherently political process that both reflects and reinforces power relations, especially the power relations of gender, race, and class.'

My purpose is to suggest historically and culturally specific analyses of the multiple realities and struggles concerning political community, citizenship and gender and the deployment of metaphors of boundary in these projects. Citizenship comes to be gendered in historically and culturally specific ways as the imagined public/private in the imagined nation/state shifts and transforms in the competitive and collaborative encounters of situated persons and collectivities. The public/private is an imagined divide which enables critical moves in law and social arrangements impacting citizenship, but does not correspond neatly with the lived experience of daily life in any state, Western or Southern. Yet, often there is a slippage between the imagined divide and lived reality in discourse and practice. Our concern as feminists is the ways in which the discourses and the practices differentially empower or disempower based on gender.

Imagining the domestic

All societies articulate culturally specific boundaries among arenas of social life. Most societies normalize and naturalize these imagined boundaries. In all societies there are continuities and discontinuities of structure, modes of operation and idioms of discourse among the articulated spheres, despite the imagined distinctions. Some societies dysfunctionalize the continuities through discourses and practices highlighting the firmness of the boundaries.

The imagined binary between public and private conflates multiple domains of social activity in such a way as to gloss gender issues, particularly by glossing the impact of systems of gendered domination across social fields. Nira Yuval-Davis (this issue) offers an alternative paradigm of three domains: state, civil society and family/kinship. I concur with Yuval-Davis, but to avoid assumptions embedded in Westerncentric civil society theory which deploys public/private in conflicting ways, I avoid the term civil society. In order to recognize diverse domestic arrangements, found in all societies, which are often glossed in the term 'kinship' (Stack, 1974, 1996), I avoid using 'kinship' to describe a sphere. The terms state and kinship are nevertheless important as much of the literature makes reference to specific state and kinship forms. I use the terminology of governmental, non-governmental (formally and informally organized) and domestic (householding arrangements) when I refer abstractly to these spheres (though I may use state and kinship when referring to specific theoretical constructs or bodies of literature).

While no imagined boundary is innocent of politics and culture, the abstraction of a domestic domain (in addition to governmental and non-governmental) is a useful analytical tool for distinguishing dynamics in householding arrangements as they impact and are impacted upon by other areas of social life. This analytical distinction opens theoretical space to consider the possible *relative* autonomy of householding arrangements, while resisting a priori conceptions about the content of that space.

Pre-state societies tend not to differentiate between government and domestic spheres. Anthropologists have theorized that this is largely because kinship is the central organizing institution in pre-state societies, structuring politics, religion, economy and society. Christine Gailey (1987) suggests that pre-state societies classify women (and men) primarily in kinship terms. Categorization of women on the basis of their gender emerges with the state, she argues, implying that it is with the state that women are discriminated against, categorically, as women.

It appears that the more hierarchically developed a society, the more dominant formal bureaucratically organized institutions are, the more disembedded political institutions are from the domestic and the more successful political institutions are in displacing domestic institutions, the more likely it is that such a society would value and institutionalize firm boundaries and discontinuities between arenas of social life. These conditions tend to hold more in state-level societies and more so in strong centralized states. If government/non-government/domestic divides emerge in state-level societies, their articulation as separate spheres concerns state projects to organize social life. The simplified binary of 'public/private' glosses the competition between state and kinship for power over resources and personnel (Sullivan, 1995). The key issue, for this paper, is the relation between government and domestic institutions. Because the boundary is about competing forms of power, the gendering of the boundary is crucial for women.

This logic suggests that the tension between kinship and state, long theorized by anthropologists as competitively coexisting institutional forms, is key to understanding not only the gendering of women as a category, but also the gendering of the 'public/private' divide. It also suggests the need for closer examination of the strength of kinship relative to the state in particular societies. In addition to the relative strength of kinship and state, there is the issue of continuities and discontinuities of structures, idioms and modes of operation between them. Governmental and domestic institutions in many societies tend to be patriarchal. Patriarchal domestic and government institutions, idioms and modes of operation help subsidize the continuities between spheres in these societies in relationship to gender issues – even though there may be different forms of patriarchy at play.

State, class and competing imaginations

Most often the boundaries we visualize are imagined by ruling élites trying to construct political communities. The seductiveness of state-subsidized boundaries, however, may naturalize them, making the divides asserted by ruling élites appear to be compulsory. This account must be seen as a story of competing class interests. Government and non-government spheres in most state societies, therefore, are arenas of operation not for 'men', but for some men, men of privileged classes. The majority of men (working class) are excluded from the government and non-government spheres, despite their imagined identification with maleness. Judith Tucker (1986: 10), for example, argued that the formalization of the 'public' sphere in Egypt excluded both women and men from disadvantaged classes. Carole Pateman (1988: 12) has argued that the separation of 'public and private' is constitutive of patriarchal liberalism, the Western contractarian vision of state/citizen relations. The fluidity between spheres, I suggest below, may be constitutive of patriarchal connectivity, a particular form of patriarchy linked with a culturally specific form of personhood and linked with the state-building enterprise in Lebanon.

Imagining kinship, imagining state in Lebanon

I take Lebanon as a case study. Lebanon is a small country of only 4 million on the Eastern shores of the Mediterranean. Still struggling to bring closure to the civil war that tore open its social fabric from 1975 to 1990, Lebanon is considered a constitutional republic, with an elected representative government, a parliament and a legally independent judiciary. Its political institutions, including its citizenship laws, in many ways are the legacy more of the French colonial mandate (1918–43) than of the Ottoman Empire under which it remained for almost 500 years (Makdisi, 1996).

Lebanon is interesting for its continuities and discontinuities with both West and South. It is a new state (independence in 1943) and an old state-level society (under consecutive state formation for several thousand years). As a Mediterranean state, it shares much history and culture with Southern Europe and North Africa. As a West Asian state, it shares much history and culture with Asia. As the only Arab society almost equally divided between Muslims and Christians, with eighteen legally recognized religious sects, its people adhere to multiple religious traditions which bridge many cultures. Because of this religious diversity, Lebanon, unlike most of the Middle Eastern states (including Israel), has no official state religion. As a patriarchal culture in which kinship is central to social life, it shares much with surrounding countries – and yet, its patriarchies are diversified by its numerous ethnic and religious cultures. As the Arab state with the highest literacy rate, educational level, per capita schools, colleges, universities, publishing houses and newspapers/magazines/journals, Lebanon boasts a relatively political conscious and engaged population.

Many have considered Lebanon the most politically open and 'democratic' of the Arab states. While lacking a woman's movement, Lebanon has produced much feminist art, literature and scholarship, as well as numerous social and political feminist activists working on behalf of women's rights in the domain of citizenship.

In Lebanon, kinship has been central to all spheres of social activity. Given the weakness of the state, Lebanese citizens have experienced kin as the anchor of their security, acting as the central metaphor for social relationships. Persons in all social classes and religious/ethnic communities regularly have justified many long- and short-term relationships in kin terms, calling each other brothers, sisters, uncle/aunt/niece/nephew, cousins in places of work, in the market place, in politics, civil society and other nongovernmental activities. In referring to each other by kin terms of address, they have evoked the expectations and obligations of kinship for instrumental and affective purposes. Through idiomatic kinship, they have incorporated kin and non-kin into familial boundaries, moralities and modes of operation. These uses of kinship have been perceived as continuous with, rather than disruptive of domestic boundaries and life. They have also been seen as continuous with rather than a challenge to political practices and norms.

The centrality of patriarchal kinship in government/nongovernment/ domestic spheres in Lebanon has been made possible by the transportation of patriarchal structures, modes of operation and idioms from domestic to other spheres. Political leaders have used kinship to mobilize their relatives into public offices. Lay people have expected their relatives to give them privileged access to the resources and services at their disposal regardless of whether the relatives were positioned to do so. In expecting kin to act as conduits to resources and services regardless of where they were situated, the Lebanese have transported the structures, modes of operation and idioms of patriarchal kinship with them into these multiple spheres.

Patriarchal kin modes of operation, in Lebanon, were produced and reproduced not only in domestic but also in government and non-government spheres. The privileging of males and elders justified in kin moralities and sanctified by religion, the hallmark of patriarchal kinship in Lebanon, was widespread in public arenas. Elites distributed resources on the basis of highly personalistic, face-to-face relationships often grounded in real or idiomatic kinship, subsidizing the control of males and elders over familial females and juniors. Political, religious, economic and social leaders often deferred to family heads in matters related to members of their families. As a result, citizens came to expect that their civic rights were conditional on the set of relationships they could mobilize. The most effective of these were based in patriarchal kinship (Joseph, 1990, 1993b). Patriarchal kin relationships, modes of operation and idioms have been socially acceptable, expected and ascendant in government and non-government spheres in Lebanon, fostering continuities that many citizens have found necessary and normal for social existence.

Patriarchal kinship, thus, has been firmly embedded within the Lebanese state. Patriarchal values, structures and processes link government, non-government and domestic spheres. Kinship has been one of the primary means of access to state and civil society resources. Kinship has been reproduced by political leaders who call upon their own kin for public positions and political support, where father follows son in political office, where relatives privilege each other to gain access to public and private resources.

The domestic as state-imagined kinship in Lebanon

Carole Pateman (1988) has suggested that liberal contractarian political theorists constructed the family as natural collectivity existing prior to the state and meriting privilege within the state. By creating the domain of the domestic, the state constructed a particular sort of family system with legal privileges, however. The domestic can be seen as a state-imagined sphere deployed to define and police householding arrangements. States regulate the age of marriage, the number and gender of spouses allowed to marry, who may inherit what and how much from whom, child custody in cases of divorce and death of parents, age and gender of who can own property or businesses, age and gender of who can travel outside the country, who can pass citizenship on to their children and spouses, who can receive employee-based benefits, who is entitled to receive public assistance as heads of families, whether having additional children offers tax benefits, other state-subsidization or penalties (Mertus, 1995; Elshtain, 1982).

Many Southern state constitutions write the family in as the basic unit of the state (Mertus, 1995; Cook, 1986 cited in Mertus, 1995). Carole Pateman (1988: 11) argued that, by locating the family in the sphere of nature (and natural law), Western classical liberal contract theory justified the creation of the 'private' (i.e. domestic) as a domain in which women could be subordinated to men by the laws of nature, outside the laws of the social contract. Despite the presumed boundary, as Julie Mertus (1995: 135) observed, the state 'intrudes upon family life to the extent that such interventions serve larger political and social goals'.

In Lebanon, as in most Middle Eastern countries, the state constitution defines 'the family' as the basic unit of society. In doing so, the state implicitly underwrites the patriarchal family as the model of kinship. Patriarchy is supported by the legal codification of patrilineality (reckoning decent through the male line) in citizenship laws. A child derives citizenship in Lebanon through her/his father. A woman cannot pass citizenship on to her children or foreign husband, except under limited circumstances. If the children have no known father (or known mother), they can obtain citizenship through their mother or independently if neither parent is known. Until recently, such children had 'ghair shar'i' (illegitimate) written on their Lebanese identity cards. Until 1960, Lebanese women lost their citizenship when they married a non-citizen. Now they are able to choose citizenship at marriage and can maintain dual citizenship. A non-Lebanese woman married to a Lebanese man can give Lebanese citizenship to her minor children if her Lebanese husband dies. Similarly, Lebanese women who regain their Lebanese citizenship after their non-national husband dies can give Lebanese citizenship to their minor children. Yet Lebanese women on their own cannot give citizenship to their children (Mogheizal, 1997).

Other legislation has also been imbued with patriarchal modalities. It was only in 1993 the Lebanese law allowed the testimony of one woman to equal the testimony of one man in court (previously two women's testimony was required to equal that of one man). And only in 1994 were women allowed to own and operate businesses independently of the permissions and formal supervision of their male kin. Punishment for crimes of honour are still discriminatory. A man is punishable only if he commits adultery at home, while a women is punishable if she commits adultery inside or outside the home. A wife can be punished for up to two years for adultery, a man only up to one year. A man is punishable for an honour crime only if he is married, but not so a woman. One witness is enough to condemn a woman for an honour crime, but additional evidence is needed for a man to be convicted (Jreisati, 1997).

While Lebanese women achieved the right to vote and the right to be elected to office in 1953, few women have held political office. The saying goes that Lebanese women come to parliament dressed only in black, meaning that they take the seats of their deceased husbands or fathers. But as one woman member of parliament acerbically noted, Lebanese men come to parliament in black as well, coming to office through implicit patrilineal succession.

The Lebanese state enshrines patriarchal kinship further by elevating religious family law to public law. The state devolves the area of family law to the eighteen formally recognized religious sects (a common practice in many colonial and some postcolonial societies). In so doing, the state sanctifies family within the domain of religious discourse as something immutable and God-given, subordinating women (and men) to the ideologies and wills of patriarchal clerics.

FEMINIST REVIEW NO 57, AUTUMN 1997

The religious courts in Lebanon regulate marriage, divorce, child custody and inheritance. Virtually all of these religious laws encode patriarchy. For most religions in Lebanon, children belong to their father and their father's family. Fathers and their families have priority over mothers and their families in child custody. In the Sunni Muslim sect, women cannot inherit. Shi'a Muslim law allows women to inherit one half as much as their brothers. Christians follow the state law which allows equal inheritance for women and men. Muslim laws generally give men a larger percentage of their deceased wife's property than women are entitled to from their deceased husband's property. Divorce in general is much easier for Muslim men than women to initiate. Sunnis and Shi'a allow plural marriages, but Druze and Christian sects prohibit polygamy. Among Christians, divorce laws vary greatly. Divorce is virtually impossible for the Catholics, while the Greek Orthodox are more flexible.

Though there is great variation among the legal codes of the Muslim and Christian sects, the general pattern is a patriarchal bias. Thus by devolving family law on to religious courts, the Lebanese state not only institutionalizes and legalizes the preferential treatment of men in sectarian codes but privileges particular forms of family. In addition, as Marie Rose Zalzal (1997) observed, the state has created non-homogeneous legal conditions for its citizens, making for a direct conflict with the constitutional codes asserting equality among citizens. It also throws family matters into the domain of non-negotiable sacred religion and into the hands of patriarchal religious clerics who relatively consistently support patriarchal kinship structures, modes of operation and idioms.

Underwriting this legal pluralism in family codes is a state-building enterprise based in sectarian pluralism. The history of the modern Lebanese state (Makdisi, 1996) – rooted in modern Ottoman and French colonial projects – is too complex a story to summarize in this paper. However, it is important to note that, by independence in 1943, the founding élite of the state had agreed to what has been called the 'National Pact' by which the major public offices and positions in government and allocation of government services would be distributed proportionally among the recognized religious sects in the country. Article 95 of the otherwise relatively secular constitution similarly calls for attention to sectarian distribution of access to the state. Political élites ('zu'ama') have often legitimated their positions in government on the basis of their being representatives of their religious communities and have used their position in government to subsidize their personal followings, based primarily in sectarian communities (Hudson, 1968). Legal pluralism in family law has been not only a concession to the powerful religious institutions, but also a basis for the reproduction of the political élite as they constituted themselves in the early course of nation/state building. Legal pluralism and its enshrining of patriarchal kinship, religious and communal structures, modes of operation and idioms has been constitutive of the Lebanese state-building project.

In reality, as Carol Stack (1974, 1996) has eloquently documented for the United States every society supports diverse forms of domestic life. The domestic, as a purposeful fiction, polices the boundaries of kinship, as part of a state-building project. The conflation of the domestic with kinship, however, not only over-privileges kinship, but underwrites specific family forms as kinship. The over-privileging of kinship also often reinforces the conflation of gender with kinship, further encoding women's delegation to the domestic sphere.

Patriarchal community and the state enterprise

Western classical liberal political theory has constructed the citizen as an individual, unencumbered by competing loyalties in the public realm. In the private realm, citizens are seen as members of collectivities – familial, ethnic, racial, religious – making for two kinds of citizenship, individualized and subnational. The citizen, in classical liberal thought, has an unmediated relationship to the state in the government sphere, but in the domestic sphere the relationship is mediated through privileged memberships in subnational collectivities. Classical liberal theory, by not recognizing the agency of the state in constructing these communities, has naturalized them – constructed them as existing prior to and relatively autonomously from the state.

In Lebanon, the state in practice has legally mandated sectarian communities by elevating religious family codes to the status of civil code and by not offering secular alternatives. In effect, a Lebanese citizen must belong to a religious sect to be married, divorced, resolve child custody and inheritance issues. In addition, the state has authorized patriarchal sectarian communities by indicating religious sect on Lebanese identity cards, basing representation in parliament on an assumed distribution of the nineteen religious sects in the population and formally and informally allocating positions in government and civil service on the basis of religious sect. Institutions operated by religious sects, such as schools, hospitals, charity organizations, youth and cultural clubs, have been entitled to government funding. Through these and other practices the Lebanese state has helped construct the very 'communities' it has assumed to have an existence prior to itself, thus constituting the state as a nation of subnational patriarchal communities defined by religious sect. This has been part of the state-building enterprise.

In this environment, some Lebanese feminist activists have looked to the state to free them from the control of their religious communities (Sharara, 1978), particularly in their lobbying for civil personal status codes (family law). While the state must and will continue to be a site for the contestation of these gendered issues, the complicity of the state in the construction of patriarchal communities these women wish to free themselves from must be made clear. The legal pluralism, discussed above as part of the state-building project of the Lebanese élite, provides the legal legitimacy for the existence of the patriarchal communities and empowers them over the daily lives of women and men.

Communities in Lebanon, in reality, have been lived as sets of specific relationships which shifted with needs and circumstances. For example, a woman may think of herself as Maronite in relationship to a Greek Orthodox, but in relationship to another Maronite may think of herself as a member of her family, village, class or nationality. And even in relation to fellow Maronites, her identity as Maronite might shift depending on the event uniting or dividing them. These different positionalities bring with them different sets of entitlements as well as liabilities.

Historically the personal relationships of Lebanese may have been primarily embedded within ethnic and religious communities. Yet almost every Lebanese has created and sustained enduring relationships across sectarian, ethnic, linguistic, racial, class and national boundaries not coterminous with imagined communal boundaries (Joseph, 1990). For example, Lebanon's civil war 1975–90 was constituted in part on the basis of religious 'communal' conflicts. Even with this heightened sectarianism, most Lebanese, urban and rural of all social classes, nevertheless continued to have relationships across religious sects. With the government non-operational during parts of the war, it was often necessary for social and political survival to maintain extensive networks with members of different militas, many of which constructed themselves in religious sectarian terms. For many Lebanese, the boundaries of the sectarian communities are irrelevant to their daily lives. Many have actively organized against sectarianism for decades.

Communities are not natural, bounded and fixed, but shifting, situational and changing phenomenon. They rarely have the same configuration or call up the same constituents for all events. Their meanings for those who claim or are assigned membership changes continually. Assigning fixed value to communities that translate into specific political rules, rights or obligations for their members is problematical, particularly for women. We can neither dissolve the categories of communities nor congeal and reify them. When they are congealed and naturalized, it is often for the purposes of state-building enterprises, as I argue for Lebanon, and often such crystallization of community impacts disproportionately on women.

The national subject and difference

The struggles over government/non-government/domestic divides can be seen partly as struggles over institutionalization of universal versus specific identities. The success of the state rests partly on the degree to which it can institutionalize national identities and subordinate (or eliminate) others. Western states invest governmental spheres with the construction of 'national' identity, the domain of the 'modernized', homogenized, the universal, in which individualized citizens are divested of particularistic status based on subnational communities to be invested with status as national subjects (Zubaida, 1989). It is the site, as Talal Asad (1993:11) observed, in which national subjects have become standardized, interchangeable with one another – the industrial model of citizenship.

Uniform, standardized national law and administration of justice then becomes necessary for the construction of the universal national citizen. While the interchangeability of 'individuals' as citizens eliminates the differences between women and men, as Carole Pateman (1988: 186) astutely observed, the lack of such interchangeability may institutionalize subnational differences. In this discourse, the domestic becomes the realm of the specific, of the subnational, racial, ethnic, religious, tribal, linguistic and familial differences – the realm of diversity. The elision of the domestic with the subnational makes the domestic synonymous with difference in many state discourses. By locating difference and subnational communities in the domestic realm, states (both Western and non-Western) set the stage for conflating difference with women's bodies.

In Lebanon, with eighteen different formally recognized religious sects governing personal status or family law, there can be no universal national subject. The deferral of family law to religious courts, the absence of civil alternatives, the patriarchal male control of sectarian institutions, the representation of citizens on the basis of religious sects, the distribution of state services and resources on the basis of religious sects and other practices discussed above have particularized the national subject. In terms of the argument of this paper, the concern is that these practices of citizenship not only particularize but gender citizens through the reproduction and valorization of patriarchal structures, modes of operation and idioms.

FEMINIST REVIEW NO 57, AUTUMN 1997

Patriarchal connectivity and the nation/state project

In naturalizing domestic boundaries, states (Western and Southern) have assumed that the citizen attains existence, personhood and identity through the subnational collectivities presumed therein. The presumed primordiality of subnational collectivities has justified the privileges negotiated for and by them around the boundary of the domestic sphere and the naturalization of the 'family' as the unit through which persons are socialized into citizenship.

In Western classical liberal discourse, citizenship is an attribute of the individual. In seeing citizenship an attribute of the individual, classical liberalism has required persons to become individuals. The 'individual', however, is an historically and culturally specific construct of self. Carole Pateman (1988: 14) has argued that the individual is a figment of modern patriarchal liberal imagination. This individualized citizen has been viewed as an autonomous, unattached, bounded, mobile, independent, contract-making, individuated, separative self.

I have suggested that there are numerous constructs of selfhood cross-culturally and in any one culture. In Lebanon, I found a construct (among other constructs) of selfhood that I have called connective. A connective self, which I have detailed theoretically and empirically elsewhere (Joseph, 1993b, 1994a, 1994b), is one that sees itself embedded in others and fosters relationality as a central charter of selfhood. This construct of selfhood, I have argued, is linked to a relational notion of rights – a notion that rights are generated in and embedded in significant relationship, which I have also described in detail elsewhere (Joseph, 1994a). With relational rights one comes to have rights by having relationships with people who have access to the desired resources and privileges. Connectivity in Lebanon, I have argued, is linked with patriarchy to create patriarchal connectivity – the construction of selves with a relatively fluid sense of boundaries, predisposed towards the privileging of males and elders and embracing that system through kinship moralities. The embedding of connectivity in patriarchy in Lebanon has served as a powerful conduit of gendered and aged privilege for men and elders (Joseph, 1993b).

Connective selfhood and patriarchal connectivity are not the only forms of selfhood and kinship systems available in Lebanon, but they are highly valorized and institutionally supported (Joseph, 1993b). They are not unique to Lebanon; relational rights are found in many Western and Southern societies (Nedelsky, 1993). Also relational rights are not the only form of rights subsidized, but are a highly institutionalized practice of rights in Lebanon (Joseph, 1990). What may be specific to Lebanon at this historical moment is the confluence of patriarchal connectivity, relational rights and the specific state-building project which subsidizes a fluidity of boundaries by subsidizing patriarchal kinship structures, modes of operation and idioms in government, non-government and domestic spheres. The fluidity of boundaries between government/non-government/domestic spheres, I suggest, may be constitutive of patriarchal connectivity in Lebanon. Patriarchal connectivity can be linked (not in a linear, mechanical manner) to the Lebanese nation/state-building enterprise.

Patriarchal connectivity meant that men in Lebanon were embedded in and identified by kin relations (Joseph, 1994b). The domestic was not viewed as an exclusively feminine domain. Under religious authority, the domestic became a sacredly sanctioned domain of gender and age-based hierarchal relationships of women and men. Recognizing men's embedding in kin relationships gives the lie to the gendering of the 'public/private' binary.

The family in Lebanon has been a porous, not bounded system. The boundaries have changed with shifting alliances, structural situations and memberships. Personal relationships have been seen as key to social, political, economic life. Family relations have flowed into the state and political relationships have become familial. The political leader has been seen as a family member, an honorary family patriarch. Fluid boundaries were culturally normative. Government/non-government/domestic flowed into each other in culturally acceptable ways. Patron-client relationships worked because of the expectations that the morality and commitments of kinship were relevant to government and non-governmental spheres. Patriarchal kinship was a key prototype for relationships in the government and non-governmental spheres. Men were relational and carried their familial model of relationships beyond the domestic domain. Citizens expected the demands of personal relationships would take precedence over civil procedure (relational rights). Hisham Sharabi (1988) has argued that, in many Arab societies, state has been subordinate to the cultural rules of familistic politics.

Patriarchal connectivity has been one (of several) culturally normative patterns for significant male and female relationships in the economic and political arena. Such relationships have been moralized in the idiom of kinship in Lebanon. Political leaders have often presented themselves as the senior patriarchs of the extended political family, calling for the loyalty, deference and service due them as heads of families. Contrary to the notion that the public is non-relational (Chodorow, 1978: 179), the public world in Lebanon has been very relational.

Citizenship in Lebanon has entailed investing in relationships giving access. Citizens have practised and experienced their rights as a matter of knowing people upon whom they can make claims and who are located in critical places of access or who can link each other to critical places of access.[2] This relational notion of rights is very different from that assumed in the classical liberal construct where rights inhere in the individualized person as parts of her or his membership – citizenship – in the political community.

This leads me to suggest that not only are there different relationships to the state because of subject positions defined by gender, ethnicity, race, religion as structural categories of society, but there are different relationships to the state based on different constructs of selfhood embodied in the meanings of the citizen person and the practice of rights linked to different meanings of the citizen person. By having to be 'individuals' or by having to be 'connective selves' persons gain or lose their rights in domestic, government and non-government arenas. The state and family-building enterprises then ramify into each other in constituting citizens and selves.

Conclusions

The 'public/private' divide, I have argued is a boundary imagined by a state imagining its people. The public/private boundary is constitutive of the will to statehood. Underwriting any imagined public/private boundary are ongoing power struggles imbued with gender, race, ethnic, religious and class conflicts. Pivotal to the struggle over the public/private are the efforts of ruling élites to consolidate state control over citizen constituencies by reconstituting prior institutions claiming citizen loyalties. Tensions between kinship, the main pre-state organizing social institution and the state are at the heart of the changing meaning and character of the public/private dynamic. For this reason, I suggest, the binary simplified a more complex set of competing and shifting categories.

While displacing the public/private with government/non-government/domestic also reifies dynamic processes and brings with it Westerncentric presumptions, it offers a provisional framework for critical analysis of domestic institutions, particularly kinship forms, as they collide and collaborate with state institutions. The interest in articulating a 'third' sphere of the domestic emerges not from a distaste for the simplicity of binaries (a third sphere adds little in and of itself), but from a desire to analyse the operations of cultural practices not adequately conceptualized by the analytical and material categories of government and non-government. The domestic is an analytical tool, a lens to bring into focus an area of critical importance for gender relations. In pre-state societies, some may argue, the 'domestic' is co-terminous with society. State-level societies, however, invest in differentiation. The degree and nature of differentiation, varying with state-building projects, has critical implications for gender.

Thus, though it is necessary to distinguish the domestic analytically it is not a bounded, autonomous sphere. It may not be autonomous not because it is subordinate to government and non-government spheres, however, but because it is embedded in them, as in the Lebanese case. The domestic is part of the Lebanese state-building enterprise. Ruling élites in Lebanon have relied upon patriarchal kinship structures, modes of operation and idioms. They have reinscribed patriarchal connectivity in the everyday practices of government by which citizens obtain access to state resources and services. They have sanctified patriarchal communities in the elevation of religious family law to public law. They have bolstered the sectarian pluralism underwriting their claims to authority by codifying legal pluralism – a legal pluralism that not only fragments the national body, but rends asunder the grounds on which women can make unified claims to civil protection from the state as national subjects. The domestic indeed shapes as well as is shaped by government (Sharabi, 1988). And unless we fashion a frame through which to view its operations, neither the relative autonomy nor the dependency of either the domestic or the government can be brought into focus.

The centrality of gender to contestations over government/non-government/ domestic boundaries suggests that gender is at the heart of state-building enterprises. Elites imagining the state and nation not only must conceptualize women as a category but must articulate the gender-specific expectations of citizenship. Though gendered notions of citizenship often appear absent from universalistic declarations of citizenship, there is no state or nation that has not differentially incorporated and entitled its female and male members. Imagined boundaries concerning 'the domestic' and its assumed 'natural' differentiation from government and non-government spheres have invariably played a role in the justifications of such differential treatment. I present the Lebanese case, not to represent 'the South' (which no case, especially the Lebanese, could do), but to complexify the interrogation of the imagined boundaries and to expose the terrain of power relations on which states, through culturally and historically specific ways, erect and gender[3] their institutions and ideologies in their will to statehood.

Notes

Suad Joseph is Professor of Anthropology and Women's Studies and Director of Women's Studies at the University of California, Davis. Her research, focusing on her native Lebanon, analyses the dynamics of gender, family, selfhood, rights and citizenship in Lebanon. She is founder of the Association for Middle East Women's Studies, and the Middle East Research Group in Anthropology. Her

FEMINIST REVIEW NO 57, AUTUMN 1997

publications include: *Muslim-Christian Conflicts: Economic, Political and Social Origins* (co-edited with Barbara Pillsbury), 1978, Westview Press; 'Gender and citizenship in Middle Eastern states' (ed.) *Middle East Reports* 1996, Vol. 26, No. 1. She has just completed editing *Intimate Selving: Gender, Self and Identity in Arab Families* and is editing a book on gender and citizenship in the Middle East.

1 I am grateful to Nira Yuval-Davis and the anonymous reviewers of *Feminist Review* for many helpful insights in the revisions of this paper.

2 See Nedelsky (1990) for a discussion of rights and relation within Western discourses and Mayer (1991) and Dwyer (1991) for a discussion of rights in Islamic and Arab discourses.

3 As well as mark by class, race, ethnicity, religion, nationality and sexuality.

References

ANDERSON, Benedict, (1983) *Imagined Communities: Reflections on the Origin and Spread of Nationalism* London: Verso.

ASAD, Talal (1993) *Genealogies of Religion: Discipline and Reasons of Power in Christianity* Baltimore, Md: Johns Hopkins University Press.

BENN, Stanley I. and GAUS, Gerald F. (1983) 'The liberal conception of the public and the private' in **S.I. Benn** and **G.F. Gaus**, editors, *Public and Private in Social Life* pp. 31–65 London: Croom Helm.

CHODOROW, Nancy (1978) *The Reproduction of Mothering: Psychoanalysis and the Sociology of Gender* Berkeley: University of California Press.

COOK, Rebecca (1986) *The Family as a Basic Unit of Social Order* 8th Commonwealth Law Conference, Oncho Rios, Jamaica, September.

DWYER, Kevin (1991) *Arab Voices: The Human Rights Debate in the Middle East* Berkeley: University of California Press.

EISENSTEIN, Zillah (1994) *The Color of Gender: Reimaging Democracy* Berkeley: University of California Press.

ELSHTAIN, Jean Bethke (1981) *Public Man, Private Woman: Women in Social and Political Thought* Princeton, NJ: Princeton University Press.

—— editor, (1982) *The Family in Political Thought* Amherst: University of Massachusetts Press.

GAILEY, Christine Ward (1987) *Kinship to Kingship: Gender Hierarchy and State Formation in the Tongan Islands* Austin: University of Texas Press.

HUDSON, Michael (1968) *The Precarious Republic: Political Modernization in Lebanon* New York: Random House.

JOSEPH, Suad (1975) 'Urban poor women in Lebanon: does poverty have public and private domains?', presented at Association of Arab-American University Graduates Annual Meeting, Chicago, October.

—— (1983) 'Working class women's networks in a sectarian state: a political paradox', *American Ethnologist* Vol 10. No. 1: 1–22.

—— (1990) 'Working the law: a Lebanese working class case', in **Daisy Dwyer**, editor *The Politics of Law in the Middle East* South Hadley, Mass.: J.F. Bergin, pp. 143–60.

—— (1993a) 'Gender and civil society: an interview with Suad Joseph', by Joe Stork, *Middle East Reports* Vol. 23, No. 4: 22–6.

—— (1993b) 'Connectivity and patriarchy among urban working class Arab families in Lebanon', *Ethos* Vol. 21, No. 4: 452–84.

—— (1994a) 'Problematizing gender and relational rights: experiences from Lebanon', *Social Politics* Vol. 1, No. 3.

—— (1994b) 'Brother/sister relationships: connectivity, love and power in the reproduction of Arab patriarchy', *American Ethnologist* Vol. 21, No. 1: 50–73.

—— (1996) 'Gender and citizenship in Middle Eastern states' *Middle East Reports*, Vol. 26, No. 1: 4–10.

—— In press 'Women between nation and state in Lebanon', in **Norma Alarcon**, **Caren Kaplan** and **Minoo Moallem** editors, *Between Women and Nation: Feminism and Global Issues* Durham: Duke University Press.

—— forthcoming. 'Civil society, the public/private, and gender in Lebanon' in **Muge Gocek** editor, *Social Constructions of Nationalism* Berkeley: University of California Press.

JREISATI, Arlette (1997) 'Gender in Lebanon's criminal code', presented at the Gender and Citizenship in Lebanon Conference, American University in Beirut, Beirut, March.

KEANE, John (1988a) *Democracy and Civil Society* London: Verso.

—— (1988b) 'Despotism and democracy: the origins and development of the distinction between civil society and the state', in **John Keane** editor, *Civil Society and the State* London: Verso.

MAKDISI, Ussama (1996) 'The modernity of sectarianism in Lebanon', *Middle East Reports* Vol. 26, No. 3: 23–6.

MAYER, Elizabeth (1991) Islam and Human Rights: Tradition and Politics Boulder, CO: Westview Press.

MERTUS, Julie (1995) 'State discriminatory family law and customary abuses', in **Julie Peters** and **Andrea Wolper** editors, *Women's Rights Human Rights: Internatinal Feminist Perspectives*. New York: Routledge.

MOGHEIZAL, Laure (1997) 'Gender and the transmission of citizenship in Lebanese law', presented at the Gender and Citizenship in Lebanon Conference, American University in Beirut, Beirut. March.

NEDELSKY, Jennifer (1990) 'Law, boundaries, and the bounded self', *Representations* No. 30: 162–89.

—— (1993) 'Reconceiving rights as relationship', *Review of Constitutional Studies* Vol 1, No 1: 1–26.

PATEMAN, Carole (1988) *The Sexual Contract* Stanford, Calif.: Stanford University Press.

PHILLIPS, Anne (1991) *Engendering Democracy* Cambridge: Polity Press.

REITER, Rayna (1975) 'Men and women in the south of France: public and private domains', in *Toward an Anthropology of Women* New York: Monthly Review Press.

ROSALDO, Michelle and LAMPHERE, Louise (1974) editors, *Women, Culture & Society* Stanford, Calif.: Stanford University Press.

SADOWSKI, Yaha (1993) 'The new orientalism and the democracy debate', *Middle East Reports* Vol. 23, No. 4: 14–21.

SELIGMAN, Adam B. (1992) *The Idea of Civil Society* New York: The Free Press.

SHARABI, Hisham (1988) *Neopatriarchy: A Theory of Distorted Change in Arab Society* New York: Oxford University Press.

SHARARA, Yolla (1978) 'Women and politics in Lebanon', *Khamsin.* No. 6: 6–32.

STACK, Carol (1974) *All Our Kin: Strategies for Survival in a Black Community* New York: Harper & Row.

—— (1996) *Call to Home: African Americans Reclaim the Rural South* New York: Basic Books.

SULLIVAN, Donna (1995) 'The public/private distinction in international human rights law', in **Julie Peters** and **Andrea Wolper** editors, *Women's Rights Human Rights: International Feminist Perspectives* New York: Routledge.

TUCKER, Judith (1986) 'Insurrectionary women: women and the State in 19th century Egypt', Middle East Reports No. 138, Vol. 16, No 1: 9–13.

VISWANATHAN, Gauri (1995) 'Ethnographic politics and the discourse of origins', *Stanford Humanities Review* Vol. 5, No. 1: 121–40.

WILLIAMS, Patricia (1991) *The Alchemy of Race and Rights: Diary of a Law Professor* Cambridge, Mass.: Harvard University Press.

YOUNG, Iris (1987) 'Impartiality and the civic public: some implications of feminist critiques of moral and political theory', in **Seyla Benhabib** and **Drucilla Cornell** editors, *Feminism as Critique* Minneapolis: University of Minnesota Press, pp. 56–76.

YUVAL-DAVIS, Nira (1997) 'Women, citizenship and difference', *Feminist Review*, No. 57: 3–26.

YUVAL-DAVIS, Nira and ANTHIAS, F. (1989) editors, *Woman-Nation-State* London: Macmillan.

ZALZAL, Marie Rose (1997) 'Personal status and sectarian law', presented at the Gender and Citizenship in Lebanon Conference, American University in Beirut, Beirut, March.

ZUBAIDA, Sami (1989) *Islam, the People and the State: Essays on Political Ideas and Movements in the Middle East* London: Routledge.

The Limits of European-ness:
Immigrant women in Fortress Europe

Helma Lutz

FEMINIST REVIEW NO 57, AUTUMN 1997, PP. 93–111

Abstract

This article is intended to contribute to the ongoing debate on the ideological, social and political formation of a New Europe. By focusing on the position of immigrant women it examines the gendered nature of the changing configurations of cultural and social European landscapes. Two features of immigrant women's positioning are the key issues of this analysis: regulations through national and European law and ideological representation. It is argued that the debate on European citizenship should be closely linked to the question of formal and substantive and also of symbolic rights. Moreover, feminists, when using the concept of difference in this context, should be aware of the power structures underlying differentiated social positions in society. European-ness will lose its exclusive character only if it provides a solid place in the symbolic order of Europe for immigrants.

Introduction

In recent years, an impressive body of literature revising the concept of citizenship from a feminist perspective has emerged. It has been argued, for example, that citizenship is not simply a 'status bestowed on those who are full members of a community' as T.H. Marshall (1950: 28) claimed, but that it is constructed both as a status *and* as a social practice (Lister, 1997a). Lister emphasizes the need for a framework in which citizenship recognizes ongoing structural constraints and their effects on women while at the same time, not reducing women to passive victims but, rather, also recognizing their active potential, their agency. While she rejects the concept of a unitary, universal woman, she suggests maintaining a 'differentiated universalism', 'which, rather than denying diversity and difference, acknowledges them' (Lister, 1997b).

Nira Yuval-Davis (1997) goes still further by stressing a concept of citizenship in which the recognition of 'difference' as a specific positioning of political actors is crucial. Her suggestion that citizenship is more than just being or not being a member of one or more communities, but is instead

FEMINIST REVIEW NO 57, AUTUMN 1997

a 'multi-tier concept' determined by factors such as gender, ethnicity or 'race', ability, class position, religion, sexuality, rural or urban background, the stage in the life-cycle, etc., is taken as a point of reference in this article. The subject of the following analysis is immigrant women's position/ing in Europe. Thus far, the debate on European multicultural citizenship has focused on (ethnic, religious, sexual) minorities' cultural rights (Bauböck, 1994; Castles, 1995; Kymlicka, 1995). Less attention has been paid to the issue of formal rights – with the positive exception of feminist researchers (see, for example, Bhabha and Shutter, 1994; Kofman, 1995, 1996; Morokvasic, 1991, 1993). It seems to me, however, that the ability of (a group of) people to act as citizens is closely linked to the formal and substantive rights they enjoy. I shall, therefore, focus on two features of immigrant women's positioning. I have called the first of these *regulations*, referring to those aspects of European and national law concerning immigrant women. The second relates to another subject which has attracted little attention in the current literature on citizenship and difference, the portrayal of immigrant women, their *representation*. By representation I refer to the ideological constructions of immigrant women in policy making and social practice. Regulations and representations are closely linked, not least in the legal systems themselves, in which criteria for exclusion from or inclusion into Europe are not infrequently based on 'racialized' gender stereotypes and assumptions. In this article I will examine the gendered nature of the changing configurations of the legal, cultural and social landscapes of Europe. I will do so by analysing the 'production' of two antagonistic categories, the 'immigrant' woman and the 'European' woman, focusing on formal regulations and cultural representations as two aspects, among others, contributing to the ongoing re-creation of this binary configuration.

The redefinition of Europe and European-ness

The 'New Europe' is emerging against the background of a changing global economy and political reorganization. With others, Balibar (1990) suggests that the fall of the Soviet Bloc and the end of the Cold War have brought into focus questions of 'what Europe is' and what are its boundaries. Before 1989, 'Europe' referred to those countries of Europe included in the then European Economic Community (EEC) along with the other parliamentary democracies of Western Europe. Since then, there has been a search for alternative organizing principles which could unify Europe, often focusing around the elusive concept of 'European civilization'. In the search for intrinsic features of 'Europe', discourses of culture, politics and space have become closely intermeshed with discourses of nationalism, racism and home ('Heimat') versus 'foreigners'/otherness (for an

Poverty and dependency, the legacy of colonial rule

Figure 1 © Roshini Kempadoo.

exploration of the ways in which the binary 'Heimat' versus 'Ausländer' operates, see Räthzel 1994, 1995). The new racist nationalism (see Lutz, Phoenix and Yuval-Davis, 1995a: 5) which is gathering force in contemporary Europe evokes notions of defending 'our' home, space, territory against 'disturbing' others (immigrants, asylum seekers, ethnic minorities). The former Yugoslavia as well as the other former socialist countries have been largely excluded from the construction of Europe. As Zarkov (1995) argues, these countries have been characterized and categorized on a sliding scale of Eastern/Oriental deviations from the Western standard model.

There is growing evidence that there has been a shift from Eurocentrism into what Philomena Essed has termed Europism (see Essed, 1995: 54). Eurocentrism is the old discourse of European superiority and domination over the South; in this discourse the term European, as Balibar (1991) has noted, referred to groups of colonizers in the colonized regions of the world. The processes of colonization, the settlement by Europeans of other parts of the globe, empire formation and the struggles against it constituted the terrain on which Europe constructed itself. In contrast, Europism is the defensive discourse of constructing a 'pure Europe' as a symbolic continent whose territory is cleansed of foreign and 'uncivilised elements'. Although Eurocentrism and Europism are constructed around the same key elements, they are distinguished by the former's territorial focus on the outside and the latter's homogenizing process from the inside. These are indications of a shift from Eurocentrism to Europism. Features of Europism can be found in what the German philosopher Jürgen Habermas (1992) has called the 'chauvinism of prosperity', which focuses on the defence of the institutions

95

Figure 2 © Roshini Kempadoo.

of the welfare state – seen as proof of self-achievement through suffering and hardship – against greedy, indigent 'outsiders'. The emergence of this 'chauvinism of prosperity' was, however, triggered or at least fed by the radical restructuring of the welfare state in many West European countries. This involved a reordering of the relation between the state and the 'citizen' with regard to their respective responsibilities.

Ideological, legal, economic and political constructions of a 'pure Europe' have used the other side of the 'Iron Curtain' as well as post-colonial and migrant labour positionings to promote images of demonic Others. The former has been transformed by developments since 1989, but the constructions and images have not disappeared; the dominant discourses now concern the lack of democratic features of Eastern European societies and doubts about their capacity to change into 'civil societies'. The latter concerns those discourses in which migrants are constructed as cultural, ethnic and religious 'others'. Both types of construction continue to exist alongside each other as themes of reference through which Europe defines itself (see Lutz, Phoenix and Yuval-Davis, 1995a).

It is through these discourses of 'racial', ethnic and national otherness, rather than through sexual difference, that the antagonism between the 'European' and the 'other' woman is emphasized. In this binary, the European woman serves as the standard against which to measure women from elsewhere. Muslim women are often constructed as the prototype of migrant women, perceived as miserable victims *par excellence*, handicapped by their culture of origin. In analysing the situation of Muslim migrant women, one generally encounters an image of Western women as triumphant in the realization of equal rights and social equality (see Lutz, 1991). The common assumption underlying this comparison is that female autonomy is generally absent from Muslim culture and through this process of 'standardization', European women become the yardstick of excellence, idealized as straightforward and independently successful beings whose gendered life has been freed of major contradictions and ambivalence.

As well as Muslim women there are numerous 'other others', portrayed as a particular kind of deviation from 'European' femininity – perhaps unconsciously functioning as counter-images or alter-egos of European feminine self-images.

The outcome of this process of construction, the image of a 'European woman', defined by the opposition between 'indigenous' and non-indigenous women, is relevant not only at the ideological level but also within legal systems and at the level of policy making. Before demonstrating in detail the legal position of migrant women, I want to contextualize the latter as a social category by drawing on historical shifts in the genesis of the term 'migrant' in Europe.

Changing landscapes: migration in Europe

Historians have recently proved that the popular image of a sedentary Europe, in which people led a stable life in the same surroundings from birth to death, is seriously flawed. European men and women have been on the move inside and outside Europe over at least the last three hundred years (see Moch, 1992). These findings are inconsistent with the common belief that Europe, contrary to the United States, Australia or Canada, has been a continent of emigration rather than immigration, a belief which helps explain why Europeans imagine themselves as sedentary, homogeneous and white. The idea still prevails that mass migration to continental Western Europe started in the 1950s with the arrival of 'guest-workers'. While it is true that the migration balance was negative for the first half of this century – in the Netherlands for example, up to 1961 there were more emigrants leaving the country than migrants arriving – it is also true that hundreds of thousands of people were on the move before, during and after the Second World War. Yet, not every movement was automatically perceived as 'migration' – at least, not in the sense attached to this term today. Turning again to the Netherlands, repatriates from Indonesia, especially those who were white and had not mixed with the 'inlanders', arrived in large numbers after the declaration of Indonesian independence in 1949. These immigrants have never been and are still not referred to as 'migrants', or as an 'ethnic minority', and they are not a target group of the Dutch minority policy (*minderhedenbeleid*). Similarly, West Germany witnessed the largest influx of immigrants of its history at a time when the country lay shattered in ruins, and unemployment rates had reached a dramatic level, receiving 12 million people over a period of twelve years, between 1949 and 1961 (see Bade, 1993). Of these, nine million were so-called ethnic Germans (Aussiedler), expelled from the East European countries where they had lived for generations (some for over 300 years), and three million were refugees from the GDR (Übersiedler). These migrants were 'white'; they were perceived as 'Germans' and granted citizenship status immediately after arrival on the basis of the German law which stresses citizenship rights based on *ius sanguinis* (literally the 'right of the blood', meaning that nationality is inherited from the parents). As the official terminology, 'Aussiedler' and 'Übersiedler', indicates, this migration process was seen as a re-settlement process of national subjects, an act of repatriation to the country where they belonged by ancestral right, their 'fatherland'. This immigration flow has hardly ceased since this time. Between 1961 and 1988 1.5 million ethnic Germans arrived in the FRG (Federal Republic of Germany) and since then the number of newcomers from German groups in Russia, Romania, Poland and so on is approximately 250,000 per year (see Rudolph and Hübner, 1993: 268; Morokvasic, 1993: 462).

In the de-colonization process after the Second World War, the collapse of the old Empires led to significant changes of state-borders and, consequently, to a re-definition of nationality. Every Empire had created its own colonial system of hierarchical citizenship, and so the question of who had to be admitted to the colonial 'motherland' became a problem for all state bureaucracies of the involved nations. It was in this context that the term 're-patriate' emerged, a category which was not neutral but implied selection criteria, based on perceived differences between those who – despite their absence – 'belonged' to the 'patria' and therefore were assumed to be capable of quick integration, and those who did not belong because of real or imagined ethnic and cultural differences. This becomes clear if we consider the way in which black colonial citizens are treated. In the Netherlands, for example, where 'national subjects' from Surinam (the former Dutch Guyana) immigrated in large numbers shortly before and after the declaration of independence in 1975, measures were taken to prevent a further influx from Surinam: after a short period of free entry, guaranteed by the Dutch state out of a sense of moral and political responsibility, the former nationals were declared foreigners and became subject to the aliens law. In Britain, the legal position of Commonwealth citizens has been subject to a number of successive legal acts (1962, 1968, 1971 and 1988). The 1971 Act differentiated between citizens from the Old 'white' Commonwealth (Canada, Australia, New Zealand) and the New 'black' Commonwealth and Pakistan. Citizens of the Old Commonwealth were allowed the right to settle in the UK free from immigration control if they were white and of 'English decent' over a specified number of generations; while primary settlement from the New Commonwealth was abolished. After 1971 family reunion was to be the only major criterion for settlement from the New Commonwealth (BMWP, 1995: 227). This means that '(post)-colonial' non-white migrants are denied the right to settle in the former colonial 'motherland'. In practice, members of two or three generations of (extended) families can be divided by nationality. Family affairs (like caring for children, illness or a funeral) can become a problem as visa permits are required (but not easily delivered). It should be noted here, however, that former colonial powers like Spain, Portugal and Italy have dealt in slightly different and more permissive ways with the immigration of their former 'subjects', particularly those from South America.

As the perceptions of the national belonging of former colonial citizens have changed over time, so have the perceptions of 'migrants'. Thirty years ago, when West and North European countries recruited migrant labourers from the Mediterranean region (Italians, Portuguese, Spaniards, Yugoslavs, Greeks, Turks and Moroccans), these people were called 'guestworkers' and their sojourn was considered to be of limited duration. From the 1980s onward their status was gradually changed to '(im)migrant', and, since the expansion of the EU and the gradual amelioration and mutual acceptance of membership rights, they have now become – with the exception of Yugoslavs, Turks and Moroccans – 'Europeans'. (The Maastricht treaty of 1992 acknowledges not only the right of free settlement for European citizens but also the right to participate in local elections.) Thus, while the (legal) status of the Southern European immigrants in North and West Europe has been improved through their integration into the European Union, the former (non-white) colonial citizens and immigrants from non-EU countries are exposed to increasing exclusion. Today, the term (im)migrant refers much more to non-European immigrants. In fact, two new categories have emerged: the European nationals and the so-called Third Country Nationals (the 'TNCs', see Bhabha and Shutter, 1994: 212).[1]

These examples demonstrate how the nation states of Europe have followed a pattern of inclusion/exclusion in their treatment of migrants by selectively integrating some while at the same time keeping others out. Skin-colour, culture and religion have served and still serve as signifiers for 'otherness', whether (im)migrants are 'citizens' or not.

FEMINIST REVIEW NO 57, AUTUMN 1997

European migration: current and future trends

The European migration is currently characterized by a number of new trends. As well as settlement and stabilization of immigrant populations originating in post-colonial migration and the 'old' guest-worker system,[2] there is evidence that, since 1989 and the opening of the borders between East and West, Europe has faced a 'new migration' (see Koser and Lutz, 1997a). This new migration has been identified in various ways: first, in terms of numbers – Fassmann and Münz (1994) suggest that four million people migrated into the EU between 1989 and 1994, while, at the same time, the outbreak of the war in the former Yugoslavia has triggered the flight of an estimated five million refugees (UN-ECE, 1995). The extent of this migration is said to outnumber any other migration in Europe since the end of the Second World War (Fassmann and Münz, 1994; Münz, 1996; King, 1993).

Other features which distinguish the 'new' migration from earlier movements include: changing migrant profiles, feminization, shifting geographies, new policy responses and changing migration strategies (Koser and Lutz, 1997a). Due to lack of space, I will define these only briefly while focusing on the one which is most relevant in the context of this article, namely feminization. By 'changing migrant profiles' commentators refer to the increase in the range of migrant 'types', among which the most significant are highly skilled workers (from East to West and vice versa), clandestine migrants and asylum seekers (see Champion, 1994; Rudolph and Hillmann, 1997). Shifting geographies are characterized by new developments in which countries of emigration become countries of immigration (as for example Southern Europe has become), while they can also be both at the same time (Russia and other East European countries – though to a different extent (see Wallace, Chloumiar and Sidorenko, 1996; Pilkington, 1997; Codagnone, 1997). New policy responses are increasingly important on political agendas. These responses carry signs of a moral panic in many European societies, where undocumented migrants and asylum seekers are represented as abusing the welfare state, committing crimes and threatening the employment of established citizens (Cornelius, Martin and Hollifield, 1994). Changing migration strategies, partly as a result of the aggressiveness of policy responses, are meant to undermine the effort of new restrictions (see Koser, 1997; Staring, 1997).

The feminization of migration, finally, is receiving more attention and is increasingly visible. First, visibility is achieved in conventional data by rejecting the assumption that women's migration motivations can be automatically reduced to family reunification, even if they use this mode of entry, and by expanding the investigation of migration data to undocumented migrants (see Phizacklea, 1997; Morokvasic, 1993; Kofman, 1996).

Second, there is an increasing movement of female migrants into the (informal) economy of highly industrialized territories like Europe. Due to a steadily growing demand for female labour in certain sectors both inside and outside the formal economy, such as the service industries, domestic work, the entertainment industries and prostitution (see Council of Europe, 1993; Weinert, 1991; AGISRA, 1990; Phizacklea, 1997), the presence of female migrants in Europe is growing. The quest for female workers is satisfied by recruiting or trafficking in women from either Third World countries or Eastern Europe. The US-American case of 'Nanny-gate' has brought to public attention a phenomenon which is 'invisible' but widespread in Europe too: indigenous European women who enter the (qualified) labour market, especially in Italy, Spain and Greece where child and elderly care facilities are lacking and the majority of husbands and fathers are still reluctant to share in 'care work', solve this problem by hiring immigrant women as domestic workers or live-in maids. Most countries in Europe have introduced measures to regularize this laobur flow through quota systems. In some countries, like France, where the payment for domestic workers is tax deductible, nearly a million families are registered as employers of domestic workers; there is also evidence, however, of large numbers of undocumented domestic workers (Anderson, quoted in Phizacklea, 1997). The number of domestic female workers in Europe is estimated to be more than a million; welfare contributions are paid for them by only some employers. This fact is due to a) the (one-year) limitation on work permits granted which most European countries have installed as part of the immigration-defence policy; b) the relatively high expenses of a legally employed worker; c) the fact that current regulations tie a domestic worker to the very employer who originally hired her and, thus, women who are (sexually) abused are forced to find a new employer at the expense of their legal employment permit. Domestic workers are forced into a situation where they are highly dependent on the good-will and the mercy of their employers. In countries like Italy, Spain and Greece and to some extent Great Britain and the Netherlands, Filipinas forming the main group of live-in maids (the Filipina self-organization talks of a total of approximately 500,000 Filipinas; see Caldo Rantzinger, Lutz and Pablo, 1996). While Italy and Spain often recruit from the territories of their former colonies (see Campani, 1993; Andall, 1997), countries like Germany and Austria profit greatly from the proximity of Eastern Europe with Polish, Hungarian, Czech and Slovakian women functioning as the available reservoir for (commuting) domestic workers (Morokvasic, 1991, 1993; Rerrich, 1996). Annie Phizacklea stresses that this development unmasks the myth of the new 'spousal egalitarianism'. 'The hiring of a full-time domestic worker means that patriarchal household and work structures can go unquestioned, women pursuing a career *and* a family need not "rock the boat"

FEMINIST REVIEW NO 57, AUTUMN 1997

and any guilt over exploitation is assuaged by the knowledge that a less for-tunate woman is being provided with work' (1997). The outcome of this development is, in fact, the maintenance of a binary division in terms of 'racialized' gender relations: the European *vis-à-vis* the 'other' woman.

These trends in current European migration not only produce increasing heterogeneity within and between the social strata of immigrant com-munities: they also contribute to the generation of several coexisting politi-cal categories, ranging from naturalized immigrants through different kinds of residence to the 'tolerated' and the 'undocumented'. These cat-egories are the outcome of political decision-making processes according to which immigration is desired at one historical point and rejected at another. They are, moreover, far from applicable to neatly separable groups, but are co-present throughout the EU.

Stabilization *and* the expansion of immigrant groups are two sides of the same coin, the ongoing diversification of European societies. In reaction to cultural and ethnic diversity, ideological constructions of 'adaptability' or 'otherness' go hand in hand with legal regulations; that is to say, for many immigrants the duration of their settlement does not lead implicitly to an improvement in their legal situation. As will be shown in the following section, this is particularly so in the case of immigrant women.

Immigrant women in the jungle of legislation and policy making

Figures on the total number of immigrant women in Europe vary sig-nificantly. A EUROSTAT report (1993–8) suggests that 14.1 million 'non-nationals' were identified in the statistics of the EU member states as resident on 1 January 1991 (undocumented residents were excluded); of these 6.4 million were females, accounting for 4 per cent of the total female population of the EU. One third of these female 'non-nationals' were citizens of another EU member state. All figures, however, have to be read with caution, because they are based on varying national defi-nitions and practices of registration. This is also the reason why reliable numbers of undocumented migrants are not available.

Talking about migrant women today means talking about an extraordi-narily heterogeneous group, encompassing significant differences in educational, social, cultural and ethnic backgrounds. There are also numerous commonalities, however, such as the issue of gaining entry to the countries of destination.

While over the last three decades legislation in several European nation states has taken into account the radical changing conjugal role-patterns between men and women and couples of the same sex by legally equating cohabitation (contracts) with marriage (as in Denmark, Sweden, The Netherlands),[3] in the case of immigrants the situation is the opposite: more than ever, marriage has become the backbone of legal entrance to the EU. After official recruitment stopped in the early 1970s, family reunification or formation has become one of the few ways of entering Europe legally.

Before 1973, Germany and France had recruited tens of thousands of women as labourers for certain industries, like electronics. In Germany, before 1973 one in five Turkish workers and one in three Yugoslavian workers was a woman (Wilpert, 1988). Female recruitment into other EU countries was also not unusual, but the majority of female labour migrants have entered the countries of destination as legally defined 'dependent spouses', often many years after their husbands were recruited to work abroad. This was, however, not the case with (post)colonial migrants, leading to immense differences between the migration patterns of colonial- and labour migrants. In the Netherlands, for example, the percentage of women from ex-colonies equalled that of men almost from the beginning; in the case of labour migrants the percentage of women increased slowly over a period of twenty years, now reaching 43–5 per cent of the respective immigrant population. Yet there are still considerable differences in the distribution of the sexes within and across the various ethnic groups throughout the EU, according to recruitment patterns or – in the case of refugees – to the history of persecution.

An expressed desire to reunify with a husband or wife is nowadays examined extensively by the immigration office and tests or interviews are carried out in which the purpose of migration is investigated. While, in the majority of European countries, the requirements for entry are (formally) sex-neutral, Britain was the only country officially applying sex-discrimination in the admission of husbands and wives, until this practice was stopped by the European Court in 1985 (Bhabha and Shutter, 1994: 76). Since the late 1960s Asian men in particular have been suspected of seeking entrance to Britain through a marriage of convenience when their main purpose was work. The Home Office assumed that the arranged marriage system was abused by men and set up an entire interrogation system to check on the primary purpose of migration of the applicants. Though, officially, this practice had to be abolished on the grounds of gender discrimination – which was done by levelling down the admission criteria for women – the majority of male Asian applicants (86 per cent in 1991 and 84 per cent in 1992) are refused entrance into Britain on the basis of the primary-purpose rule (Bhabha and Shutter, 1994: 80). Moreover, British immigration practices contain numerous exemplifications of the observation that gendered stereotypes about the 'cultural background' of the applicant serve as assessment criteria in the admission procedure – the virginity test[4] being only one absurd example among many others (for an excellent description and analysis, see Bhabha and Shutter, 1994). In Germany, until 1991, a marriage had to have a minimum duration of one year (three years in Bavaria and Baden-Württemberg) before an application for family reunification could be made. This is in sharp contrast to family legislation according to which a marriage is considered *broken* if spouses live apart for a period of one year.

Over the last few years, the prerequisites for a spouse's entrance have been tightened in many countries of the EU. The primary resident is supposed to prove a legal uninterrupted abode of five to eight years, to have an income at his/her disposal equal to 70 per cent of the officially fixed national minimum income and an employment contract of one year in advance. Furthermore, the requirements concerning housing conditions have been extended to include sufficient proof regarding the size of the future couple's home. Another condition for permission to enter is that the couple must prove the quality of their relationship, namely that the marriage was not motivated by considerations other than affection and love, thereby introducing the romantically idealized love-marriage as a yardstick of legality. Intimate questions about sex life as well as the production of love letters can be part of the investigation process (Bhabha and Shutter, 1994: 80). A marriage can be declared illegal if the immigration office has reason to believe that it is based on false (material) motives. In Germany and in the Netherlands a dependent spouse is granted an independent residence status one (NL) to four years (G) after the consummation of the marriage (Kang, 1996: 11). In the event that the marriage breaks up before this or if the husband dies, women are left in a difficult and vulnerable situation: they can ask for an independent residence status on humanitarian grounds, but the criteria for recognition differ greatly from one country to another and even between municipalities inside a state. The decision is up to the local immigration office which decides if an application has 'the chance' to be recognized; otherwise the applicant is not granted welfare aid and her health insurance is not covered. A consequence of the lack of a residence permit is that women cannot apply for paid work. A further peculiarity of the family unification regulations is the receiving states' use of the nuclear family pattern, defining a family as consisting of a husband, his wife and their biological children. For some immigrant groups this has led to the isolation of women from their family networks. 'Social parenthood' (custody and care for children by the extended family, including nephews and nieces) or the active involvement of grandmothers in childcare, which are features of many immigrant groups' cultures, are not accepted by the current regulations.[5] Thus, the regulations force immigrants into a 'Western' model of nuclear family life, one which was not necessarily theirs before emigration. As the influx of new migrants is and will stay significant, the isolation from family members is still an important issue for young migrants, though it is also true that in many cases, more than for many second- and third-generation immigrants, new forms of the extended family are reconstituted in Europe.

Looking at these regulations from an analytical point of view, two features are noticeable. First, the 'male bread-winner principle', which is under pressure or fading away in the indigenous population, is reinforced through the aliens' law. It thereby produces and widens the gap between the role patterns and lifestyles of the so-called modern indigenous and the so-called traditional immigrant population. This also applies to another 'traditional' institution, marriage. We can state that using marriage as a 'gatekeeper' in immigration law not only creates inequalities between indigenous and immigrant men and women, but contributes – on an ideological level – to the reinforcement of static perceptions: immigrants are bound to traditions whereas the 'native Europeans' are increasingly shaking off the yoke of repressive old-fashioned lifestyles. In its current form, the breadwinner and marriage principle discriminate against a large group of immigrant women, those who are dependent on their spouses' legal status. Numerous reports have argued that these laws put women into a deeply vulnerable position which can be easily misused and exploited by men. It is therefore not an exaggeration to state that only in those cases where the marriage works is the law *not* an obstacle. In many other cases, patriarchal habits are reinforced by the legislation of the countries of immigration. In this respect very low divorce rates among the non-European labour immigrants (Turks and Moroccans) – which are usually interpreted as a cultural feature of these groups – are also an indication of the law's impact on the private sphere (see Nauck, 1988). Finally, as the majority of the European countries do not recognize homosexual partnership as the equivalent of heterosexual partnership, the family unification of homosexuals is legally virtually impossible.

These and other aspects contribute to what can be called a 'jungle' situation: in the majority of the European member states immigration laws have been changed frequently, often once a year. Few immigrants can keep pace with these changes in regulations. Since the ratification of the 'Schengen Treaty'[6] there is growing evidence that harmonization of the member states often means taking over the most restrictive legislation from those countries where it has proved implementable.

The emphasis on the legal situation laid out in this section – where regulations concerning asylum seekers and refugees were not covered – is not aimed at drawing a Machiavellian picture of Fortress Europe. Some people

FEMINIST REVIEW NO 57, AUTUMN 1997

are, indeed, creative in overcoming these rules and regulations. Yet, besides absorbing large amounts of time and energy and often being humiliating for the people involved, the rules also have an impact on the indigenous population by reinforcing prevailing ideas that legal weakness implies weak people. Such images of misery tend to survive even when immigrants acquire permanent status. At the same time, immigrants are ambivalently demonized as threatening.

The division of Europe into those with and without full citizenship rights is not only an outcome of the fear of losing control. It also serves the urgent need of creating a consistent image of what it means to be 'European'. In the face of controversies within and between different EU nations about the advantages of European integration, and the tremendous social disparities within European societies (between Northern and Southern Europe, North and South Italy or East and West Germany) the pressure to harmonize the EU at the ideological level is growing. In other words, as *the* European does not yet exist, the making of 'the European' is not merely a challenge for politicians, economists, lawyers and bureaucrats but also has to be expressed in the creation of an imaginative representation.[7]

The limits of European-ness

In this article I have stressed obstacles to the inclusion of immigrant women in European society, central to the question of whether or not migrants will be granted the status of Europe's citizens. There are some indications that – in the long run – formal citizenship may be within the present non-citizens' reach. Most European countries combine two basic principles in the allocation of formal citizenship; citizenship is inherited from the parents (*ius sanguinis*) and/or it is granted to persons born on the country's territory (*ius solis*). Many European countries apply a mixture of these principles, granting citizenship to ex-nationals from former colonies if they applied for it within a certain period of time. In France the children of labour migrants born in the country were naturalized by birth (this law is presently under pressure). First-generation non-European (labour) migrants, however, have been excluded from nationality status in many European countries (The Netherlands, Germany, Austria, Switzerland, France, Belgium, some Nordic countries, Greece). It seems likely that in the future more European states will grant formal citizenship to – at least – second-generation settlers. Although this would obviously represent progress, it does not make immigrants automatically into Europe's 'citizens'. Instead, it assigns to them the nationality of the particular European nation state in which they happen to live. If one of these states introduces special restrictions against a particular group of citizens, as the French government did in the summer of 1995 with regard to the 'Arab population', then EU citizenship does not offer particular security. As there is no European institution taking care of the security of immigrant citizens, every state is its own sovereign and can do with its immigrants what it considers adequate. As long as the sovereignty of the nation states of Europe, positioned *vis-à-vis* Europe as symbolic and politico-economic unions, is a source of ambiguity and contradictions, 'European-ness' will stay a symbolic identity, in danger of symbolizing whiteness, Christianity, enlightenment and modernity.

Returning to feminist debates about citizenship, the analysis of this article suggests that 'difference' is not merely another addition to the concept of citizenship, but that citizenship is constituted by difference. When feminists argue for the acknowledgement of difference, they have in mind something other than the difference laid out in this article; that is to say, difference can be defined in both positive and negative terms, it can be constructed as a means of both ex- and in-clusion. Thus difference is not neutral or innocent, it has many facets and faces, each connected to a specific form of power relations. Any sound analysis of citizenship has to be aware of the power structures embedded in the use of a certain terminology and the concepts involved. In the light of this, it is no longer possible to make claims from a feminist perspective without recognizing that (groups of) women are positioned differently towards each other and that they face different opportunities as well as structural constraints in performing their agency.

Notes

Helma Lutz is a sociologist and currently professor in General Education and Women's Studies at the Johann-Wolfgang Goethe University of Frankfurt, Germany. The research upon which this paper is based was carried out in 1994 on behalf of the Council of Europe, Steering Committee for Equality between Women and Men (see Lutz, 1994). I would like to thank Gail Lewis, Pnina Werbner, Lale Yalcin-Heckmann, Nira Yuval-Davis, Dubravka Zarkov and the anonymous reviewers for their helpful comments on an earlier version of this article. I am very grateful to Liz Gooster for tidying up my English.

1 Administrative and everyday language in Gemany, however, still talks of foreigners, *Ausländer*; while Dutch policy makers talk of ethnic minorities or *allochtonen*, but everyday discourse still refers to *buitenlanders*, foreigners.

2 In several West European countries, among them Germany, a 'new' guest-worker system has been applied recently. Since 1990, as a result of bilateral agreements between Germany and predominantly East European countries like Poland,

Hungary and the Czech Republic, tens of thousands of temporary work permits have been issued (see Rudolph, 1996).

3 However, in the case of adoption marriage is still required.

4 In 1978 a virginity test (vaginal examination) was carried out on Asian brides and to a lesser extent on women coming from Nigeria by the immigration officers as a measure for the detection of false marriages. This test, based on the assumption that according to Hindu and Muslim culture young women have to start married life as virgins, was abolished after international protest (see Parmar, 1982: 245).

5 Morokvasic describes the result of a German case in which an exception was made, but on a temporary basis. 'According to a decision of an administrative court in Mannheim, Germany (reg.no. 13S268/90) a Turkish grandmother was to be expelled from the country. She was admitted to take care of her grandchildren who, when they turned nine and eleven, were considered to be "old enough to be taken care of by another person". It was argued that "the public interest in limiting immigration is of more importance than the special relationship between the grandmother and the children that has developed over the years"' (Morokvasic, 1991: 74).

6 The Schengen-Treaty was first signed in 1985 by France, Germany and the Benelux countries. It is aimed at regulating common visa politics throughout the Schengen territory and controlling entry and movement of non-EU citizens including asylum seekers by a common electronic database system. Next to the five original states, the treaty has been signed by Spain, Italy, Greece and Austria but is not carried out by all of them (state of art, January 1997).

7 I am not saying that there is a central brain behind this creation; the image is rather a discursive product born out of many policies and policy makers.

References

AGISRA (1990) *Frauenhandel und Prostitution – eine Bestandsaufnahme* München: Beck.

ANDALL, Jaqueline (1997) 'Catholic and state constructions of domestic workers: the case of Cape Verdean women in Rome in the 1970s', in **Koser** and **Lutz** (1997b).

BADE, Klaus J. (1993) editor, *Deutsche im Ausland – Fremde in Deutschland* München: Beck.

BALIBAR, Etienne (1990) 'The nation form – history and ideology', *Review* Vol. XIII, No. 3: 329–61.

—— (1991) 'Es gibt keinen Staat in Europa: racism and politics in Europe today', *New Left Review* No. 186: 5–19.

BAUBÖCK, Rainer (1994) *Transnational Citizenship* Aldershot: Elgar.

BHABHA, Jacqueline and SHUTTER, Sue (1994) *Women's Movement: Women under Immmigration, Nationality and Refugee Law* Stoke-on-Trent: Trentham Books.

BMWP, The Black and Migrant Women's Project (for the European Women's Lobby) (1995) *Confronting the Fortress: Black and Migrant Women in the European Union* Brussels: The European Parliament.

CALDO RATZINGER, Agnes, LUTZ, Helma and PABLO, Marissa (1996) 'Das DH-Phänomen' in *Frauen in der einen Welt* Vol. 7, No. 2: 101–9.

CAMPANI, Giovanna (1993) 'Labour markets and family networks: Filipino women in Italy', in **Rudolph** and **Morokvasic** (1993).

CASTLES, Steven (1995) 'Democracy and multicultural citizenship. Australian debates and their relevance for Western Europe', in **Bauböck, R.** editor, *From Aliens to Citizens. Redefining the Status of Immigrants in Europe* Aldershot: Avebury.

CHAMPION, A.G. (1994) 'International migration and demographic change in the developed world', *Urban Studies* Vol. 31, No. 4–5: 653–77.

CODAGNONE, Cristiano (1997) 'The new migration in Russia', in **Koser** and **Lutz** (1997b).

CORNELIUS, W.A., MARTIN, P.L. and HOLLIFIELD, J.F. (1994) editors, *Controlling Immigration: A Global Perspective* Stanford, Calif.: Stanford University Press.

COUNCIL of EUROPE (1993) *The Council of Europe's Work on Violence against Women* Strasbourg.

ESSED, Philomena (1995) 'Gender, migration and cross-ethnic coalition building' in **Lutz, Phoenix** and **Yuval-Davis** (1995b).

EUROSTAT (1993–8) *Rapid Reports. Population and Social Conditions: Female Population by Citizenship in the European Community* Luxembourg.

FASSMANN, Heinz and MÜNZ, Rainer (1994) 'European East-West migration, 1945–1992', *International Migration Review* No.3: 520–38.

HABERMAS, Jürgen (1992) 'Citizenship and national identity: some reflections on the future of Europe' *Praxis International* Vol.12, No 1: 1–19.

KANG, Chong-Sook (1996) '40 Jahre Migrantinnen in Deutschland', in *Beiträge zur Feministischen Theorie und Praxis* Vol. 19, No. 42: 9–16.

KING, Russel (1993) editor, *The New Geography of European Migrations* London: Belhaven.

KOFMAN, Eleonore (1995) 'Citizenship for some but not for others: spaces of citizenship in contemporary Europe', *Political Geography* Vol. 14, No. 2: 121–37.

—— (1996) 'Female "birds of passage" a decade later: immigration, gender and class in Europe', unpublished paper presented at Gender and Global Reconstructuring, San Diego, California

KOSER, Khalid (1997) 'Out of the frying pan into the fire: a case study of illegality among asylum seekers' in **Koser** and **Lutz** (1997b).

KOSER, Khalid and LUTZ, Helma (1997a) 'The new migration in Europe: contexts, constructions and realities' in **Koser** and **Lutz** (1997b).

—— and —— (1997b) editors, *The New Migration in Europe: Social Constructions and Social Realities* Basingstoke: Macmillan, in press.

KYMLICKA, Will (1995) *Multicultural Citizenship* Oxford: Oxford University Press.

LISTER, Ruth (1997a) *Citizenship: Feminist Perspectives* Basingstoke: Macmillan.

—— (1997b) 'Citizenship: towards a feminist synthesis' *Feminist Review* No. 57: 28–48.

LUTZ, Helma (1991) *Migrant Women of 'Islamic Background': Images and Self-images* Occasional Paper 11, Amsterdam: MERA.

—— (1994) *Obstacles to Equal Opportunities in Society by Immigrant Women, with Particular Reference to the Netherlands, the United Kingdom, Germany and the Nordic Countries*, Report for the Council of Europe, Steering Committee for Equality between Women and Men (CDEG), Strasbourg.

LUTZ, Helma; PHOENIX, Ann and YUVAL-DAVIS, Nira (1995a) 'Nationalism, racism and gender – European crossfires' in **Lutz, Phoenix** and **Yuval-Davis** (1995b).

——, —— and —— (1995b) editors, *Crossfires: Nationalism, Racism and Gender in Europe* London: Pluto Press.

MARSHALL, T.H. (1950) *Citizenship and Social Class* Cambridge: Cambridge University Press.

MOCH, Leslie Page (1992) *Moving Europeans* Bloomington & Indiana: Indiana University Press.

MOROKVASIC, Mirjana (1991) 'Fortress Europe and migrant women', *Feminist Review*, Vol.39, No. 4: 69–84.

—— (1993) 'In and out of the labour market: immigrant and minority women in Europe', *New Community* Vol. 19, No. 3: 459–83.

MÜNZ, Rainer (1996) 'A continent of migration: European mass migration in the twentieth century' *New Community* Vol. 22, No. 2: 201–26.

NAUCK, Bernhard (1988) 'Zwanzig Jahre Migrantenfamilien in der Bundes-republik' in **Nave-Herz, Rosemarie,** editor *Wandel und Kontinuität der Familie in der Bundesrepublik Deutschland* Stuttgart: Enke-Verlag, 279–97.

PARMAR, Pratibha (1982) 'Gender, race and class. Asian women in resistance' in Centre for Contemporary Cultural Studies, editor *The Empire Strikes Back* London: Hutchinson, 236–75.

PHIZACKLEA, Annie (1997) 'Migration and globalisation: a feminist perspective', in **Koser** and **Lutz** (1997b).

PILKINGTON, Hilary (1997) 'Going home? The implications of forced migration for national identity formation in post-Soviet Russia' in **Koser** and **Lutz** (1997b).

RERRICH, Maria (1996) 'Modernizing the patriarchal family in West Germany', *European Journal of Women's Studies* Vol.3, No.1: 27–37.

RÄTHZEL, Nora (1994) 'Harmonious heimat and disturbing "ausländer"', *Feminist Psychology* Vol.4, No.1: 81–98.

—— (1995) 'Nationalism and gender in West Europe: the German case' in **Lutz, Phoenix** and **Yuval-Davis** (1995b).

RUDOLPH, Hedwig (1996) 'The new gastarbeiter system in Germany', *New Community* Vol. 22, No. 2: 287–300.

RUDOLPH, Hedwig and HILLMANN, Felicitas (1997) 'The invisible hands need visible heads: managers, experts and professionals from Western countries in Poland' in **Koser** and **Lutz** (1997b).

RUDOLPH, Hedwig and HÜBNER, Sabine (1993) 'Repatriates – guest workers – immigrants: legacies and challenges for German politics' in **Rudolph** and **Morokvasic** (1993).

RUDOLPH, Hedwig and MOROKVAC, Mirjana (1993) editors, *Bridging States and Markets: International Migration in the Early 1990s* Berlin: Edition Sigma.

STARING, Richard (1997) 'Scenes from a fake marriage: notes on the flip side of embeddedness' in **Koser** and **Lutz** (1997b).

UN-ECE (1995) 'Population Trends and Population-related issues' in *Countries in Transition: The Need for International Assistance* Geneva: UN, Population Activities Unit.

WALLACE, Claire, CHMOULIAR, Oxana and SIDORENKO, Elena (1996) 'The Eastern frontier of Western Europe: mobility in the buffer zone', *New Community* Vol. 22, No. 2: 259–86.

WEINERT, Peter (1991) *Foreign Female Domestic Workers: Help Wanted!* Geneva: International Labour Organisation (ILO).

WILPERT, Czarina (1988) 'Migrant women and their daughters: two generations of Turkish women in the Federal Republic of Germany', *International Migration Today* Vol. 2 Paris: UNESCO.

YUVAL-DAVIS, Nira (1997) 'Women, citizenship and difference' *Feminist Review* No. 57: 4–27.

ZARKOV, Dubravka (1995) 'Gender, orientalism and the history of ethnic hatred in the former Yugoslavia' in **Lutz, Phoenix** and **Yuval-Davis** (1995b).

Negotiating Citizenship:
The case of foreign domestic workers in Canada

Daiva Stasiulis and Abigail B. Bakan

FEMINIST REVIEW NO 57, AUTUMN 1997, PP. 112–139

Abstract

This paper argues that most conceptualizations of citizenship limit the purview of the discourse to static categories. 'Citizenship' is commonly seen as an ideal type, presuming a largely legal relationship between an inidividual and a single nation-state – more precisely only one type of nation-state, the advanced capitalist post-war model. Alternatively, we suggest a re-conceptualization of citizenship as a *negotiated relationship*, one which is subject therefore to change, and acted upon collectively within social, political and economic relations of conflict. This dynamic process of negotiation takes place within a context which is shaped by gendered, racial and class structures and ideologies; it also involves international hierarchies among states. Citizenship is therefore negotiated on global as well as national levels. This conceptualization is demonstrated by way of identifying one particular set of experiences of negotiated citizenship, involving foreign domestic workers in Canada. As non-citizens originating from Third World conditions, this is a case involving women of colour workers, highly prone to abusive conditions, and under the direction of employers who are more affluent First World citizens and pre-dominantly white women. Original survey data based on interviews with Caribbean and Filipino domestic workers in Canada are used to demonstrate the varied, creative and effective strategies of two distinctive groups of non-citizens as they attempt to negotiate citizenship rights in restrictive national and international conditions.

Keywords

domestics; citizenship; gender; Canada; Philippines; Caribbean

In recent years, the liberal project of building national societies of formally equal, rights-bearing citizens has increasingly been challenged and dis-credited. Governments have implemented dramatic restructuring policies in both the North and the South, while global pressures for international migration have increased. Polarization between different populations has augmented, notably between international business and the growing populations of low income and jobless 'others'. Ideologies such as

Keynesianism, which supported the post-World War II expansion of welfare services as citizenship entitlements have been replaced by neo-liberal clarion calls for deficit-reduction and global competitiveness. In line with these trends, policy makers across the political spectrum are seeking new definitions of state/citizen relations, emphasizing responsibilities rather than rights of citizens. Feminist, Marxist, liberal and social movement theorists are reformulating citizenship in relation to these changing conditions of a post-cold war era (for summaries of contemporary debates on citizenship, see Andrews, 1991; Bulmer and Rees, 1996; Kymlicka and Norman 1994; and Yuval-Davis, 1996).

This paper contributes to this debate in two separate but related ways. First, it argues that most conceptualizations of citizenship limit the purview of the discourse to static categories. 'Citizenship' is commonly seen as an ideal type, presuming a largely juridical relationship between an individual and a single nation-state – more precisely only one type of nation-state, the advanced post-war capitalist model. While this ideal type is sometimes understood as a relationship individually obtained and passively granted by a given state to an individual, the relationship is usually understood as a static one. The citizenship experience tends to be rendered 'thing-like', objectified as something one is granted or not granted. Alternatively, we suggest a re-conceptualization of citizenship as a *negotiated relationship*. Subject to change, it is acted upon collectively, or among individuals existing within social, political, and economic relations of collective conflict, which are shaped by gendered, racial, class and internationally based state hierarchies. Citizenship is therefore negotiated on the international as well as national levels.

Second, in this paper this new conceptualization is demonstrated by way of identifying one particular set of experiences of negotiated citizenship, involving foreign domestic workers in Canada. This example draws on a case study of non-citizen women of colour working within a gendered, highly vulnerable economy of sexualized, racialized service. In Canada, they are non-citizens originating from Third World conditions, now working for employers who are First World citizens and predominantly white women.[1] Though they retain formal, legal citizenship from their nations of origin, the capacity of their home states to act on their behalf within Canada is rendered ineffectual. As Bhabha (1996) and others (Jonas, 1996; Joppke, 1997) have argued, international conventions on human, migrant and refugee rights are markedly vague and non-binding, and there is an absence of expectations of enforcement beyond what sovereign states are willing to concede. One result is that the national, territorially based sovereignty of receiving states regarding policies towards non-citizens is virtually unchallenged. The minimalist nature of the encroachment on territorial sovereignty in international human rights conventions is reinforced by the centrality of border control to state power (Bhaba, 1996: 6). To this must be added constraints on Third World state 'interference' in First World states' treatment of migrant non-citizens arising out of the structural inequality between nations in the North and South. The increased reliance of Third World labour-exporting countries on the remittances earned from their overseas nationals makes the governments of these states reluctant to intervene to arrest their mistreatment by First World labour-importing countries.

The complexity of the process of negotiation of citizenship in this case study is demonstrated in stark relief. Relations of citizenship and non-citizenship are shown to be mediated and influenced by conditions of global capitalism, as well as by class exploitation, racism and sexism within and beyond Canada's borders. Citizenship and non-citizenship are perceived on a spectrum of variable rights and denial of rights, negotiated in a continual and dynamic process in which the active agency of the non-citizen is profiled. This perspective challenges the more common understanding of citizenship, where emphasis is placed on the granting or denial by nation-states of legal citizenship status to passive recipients.

Reconceptualizing citizenship

Current debates on citizenship have commonly taken as their point of departure the seminal work of T.H. Marshall (1950). Analytically, Marshall's framework presumes an evolutionary expansion of citizenship rights. Historically, it is based on the experience of post-World War Two Britain and the development of the modern welfare state. Such a perspective pre-figured the linear and Eurocentric view put forward by modernization theory in the development literature, as it was classically presented by W. W. Rostow (1960) in his *The Stages of Economic Growth: A Non-Communist Manifesto*. Similarly drawing on Britain as the basis of a universal model, Marshall generalized from an exception to define a rule. Contemporary critics have not been reticent to challenge the basic parameters of Marshall's perspective on these grounds (Brubaker, 1989; Bottomore, 1992).

Others have disputed the premise of Marshall's work for its presumption of the emergence of equality of citizenship rights within post-war Britain itself, blurring, in particular, the importance of class, ethnicity and gender as differentiating elements (Turner, 1990). There are many important critical insights offered in these contributions. Feminists such as Carole Pateman (1988), Mary Dietz (1992) and Anne Phillips (1991), for instance, have debunked the liberal notion of the universal citizen which valorized the attributes of the white, European, propertied male to the exclusion and devalorization of all others. A number of other theorists have given substance to arguments for a 'differentiated citizenship' to counter discrimination inherent in equal treatment which suppresses the values and identities of national, cultural, religious, racial and sexual orientation groups (see Modood, 1994; Parekh, 1991/2; Young, 1990). Within both the Marshallian and post-Marshallian literature, however, a common theme tends to be repeated, one with which our argument takes issue.

Citizenship is commonly perceived as an ideal type, either in the form of a static relationship of an abstract individual to an abstract state or as a thing-like legal status, granted to 'deserving' individuals on the basis of achievement, natural attributes or accident of birth. The assumption is that the state is, or should be, a neutral and fair arbiter of rights based on objective criteria; consistent with modern liberal ideology, the individual is perceived abstractly, subject to fair and equal conditions of access to citizenship rights. This conceptualization, while an ideal, is not artificial; it is a historically constructed feature of modern state ideology bearing and reflecting real, lived consequences. It is therefore highly tenacious and widely accepted as a real condition rather than an ideological construct. The idea of 'citizenship' itself is a politically and socially constructed expression of the development of the advanced capitalist nation-state. We can concur with Stephen Howe when he summarizes: 'the origin of the citizen ideal . . . envisaged a state which was not the personal property of an individual, or an aristocracy or a clique but in which government is the public business of all citizens and has as its aim the common good' (Howe, 1991: 125). In reality, however, women, slaves, colonial subjects, immigrants from certain countries, religious, racial and ethnic minorities, and conquered indigenous peoples were excluded historically from the ideal image of the citizen, and from the rights accorded to the ideal citizen (see Beaud, 1983; Ringer, 1992; Holt, 1992).

Under conditions of contemporary capitalist globalization, this liberal republican ideal, even as just an ideal, is increasingly relegated to outside the experience of 'actually existing liberal democracy' (Stasiulis, 1996a). While Marshall's evolutionary model seemed to 'fit' the politically and socially constructed notion of the liberal democratic state during the years of post-war expansion, his view of that state was in itself historically limited and partial. The realities and legacies of the various and widespread non-citizenship experiences, within Britain and internationally, do not figure centrally in Marshall's explanatory model. Though class exploitation was a feature of Marshall's analysis, his view of class was itself static, and there was no conception of class relationships on an

FEMINIST REVIEW NO 57, AUTUMN 1997

international scale (Marshall and Bottomore, 1992: 17–27). T.H. Marshall's notion of an evolutionary expansion of civil, political and social rights as the defining feature of citizenship is historically rooted in the development of modern capitalism. On this, Marshall himself was explicit. Civil rights are seen to be a feature of eighteenth-century capitalist development; political rights of the nineteenth century; and social rights of the twentieth century. As we approach the end of this same twentieth century, however, rather than seeing an evolution of increasing citizenship rights, or of increasing numbers of beneficiaries of such rights, it may be more appropriate to identify counter-evolutionary characteristics.

The ideal of citizenship is increasingly, in other words, being revealed to be what it is – more ideal than real. There are growing indications of the failure of the citizenship ideal to be taken up even as a model in contemporary conditions. These include the decline of the welfare state and stubbornly high unemployment rates in Europe and North America (Denitch, 1996; Miliband, 1996), the failure of structural adjustment policies in developing nations to meet the needs of the vast majority of the populations, and the failure of the once 'newly' industrializing countries (NICs) and of post-Stalinist Eastern bloc states to evolve into liberal democratic welfare states. Following from a Gramscian notion of ideological hegemony, in order for an ideal type to be experienced as 'real', it needs at least an element, even if partial or mixed, that is consistent with that experience. As the basis of such experience declines, the ideal type appears increasingly fictive (Gramsci, 1971).

As capitalism faces conditions of chronic and deeply rooted crisis on an international scale, the naked drive towards profit maximization rather than raising living standards, and towards balancing state budgets rather than delivering state services, is increasingly accepted as the bottom line in global policy making and statecraft. There is an extensive literature on the nature of the current global crisis of capitalism and its relationship to national governments. While there is considerable debate regarding the root causes of the crisis, and similarly divergent conclusions concerning the parameters of human action to intervene in hopes of a reversal, there is also increasingly common ground on the issue of the extensive damage the crisis has forced upon the majority of populations internationally (see Bauzon, 1992; Callinicos et al., 1994; Cox et al., 1995; Harman, 1995; Harris, 1987; Manor, 1991).

The view of citizenship as an ideal type associated with one type of state tends to limit our understanding of forms of inequality and modes of contestation for rights by groups which lack rights-bearing forms of membership in the territorial nation-state where they are working and residing, often for considerable lengths of time. In the view argued here, global processes of negotiation, mediated, contested or limited by the restrictions of gatekeepers to citizenship, and the reality of an uneven hierarchy among states in the world system, become central features. Our formulation regarding the negotiated, collective and social-relational character of citizenship parallels an argument put forward by E.P. Thompson in his preface to *The Making of the English Working Class* (1963: 9–14). Situating his path-breaking historical outline of the emergence of a mass working class, Thompson took issue with the notion of class as a 'thing' rather than a relationship. '[W]e cannot understand class unless we see it as a social and cultural formation, arising from processes which can only be studied as they work themselves out over a considerable historical period' (1963: 10–11).

If we substitute the word 'citizenship' for 'class' in the above, although the parallel is not an exact one, a conclusion can be drawn similar to that reached by Thompson. Citizenship is commonly taken to be an ideal type, similar to a thing. We often presume that there is an ideal of citizenship which is fair, inclusive and, if not necessarily fully universal, at least constructed in such a manner that it could be reformed or adapted to incorporate differences in an egalitarian manner. This notion of citizenship is as an ideological construct at best, rather than a lived reality. For those scholars (Pateman, 1988; Turner, 1990; Phillips, 1991) who have effectively challenged the Marshallian notion of evolutionary, universalistic citizenship, several important aspects of the ideal type have been unpacked, exposed and analysed. Further, citizenship as a relationship negotiated between an individual and the state, including the relationship between the realm of the private and the public, has been usefully explained (Pateman, 1988; Phillips, 1991). The full range of social relations inscribed in the relational character of citizenship have not, however, been explored. Understanding citizenship and non-citizenship in terms of a spectrum of negotiated relationships as we perceive it is not limited to the issue of whether citizens should be defined as individuals or groups (Turner, 1990).

Even within the critical literature, the historically specific, variable and often contradictory dynamics of the citizenship process are obfuscated or relegated to the background. Our perspective attempts to bring the dynamic, active and continually negotiated complexity of relationships that comprise the citizenship/non-citizenship spectrum into focus, both within and beyond national boundaries. Such a perspective emphasizes specific historical constraints, social conflict and negotiation, and uses the global, rather than the national, setting as its starting point.

As elaborated below, citizenship is itself a nodal point for the intersection of many other social relations. Not unlike a Thompsonian view of class,

FEMINIST REVIEW NO 57, AUTUMN 1997

citizenship exists specifically, historically, and changes continually as relationships are negotiated and re-negotiated in variable national and international conditions. Further, citizenship and non-citizenship, like conflicting classes, emerge simultaneously. However, the analogy is not an exact one. Unlike antagonistic classes, which depend directly on one another in their formation, and develop over time in a context of divergent material interests, citizenship and non-citizenship are usually mediated and socially constructed to work as oppositional by the border-control mechanisms, laws and discourses of nation-states. For example, the maintenance of the ideal type of liberal citizenship relies upon the creation of its opposite, the derogatory ideal of the dangerous, criminal, economically burdensome non-citizen (see Barratt, 1990; Bakan and Stasiulis, 1995).

In contemporary conditions of global crisis and restructuring, tendencies towards nominal or partial recognition of universal human rights, and trans-border citizenship rights, have coincided with tightening restrictions on the rights of new immigrants. These trends are contradictory and create a dynamic terrain of struggle. New immigrants, particularly those from poor Third World origins, are compelled to struggle to obtain even minimal citizenship rights from reluctant host states and among populations encouraged to scapegoat those seeking permanent status and full equality. The tendency to assume that citizenship is a static ideal type, or linear condition or status, has led some contemporary theorists, incorrectly in our view, to focus on only one or another of these trends in abstraction from the wider dimensions. For example, while Yasemin Soysal (1994) accurately identifies one pattern of rights expansion for non-citizens in the case of European guest workers, these rights have not unfolded according to some 'more universal' conception of citizenship. Rather they have been negotiated on the grounds of permanent residence through state, social movement and domestic constitutional politics, where the nation-states have continued to play the central role. Moreover, the focus on the guest workers of the 1960s ignores the trend in other less permanent forms of migration which presents a greater challenge for forging principles of post-national rights. Temporary and what Rodriguez (1996: 23) terms 'autonomous international migration' – taking place independently of intergovernmental agreements by workers, their families and communities – has become a prevalent and important means of survival for trans-border families and has made transnational communities a growing reality. Post-national theorists such as Soysal move from emphasizing the weakening of citizenship rights at the national level to projecting an expansion of citizenship rights at the global level. While the former is accurate, the latter does not follow. Similarly, others have attempted to 'save' citizenship from the failure of its implementation. Hence, going in the opposite direction from Soysal, some liberal and left theorists have strongly defended national state boundaries as a means of defining the borders of citizenship for membership within ethno-national communities (Kymlicka, 1995; Miller, 1994; Taylor, 1992; for a critique, see Stasiulis, 1996a).[2] What these post-Marshallian re-conceptualizations continue to mirror is the view of citizenship as a linear, static, thing-like status which is earned by or bestowed upon individuals or groups.

Alternatively, we maintain that citizenship is negotiated, and is therefore unstable, constructed and re-constructed historically across as well as within geo-political borders. States attempt to regulate access of different individuals and groups to various forms of rights and obligations, and to impose various forms of responsibilities and hardships upon individuals and groups. From the perspective argued here, citizenship and non-citizenship (and various intermediary categories such as non-citizen residency) emerge simultaneously, defined and re-defined according to a dynamic process of struggle and negotiation. Rather than presuming there is an active state and a passive citizenry, or an active number of states and a passive number of bodies of citizens, our view sees citizenship and non-citizenship in a variable spectrum of rights and mechanisms to deny such rights. It is a process which renders legal and legitimate discriminations based on whether individuals embody capital (e.g., as transnational capitalists benefiting from wealth creation in the NICs) or poverty (e.g., of the majority of those living in developing nations), as well as the dominant race/ethnicity and gender.

While this argument is particularly relevant in identifying the contradictions between the citizenship ideal and the reality of a declining level of access to citizenship rights in the contemporary conjuncture of the world system, it also sheds light on the historic development of citizenship in advanced capitalist liberal democracies. As we have stated elsewhere, we maintain that citizenship has to be reconceptualized in ways that:

> simultaneously reflect both global and national relations of power . . . [T]he acceptance of the regulatory authority of hegemonic states in determining access to citizenship rights is not only reflected in the racialized and gendered definition of who is and who is not suitable to obtain such rights. It is also apparent in the assumption of the non-hegemonic status of third world states. . . . The unequal distribution of citizenship rights within the advanced liberal democracies, principally along the lines of class, race and gender inequalities, become blurred and recede in importance when considered in counterposition to societies where far greater proportions of citizens suffer from chronic poverty and privation.
>
> (Bakan and Stasiulis, 1994: 26–8).

FEMINIST REVIEW NO 57, AUTUMN 1997

The particular case of foreign domestic workers in Canada is considered from this analytical starting point.

Negotiating citizenship: the case of foreign domestic workers in Canada

The selection of this particular case study is relevant in demonstrating the value of such a perspective. First, Canada in the post-World War Two era earned a reputation as one of the most advanced welfare states worldwide. In recent years, Canada has been identified by the United Nations human development index (HDI) as the 'best country in the world to live'. Since 1990, when the United Nations Human Development Index (HDI) was introduced, Canada has consistently been among the top three of Canada, the US and Japan; it is currently ranked number one (United Nations Development Programme, 1995: 18–19). Canada is rated number one in the world according to the following definition of human development:

> Human development is a process of enlarging people's choices. . . . [T]he three essential [choices] are for people to lead a long and healthy life, to acquire knowledge and to have access to resources needed for a decent standard of living.
>
> (United Nations Development Programme, 1995: 11).

Political, economic and social freedom, self-respect and guaranteed human rights are further identified as necessary features of human development. Citizenship rights in Canada may therefore appropriately be considered among the 'best' that liberal democratic capitalism can offer in the current period. The experience of 'lived' citizenship/non-citizenship rights in Canada, and how they are negotiated, may suggest the boundaries of such experiences in contemporary capitalism in general. What is not addressed in the UN Human Development ranking is that Canada in the 1990s, like other liberal democratic states internationally, has not been immune to the conditions of global crisis. Despite the advent in 1982 of a new and controversial Constitution, including a Charter of Rights and Freedoms, and regardless of the political party in office at both the federal and provincial levels, social services, the rights of immigrants and visible minorities, working women's access to public childcare and other historic provisions of the welfare state have been in continual decline (Mandel, 1994; Fudge and Glasbeek, 1992; Giles and Arat-Koc, 1994; Cameron and Smith, 1992). It is significant that, when indicators of women's welfare are factored into the United Nations HDI, Canada's 1995 rating falls to ninth place.

The second reason for the selection of this case study, however, goes beyond simply the choice of Canada. The specific experience of foreign domestic workers within Canada – more specifically Canada's largest and most multicultural city, Metropolitan Toronto – suggests that the best place in the world to live is hardly the best for all. Regulated under separate federal state legislative policy, foreign domestic workers in Canada suffer conditions of institutionalized and profound discrimination. Foreign domestic workers in Canada form part of the international migration and employment in private homes of poor Third World female workers, in a process which represents the under-belly of globalization (Chang and Ling, 1996). The scale of female-domestic-worker migration from poorer to richer countries is growing, contributing to an overall pattern of a growing proportion of female migrants that is particularly marked within Asian migration (Lim and Oishi, 1996). These workers are increasingly recognized by the international community not only to account for the majority of female temporary worker migrants from poorer to richer countries, but, along with sex trade workers, also to represent the most widely exploited and abused of migrant workers (United Nations, 1996). The systematic reproduction of migrant domestics as non-citizens within the territories where they work and reside renders them in any meaningful sense stateless as far as access to state protection of their rights is concerned. This is despite the formal retention of legal citizenship status accorded by their home country. This process of construction as non-citizens is also central to maintaining their vulnerability to abuse, violence and human rights violations.

The most recent policy formulation governing the recruitment and conditions of domestic workers in Canada, called the Live-in Caregiver Programme, was developed in 1992. Institutionalized discrimination against foreign domestic workers in Canada, however, has a historical lineage. Even during the period of Canadian post-war welfare state expansion, an explicitly racist immigration policy was maintained (Bolaria and Li, 1988; Stasiulis, 1996c). Foreign domestic workers in Canada have experienced a condition characteristic of domestic workers internationally, one that continued before, during and after the post-war expansionary period: foreign domestic workers suffer particularly harsh discrimination and vulnerability, uncharacteristic of most forms of labour in other service sectors or industry (Bakan and Stasiulis, 1997; Daenzer, 1993; Giles and Arat-Koc, 1994; Stasiulis, 1996b).

Two particular features mark the current legislation governing foreign domestic workers in Canada: 1) they are compelled by law to live in the homes of their employers for a minimum of two years out of a three-year period; and 2) while employed as domestic workers they are legally classified as temporary workers, subject to deportation upon termination of their contracted labour as live-in domestics. The vast majority are women

Figure 1 Filipino migrant women in Canada demonstrate against Canadian immigration restrictions, 1996.
Photo credit: Pura Velasco

of Third World origins, now principally from the Philippines, formerly principally from the Caribbean, who work as domestics in Canada in hopes of obtaining permanent settlement for themselves and their families. Their aim is therefore to negotiate increasing citizenship rights, but in order to do so they fill one of the most vulnerable non-citizenship niches constructed on an international scale.

Foreign domestic workers in Canada are admitted to the country under a national, and therefore federally regulated, policy. Labour legislation, however, falls within the jurisdiction of provincial states. The result is that there are no common labour laws governing their working conditions across the country, and provincial standards vary widely. Even in Ontario, the province with the greatest level of labour protection for domestic workers, the limited rights that are available operate through a complaint-driven process. These non-citizen women of colour therefore have the 'right', in certain limited instances, to demand fair terms of employment from their employers, who are usually white and female, or an employing male/female couple, and of considerable economic means. The employers also act as their landladies/landlords and control the right of foreign domestic workers to stay in Canada. The result of this institutionalized asymmetry in power between live-in foreign worker and citizen employer is that, in all provinces where studies have been conducted, cases of domestic-worker abuse ranging from unpaid overtime to sexual harassment and assault have been reported (Bakan and Stasiulis, 1997 forthcoming).

Foreign domestic workers generally continue to apply for such jobs and to accept such conditions because there is a carrot as well as a stick attached to the legislative policy. Those who endure two years of virtually indentured labour within a three-year period after arrival are entitled to apply for permanent residence in Canada. If successful in obtaining the right to permanent residency, or landed immigrant status, all of the rights accorded other workers apply, approximating full legal citizenship rights with the exception of the right to vote and hold certain civil service positions. After a period of three more years, landed immigrants are eligible to apply for full legal citizenship.

The Canadian government and private employment agencies insist that the foreign domestic worker policy increases the opportunity for the advancement of citizenship rights for poor Third World women migrants. In fact, the LCP has been portrayed ideologically as a form of foreign aid (Arat-Koc, 1992: 238–9). In reality, this policy serves to counterpose the citizenship rights of the employing families – usually white, relatively wealthy professional couples with two or more pre-school-age children – to the restriction of citizenship rights of Third World women. In the absence of a national child-care policy which might provide affordable public child care, the Canadian state 'subsidizes' a privatized child-care service for its wealthier citizens, through recourse to immigration control. In effect, the cost of this subsidized citizenship entitlement is borne by the poor, Third World female non-citizen.

From 1955, when Canada instituted its first official foreign domestic worker policy, until the mid-1970s, Caribbean women held the dubious honour of being formally ranked high on the list of most favoured domestic workers. Indeed, the job of live-in domestic worker, and particularly live-in child-care worker or nanny, was widely associated with a socially constructed stereotype of the West Indian woman.[3] The demand for in-home domestic care has continued to be filled by the labour of foreign women. However, the trend shifted through the 1980s away from the Caribbean region towards recruitment from the Philippines. Despite an historic bias against Asian immigration, for the purposes of domestic service the stereotype now turned away from West Indian women to favour Filipinas.[4] Unofficially, gatekeepers shifted their preference to Filipinas in an effort to undercut the organizing campaigns of Caribbean domestic workers attempting to increase their citizenship rights within Canada (Bakan and Stasiulis, 1995). Officially, the 1992 Live-in Caregiver Program (LCP) imposed novel and intensified barriers to entry, such as stricter educational and training eligibility criteria, for all domestic workers from the Third World, regardless of their particular region or country of origin. The combined effect was that the gatekeepers began to secure the locks,

FEMINIST REVIEW NO 57, AUTUMN 1997

limiting or restricting entry to Canadian residence or citizenship for Caribbean and Filipino female migrants to Canadian residence or citizenship.

Recent statistics confirm the discriminatory biases in the new policy (interview, Linda MacDougall, 1996). A precipitous drop in numbers of migrants to approximately one-fifth of the pre-LCP annual figure demonstrates the limiting of an important source of legal entry and acquisition of Canadian residence and citizenship for Third World women. This is particularly the case for West Indian and Filipino women who have historically comprised the largest concentrations of foreign domestic workers from developing countries. Collectively, Caribbean and Filipino women have been compelled by restrictive Canadian state policy and wider international pressures to devise distinct strategies to negotiate their way through these labyrinthine barriers.

Strategies for negotiating citizenship compared: the experiences of West Indian and Filipino domestic workers in Canada

Based on a survey of foreign domestic workers living in Toronto, the remainder of this paper offers a comparative analysis of the experiences of women currently working in the homes of wealthy Canadian families. The survey was designed to investigate the negotiating strategies of two distinct groups of women of colour attempting to challenge the myriad barriers to citizenship for foreign domestic workers in Canada. The data are drawn from fifty questionnaires, twenty-five from interviews conducted with live-in domestics from the Caribbean and twenty-five with those who have originated from the Philippines.[5] Country of origin was determined by birthplace.

The results provide the basis for a comparison of the distinct experiences of negotiating citizenship relationships among two groups of women of colour in Canada. Because the study is numerically small, it is of qualitative rather than quantitative significance. However, the Caribbean and the Philippines are not arbitrary reference points in terms of the general experience of Third World migration. Both the English-speaking island states of the Caribbean and the Philippines have long histories of colonialism and neo-colonialism, a recent history of debt-based dependency through International Monetary Fund and US-government-supported structural adjustment policies and recent or long-term experiences of emigration as a strategy for economic survival (McAfee, 1991; Beltran and de Dios, 1992). The efforts of Canada to take advantage of large pools of women workers of colour who are compelled by conditions of poverty and chronic unemployment in their countries of origin to accept labour conditions spurned by those who have other options is directly related to these global realities.

Survey data of this nature are necessarily based on generalizing collective patterns of social negotiation, rather than isolated individual experiences. While the size of the sample is small in terms of statistical trends, it is substantially larger than an approach based on individual life histories. The study effectively highlights the pathways of negotiation of distinctive groupings of non-citizen women. These are workers who are treated as temporary visitors and, though providing labour in serious demand, they are designated as menial servants by employers and the Canadian state. What are revealed are the dynamic, creative and effective attempts of noncitizen Third World women to enter Canada and, once arrived, to overcome demonstrable barriers to the attainment of citizenship rights, not only in the legal sense of the term but also in terms of the wider context of rights discussed above.

Survey findings: immigration status

The survey data reveal a commonality of conditions of work among the two groups of women working as live-in domestic employees of Canadian families. Faced with the threat of deportation for non-fulfilment of duties, domestic workers who live with their employers work long hours for low pay in very isolated and highly regulated conditions.

Regarding their immigration experience and statuses, however, there was a divergence of experience among the two groups of women interviewed. Among the West Indian women, twenty out of twenty-five responded to a question about place of work immediately prior to working as a domestic in Canada (Q7).[6] Of these, all but two (who had worked in Europe) had worked in the West Indies immediately before coming to Canada. Among the Filipinas, twenty-three responded to this question; only eleven of these came directly from the Philippines. The rest had worked in the Middle East, Asia and Europe immediately prior to coming to Canada to work.

This divergent finding reflects two different structures of migration for the two groups of women and two distinct strategies for negotiating the global restrictions to migration faced by Third World workers seeking First World residence. The migration of Caribbean women to Canada reflects historical country/region to country imperial ties. In contrast, Philippine migration reflects the aggressive marketing of labour for export on the part of various Philippine governments (from Marcos to Aquino to Ramos). The latter

FEMINIST REVIEW NO 57, AUTUMN 1997

process has had the unintentional effect of rendering unskilled or deskilled Filipino women experienced international migrants (see Bakan, 1987).

Negotiating citizenship involves making one's way through the selection processes of various gatekeepers. There is a notable preference among domestic placement agencies in Canada to recruit Filipinas from outside Manila; moreover, the experience requirement of the LCP in Canada would tend to lend favour to those who had previously done domestic service. This trend is reflected in the survey findings, which is notable given the small size of the sample. In contrast, West Indian women in search of domestic service as a means of emigrating are not on the most favoured list in Canada, or in any other country. Among the West Indian domestics, ten entered Canada as domestic workers on either the FDM or the LCP, and therefore had been legally admitted as foreign live-in domestic workers; fourteen entered Canada as visitors, and one claimed asylum as a refugee (Q15). It is, however, illegal to work in Canada while on a visitor visa, and refugee status is almost never granted to those who claim the need for asylum from the West Indies. Refugee claimants can work only with a separately issued work permit. Therefore, the majority of the West Indian respondents entered into domestic service in Canada as undocumented migrant workers. Among the Filipinas, twenty-three had entered Canada on the FDM or LCP programmes as foreign domestic workers, while only two entered as visitors.

The divergent patterns of entry into Canada and subsequent legal status for the two groups indicates more restrictive access for West Indian women versus Filipinas in current conditions. The high number of undocumented (visitor) workers among West Indian women reflects the official disfavour among gatekeepers in Canada towards these applicants. Such anti-black bias compels more and more West Indian women to enter the country as visitors and work without any formal status in the country. This is a pattern of undocumented personal service that is widespread in other countries such as the United States and Italy. Despite increasing restrictions, Filipino applicants, however, are currently considered in a racist stereotype to be 'good servants', and therefore find it easier, or at least possible, to pass through Canada's closely guarded gates. This is conditional, however, on their willingness to work as maids and nannies, arrive on temporary visas and live with their employers.

In response to another question regarding current immigration status within Canada, the picture changed somewhat (Q16). Among the West Indian domestic workers, sixteen had temporary or unidentified status within the country at the time of the interview, whereas nine had obtained landed immigrant status or actual legal citizenship. Among the Filipino domestic workers, nineteen were legal temporary workers, whereas only six had obtained landed immigrant status.

The notable feature here is that historically it has been unusual for any worker to accept live-in domestic service in Canada unless they are temporary workers. The implication is that the economy in Canada today is so restrictive for workers in general, and for 'unskilled' immigrant workers of colour in particular, that even those who are legally eligible to leave live-in domestic service are faced with few or no other options. The numbers here are not large enough to maintain an argument for a new general trend, and this is not our claim. The fact, however, that some West Indian women workers, for whom the general community network of contacts and support is older and therefore potentially more extensive than for the more recent Filipino workers, are continuing to work at least partially as live-in domestic servants (see below), despite having obtained landed immigrant or citizenship status, is a new and highly unusual phenomenon within the post-war Canadian work-force.

Regarding immigration status, then, the spectrum that is revealed is a skewed one. First, the findings suggest that there are more West Indian women than Filipinas who have legal rights to work in other occupations yet who remain working as domestics. Second, there are also apparently more illegal or undocumented domestic workers among the West Indian sample.

These findings have implications for the live-in requirement of the LCP. The LCP obliges foreign domestics to work and live in their employers' home for two years if they are to be eligible to apply for permanent residence in Canada. Domestic workers will commonly share an apartment for weekend use in order to obtain some privacy and time away from what are often twenty-four-hour, on-call obligations. Those who are illegal, however, and have no hopes of obtaining permanent legal status, would feel no obligation to live in their employers' homes to meet the FDM/LCP regulation. Those who are landed immigrants or citizens, would be released from this requirement and would normally be seeking an alternative to domestic service.

Among the West Indian domestics, of the twenty-four who responded to this question, only four lived with their employer during the entire seven-day week (Q28). Thirteen lived with their employer during the five- or six-day working week only; five lived out; and two had 'other' living arrangements. Among the Filipinas, of the twenty-four who responded, only six lived with their employer all week. Sixteen lived with their employer during the working week only; and two lived out. Regarding the live-in requirement of the FDM/LCP, the survey suggests that both

Figure 2 March for Bread and Roses, Jobs and Justice: immigrant women marching for recognition of their rights in Canada.
Photo credit: Pura Velasco

employers and domestics are inclined to bend the full-time live-in rule. This represents an important finding about the collective negotiating strategies of foreign domestic workers, for whom the live-in requirement has been identified as one of the most oppressive features of the regulated policy.

Research internationally and over historical time has found that the single greatest feature of domestic workers' ability to negotiate or bargain for improvements in the generally oppressive conditions of domestic service is the ability to live out, away from the dictates of the employing family (Romero, 1992: 139ff; Bakan and Stasiulis, 1997 forthcoming). Among both the Caribbean and Filipino domestic workers, the attraction of obtaining a private part-time residence is clear. In spite of the threat of dire consequences, including deportation, the rate of success in obtaining some degree of live-out arrangement represents a notable accomplishment in negotiating citizenship rights for this non-citizen population.

According to government explanations, the LCP exists due to a chronic shortage of labour from the Canadian market willing to provide live-in domestic service. The LCP was designed in 1992, following the earlier Foreign Domestic Movement (FDM) policy of 1981, to address the purported need to recruit workers from outside of the country for the sole purpose of filling this niche in the labour market. These findings, however, suggest a different picture. From the standpoint of the employers, demand for live-in service is generally assumed to be high among those with small children, or in some cases elderly parents, who require care during all hours of the day and night. In the context of declining real incomes for the majority of income-earners, however, employers may in fact be more concerned to hire domestic workers who are willing to work for low wages and are subject to minimal regulation – whether they are live-in or live-out.

The quality of accommodation reported by the domestic workers from both groups suggests a further reason why attempting to live out at least part of the week is attractive. Among the West Indian domestics, eleven of twenty-five who responded reported their room in their employers' house was in the basement (Q29); only seven of twenty-five had their own telephone (Q30D); ten of twenty-four who responded had no lock on their door (Q30E). Among the Filipino domestics, sixteen of twenty-four who responded had a basement room; sixteen of twenty-three had their own telephone; and fully eighteen of twenty-five had no lock on their door. When asked what changes they would like to see in the LCP (Q36F), eighteen of twenty-five West Indian domestics and sixteen of twenty-three Filipinas who responded said they would like to see changes in the live-in requirement.

Remittances and family support

The survey indicated the importance for both groups of workers of financially supporting family members back home. This is an important element of the negotiating strategy of immigrant communities, particularly of women for whom compensatory paid work sufficient to support their families is limited relative to men's in virtually every country in the world. The interviewees were asked to rank the importance, on a five-point scale from 'very important' to 'not important at all', of a number of factors considered in their decision to come to Canada as a domestic worker (see Table 1; note that each question was ranked separately).

Clearly, for a significant number of women workers, the decision to come to Canada was largely linked to their family's financial and social welfare. Another open-ended question asked 'What are the major things you have gained, or hope to gain, in becoming a live-in domestic worker in Canada?' (Q31). The largest number of West Indian domestics first mentioned furthering their education (ten of twenty-five who responded); the second most common answer was about integrating with others or getting to

Table 1 *Percentage of those who answered 'important' or 'very important'*

	Immigration to Canada[7]	Bring family to Canada[8]	Money for home[9]
WI	96	60	70.8
Fil.	80	72	76

know Canada (eight responses); and the remaining responses were about raising their standard of living, acquiring landed immigrant status, or bringing family to Canada.

The Filipino responses were different. Here, sending money home was the most common goal first mentioned (ten of twenty who responded); after this, the most common answers focused on bringing their family to Canada (six responses); and the remaining answers were scattered among educating their children, improving their standard of living or gaining a better job.

The role of remittances figures more highly in the concerns of the Filipina domestics interviewed than among the West Indians. In both cases, remittances are important, but the relative weight is different. When asked directly in another question, 'For your family back home, how important do you feel it is that you send them money from your work in Canada' (Q25), among twenty-one West Indians responding to this question, ten said 'very important'; four said 'important'; two said it was a neutral issue; four said 'not very important' and for one it was 'not important at all'. Out of twenty-five Filipinas who answered this question, eighteen said 'very important'; one said 'important'; five said it was a neutral issue; and one said 'not important at all'.

This variation in emphasis could be understood as at least partially due to the more recent migration flow of Filipinos to Canada, with more dependants remaining back home in need of overseas support. Further, the Philippine government is highly dependent upon overseas remittances as the main source of foreign currency. There is a massive network of state and private interests encouraging overseas work for this purpose (Heyzer *et al.*, 1994). The Ramos government calls female overseas workers 'the new heroines' of the Philippines. Originally viewed as a temporary answer to the Philippines' unemployment and severe balance of payments problems, labour export, and in particular international trafficking in female domestics and entertainers, has become an integral aspect of the Philippine economy.

Despite this difference, an interesting similarity regarding remittance payments was also indicated in the survey. In answer to the question, 'To whom do you generally send remittance cheques?' (Q24), among twenty West Indian respondents, only three stated that money was sent to their husbands. Other responses included their mother (nine); combinations of relatives (six); or another relative or person (two). Among the twenty-three Filipino respondents who answered this question, only six stated that they sent money to their husbands. Other responses were their mother (nine); combinations of relatives (three); another relative or person (three); and eldest daughter (two).

Of note is the fact that, among both groups of women, more directed their remittance cheques to their mothers than to their husbands, and more to other relatives in general than to their husbands. This is despite quite divergent marital patterns among the two samples (Q18). Of twenty-five West Indian domestics who answered this question, only three were in the category of married/partner prior to arrival in Canada; one described herself in the category of separated/divorced/widowed; and twenty-one stated they had never married. Among the twenty-five Filipinas who responded, roughly half (twelve) identified themselves as married/partner; two in the separated/divorced/widowed category; and eleven stated that they had never married. Therefore, there were a larger number of married/partnered Filipinas compared to the West Indian women.

This is a finding consistent with the divergent cultural norms related to the institution of marriage. In the Philippines, the majority of the population are practising Catholics and formal legal marriage is commonly expected of young women. In the West Indies, on the other hand, there is a common tradition of unions without formal marriage, and single-parent families headed by women are far from unusual (Eviota, 1992; Momsen, 1993). In both groups, however, husbands were notably not the principal recipients of the remittance cheques.

This cross-cultural similarity in remittance patterns conforms to worldwide observations that women tend to work to support the basic needs of their families rather than for personal consumption. Moreover, it implies that there is no automatic presumption that their male partners or spouses will distribute their earnings in accordance with the wishes of the women migrant wage-earners. As a strategy for negotiating citizenship, the financial independence of women workers and women-centred networks are therefore important factors in the process. This finding adds emphasis to the importance of considering female migration patterns distinctly from male migration patterns and marital relations, even when considerations of family support as a motivation for immigration are highlighted (Miller Mattei, 1996).

Conclusion

In contrast to theorists such as Soysal (1994) and Jacobsen (1996) who see a trend in the emergence of deterritorialized post-national rights for non-citizens, our analysis of one augmented form of transnationalized female labour – migrant domestic workers – indicates the tenacity of national, territorially based sovereignty to restrict rights to individuals originating from outside a nation-state's borders. Without denying that emergent forms of trans-border, regional (e.g. European) citizenship can function as a guarantee of further privilege for transnational business people and of mobility rights for some workers of designated 'appropriate' nationalities, 'control over which non-citizens can have access to the territory is a defining characteristic of the modern state, and states in the twentieth century have guarded their borders with increasing jealousy' (Bhabha, 1996: 6)[10].

Canada's immigration programme for foreign domestic workers, which institutionalizes *de facto* temporary statelessness for Third World poor women is informed by the same logic as California's Proposition 187, which, 'if implemented would deny public school education, health care and other public benefits to undocumented immigrants and their children' (Hondagneu-Sotelo, 1995: 185). Wealthier states, whose own capacities to deliver on benefits associated with social citizenship have declined in obeisance to the dictates of transnational capital and neo-liberal deficit-cutting logics, are increasingly 'wanting a labor force without human beings' (ibid.: 184), secure in the knowledge of vast reserves of labour willing to migrate from desperately poor countries. Those immigrants seeking to attain increasing citizenship rights through the migration process are therefore under considerable pressure to find creative and collectively effective negotiating strategies in face of increasingly severe restrictions on permanent, non-discriminatory and accessible citizenship rights. While becoming revealed as more a mirage than real, the status of fully recognized citizen of the advanced capitalist nation-state is still no less coveted. This is particularly the case for Third World migrant workers given the existence of large wage differentials between labour-sending and labour-receiving countries.

Other theorists have raised the possibility that, when considering the link between citizenship and international migration of various sorts (refugees, temporary workers, generally those counterposed to global capitalists), we are witnessing the constitution of new forms of global and regional apartheid (Richmond, 1994; Balibar, 1996: 362–3). Rendered largely invisible as a result of their performance of work in the private sphere of the family-household, migrant domestic workers are generally exempted from societal-level employment standards and other forms of protective labour, social security and human rights legislation. Wide-scale exploitation of Third World women domestic workers, through their construction as non-citizens, is an intrinsic aspect of globalization. It is in this context that the creative negotiating strategies of Canada's domestic workers take on international significance.

Our survey of Caribbean and Filipino women domestic workers in Toronto reveals some of the motivations and strategies of those who have the most to gain by obtaining full Canadian citizenship rights, and who risk the most if that goal is not obtained. Thus, Caribbean women who have been virtually shut out of the formal immigration routes to Canadian citizenship, bypass official channels and, as undocumented workers, also are *less* likely than Filipino domestics to acquiesce to the harsh live-in requirement of the official programme.

While the non-citizenship status of foreign domestics is negotiated through transactions involving many stakeholders in the global exploitation of Third World female domestics (sending and receiving countries, the IMF, the World Bank, citizen-employers and a host of intermediaries), these women are far from passive. They reveal the transformative power of human agency, of ordinary people, including highly exploited and undocumented migrants. They work to negotiate a measure of dignity as well as economic well-being. Through their transnational remittances, and initiation of networks of migration, these migrant women actively develop transnational ties and support transnational families and communities. There is also increasing evidence that migrant domestic workers are collectively contesting the limitations on their human and worker rights through global networking and involvement in increasingly internationalized and multi-focused social movements (Velasco, 1997; Bakan and Stasiulis, 1997 forthcoming).

Notes

Daiva Stasiulis and Abigail B. Bakan have been conducting joint research on women of colour, work and citizenship since 1991. Publications from this research have appeared in *Signs, Science and Society*, several edited books, and will appear in two forthcoming books: *Not One of the Family: Foreign Domestic Workers in Canada* (University of Toronto Press, publication date June 1997) and *Negotiating Citizenship: Filipino and West Indian Domestic Workers and Nurses in Canada* (Macmillan Press, expected 1998).

Abigail B. Bakan is Associate Professor of Political Studies at Queen's University, in Kingston, Canada, where she has been a Queen's National Scholar since 1985. She has conducted extensive research on the Caribbean female migration to Canada and contemporary issues of political theory. Other publications include *Ideology and Class Conflict in Jamaica: The Politics of Rebellion* (McGill Queen's University Press, 1990) and *Imperial Power and Regional Trade: The Caribbean Basin Initiative* (edited with David Cox and Colin Leys) (Wilfrid Laurier University Press, 1993).

Daiva Stasiulis is Professor of Sociology at Carleton University in Ottawa, Canada, where she has taught since 1983. She has published extensively on issues of racism, the politics and policies of anti-racism and multiculturalism, feminism and

FEMINIST REVIEW NO 57, AUTUMN 1997

difference. In May 1996, she chaired the United Nations Expert Group Meeting on Violence Against Migrant Women Workers, held in Manila. Her publications include *Unsettling Settler Societies: Articulations of Gender, Race, Ethnicity and Class* (edited with Nira Yuval-Davis) (Sage, 1995).

Earlier drafts of this paper were presented at the 'Women, Citizenship and Difference' conference, 18 July 1996, University of Greenwich, London, and the Society for Caribbean Studies, London, 3–6 July 1996 (Bakan and Stasiulis, 1996a, 1996b). It is part of a larger study directed by the authors and funded by the Social Sciences and Humanities Research Council of Canada, entitled 'Women of Colour, Work and Citizenship: West Indian and Filipino Domestic Workers and Registered Nurses in Toronto'. For further elaboration of findings from this study, see Bakan and Stasiulis (1994, 1995, 1996c, 1997). All works published in this study are equally and jointly authored.

1 We are aware of the potentially over-simplified implication of the terms 'First World' and 'Third World' and 'North' and 'South'. However, we take as given an international hierarchy of economic and political power among nation-states in the world system, which has seen an increasing gap between the more developed and less developed nations over recent decades. With due recognition of the risk of oversimplification, for the purposes of this argument, therefore, we think the usage of these terms is appropriate.

2 There are alternative views which recognize the need for increased rights and freedoms of immigrants as against national law See, for example, Baubock (1994), Jacobsen (1996) and Soysal (1994).

3 While this was recognized by the willingly co-operative governments of the English Caribbean – and by thousands of Caribbean women themselves – as an opportunity to migrate abroad in search of better prospects, the policy was not constructed on altruistic grounds Instead, favouring women from the British West Indies was a reflection of Canada's historic legacy of imperialist interests in the region (Bakan, Cox and Leys, 1993; Tennyson, 1990; Levitt and McIntyre, 1967; Chodos, 1977).

4 Note that the term 'Filipina' is a noun (plural: Filipinas), referring to a woman who lives in or originates from the Philippines. 'Filipino' is a gender-neutral adjective referring to those who live in or originate from the Philippines.

5 The interviews were conducted by women research assistants of the same regional or national origins as the interviewees They were conducted face-to-face or by telephone through individual interviews of about ninety minutes. The sample was selected through a snow-ball approach of community contacts. No more than three names were suggested by each interviewee, among whom no more than one name was subsequently interviewed. Interviewees were asked to respond to all questions, though it was not uncommon for some questions to be declined a response. The fifty interviews took place between 1994 and 1995, after the new LCP legislation was enacted. Some of the interviewees arrived in Canada under the previous FDM and others by other means elaborated further

in the article. We would like to acknowledge the contributions of Maria Leynes, Marcia Williams and Claudine Charley whose work as reseach assistants was invaluable to this project.

6 The reference 'Q' followed by a number refers to the question number of the interview schedule. This paper is only a partial interpretation of findings. The survey questionnaire is available on request from the authors.

7 Question 12A 'I wanted to immigrate to Canada.' Twenty-five West Indian and twenty-five Filipino workers responded to this question.

8 Question 12B 'I wanted to bring over my family or certain family members to Canada.' Twenty-five West Indian and twenty-five Filipino workers responded to this question.

9 Question 12H 'I wanted to be able to earn money to send back home.' Twenty-four West Indian and twenty-five Filipino workers responded to this question.

10 The seeming instance of post-national membership offered by European citizenship actually discriminates against third country nationals (nationals of non-EC states who have acquired legal permanent resident status in an EC country), and thus reinforces an equivalence between citizenship and nationality (Hollifield, 1994: 167)

References

ANDREWS, Geoff (1991) editor, *Citizenship* London: Lawrence & Wishart.

ARAT-KOC, Sedef (1992) 'Immigration policies, migrant domestic workers and the definition of citizenship in Canada', in **Vic Satzewich** editor, *Deconstructing A Nation: Immigration, Multiculturalism and Racism in '90s Canada* Halifax: Fernwood.

BAKAN, Abigail (1987) 'The international market for female labour and individual deskilling: West Indian women workers in Toronto', *North/South: Canadian Journal of Latin American and Caribbean Studies* Vol. 12, No. 24.

BAKAN, Abigail B. and STASIULIS, Daiva (1994) 'Foreign domestic worker policy in Canada and the social boundaries of citizenship', *Science and Society* Vol. 58, No. 1: 7–33.

—— and —— (1995) 'Making the match: domestic placement agencies and the racialization of women's work', *Signs: Journal of Women in Culture and Society* Vol. 20, No. 2: 303–35.

—— and —— (1996a) 'Negotiating the citizenship labyrinth: legal strategies and extra-legal empowerment of foreign domestic workers', paper delivered at the Women, Citizenship and Difference Conference, University of Greenwich, London, 18 July.

—— and —— (1996b) 'Domestic workers in Canada: Caribbean and Filipino diasporas compared', paper presented to the Society for Caribbean Studies, London, 3–6 July.

—— and —— (1996c) 'Structural adjustment, citizenship, and foreign domestic labour', in **Isabella Bakker** editor, *Rethinking Restructuring: Gender and Change in Canada* Toronto: University of Toronto Press.

—— and —— (1997 forthcoming) editors, *Not One of the Family: Foreign Domestic Workers in Canada* Toronto: University of Toronto Press.

—— and —— (forthcoming) 'Working the labyrinth: legal strategies and extralegal empowerment of foreign domestic workers', in **Radha Jhappan** editor, *Women's Legal Strategies* Toronto: University of Toronto Press.

BAKAN, Abigail B., COX, David and LEYS, Colin (1993) editors, *Imperial Power and Regional Trade: The Caribbean Basin Initiative* Waterloo: Wilfrid Laurier University Press.

BALIBAR, Etienne (1996) 'Is European citizenship possible?', *Public Culture* No. 8: 355–76.

BARRATT, Harold (1990) 'West Indians in Canada: adapting to the host society', in **Tennyson** (1990).

BAUBOCK, Rainer (1994) *Transnational Citizenship: Membership and Rights in International Migration* Brookfield, Vermont: Edward Elgar.

BAUZON, Kenneth E. (1992) editor, *Development and Democratization in the Third World: Myths, Hopes and Realities* Washington, DC: Crane Russank, Taylor & Frances.

BEAUD, Michel (1983) *A History of Capitalism, 1500–1980* New York: Monthly Review Press.

BELTRAN, Ruby Palma and DE DIOS, Aurora Javate (1992) editors, *Filipino Overseas Contract Workers: At What Cost?* Manila: Women in Development Foundation and Goodwill Trading.

BHABHA, Jacqueline (1996) 'Embodied rights: gender persecution, state sovereignty, and refugees', *Public Culture* No. 9: 3–32.

BOLARIA, B. SINGH and LI, PETER S. (1988) (2nd edn) *Racial Oppression in Canada* Toronto: Garamond.

BOTTOMORE, Tom (1992) 'Citizenship and social class, forty years on' in **Marshall** and **Bottomore** (1992).

BRUBAKER, W. Rogers (1989) *Immigration and the Politics of Citizenship in Europe and North America* New York: University Press of America.

BULMER, Martin and REES, Anthony (1996) editors, *Citizenship Today: the Contemporary Relevance of T.H. Marshall* London: UCL Press.

CALLINICOS, Alex *et al.* (1994) *Marxism and the New Imperialism* London: Bookmarks.

CAMERON, Duncan and SMITH, Miriam (1992) editors, *Constitutional Politics* Toronto: Lorimer.

CHANG, Kimberly and LING, L.H.M. (1996) 'Globalization and its intimate other: Filipina domestic workers in Hong Kong', paper prepared for the International Studies Association, San Diego, CA, 16–21 April.

CHODOS, Robert (1977) *The Caribbean Connection* Toronto: James Lorimer.

COX, Robert *et al.* (1995) *International Political Economy: Understanding Global Disorder* Halifax: Fernwood.

DAENZER, Patricia (1993) *Regulating Class Privilege: Immigrant Servants in Canada, 1940s–1990s* Toronto: Canadian Scholars Press.

DENITCH, Bogdan (1996) 'Democracy and the new world order: dilemmas and conflicts', *Social Justice* Vol. 23, Nos 1–2: 21–38.

DIETZ, Mary (1992) 'Context is all: feminism and theories of citizenship' in **Chantal Mouffe** editor, *Dimensions of Radical Democracy: Pluralism, Citizenship and Community* London: Routledge.

EVIOTA, Elizabeth Uy (1992) *The Political Economy of Gender: Women and the Sexual Division of Labour* London: Zed Books.

FUDGE, Judy and GLASBEEK, Harry (1992) 'The politics of rights: a politics with little class', *Social and Legal Studies* Vol. 1, No. 45.

GILES, Wenona and ARAT-KOC, Sedef (1994) editors, *Maid in the Market: Women's Paid Domestic Labour* Halifax: Fernwood.

GRAMSCI, Antonio (1971) *Selections from the Prison Notebooks,* ed. and trans. Q. Hoare and G.N. Smith New York: International Publishers.

HARMAN, Chris (1995) *Economics of the Madhouse: Capitalism and the Market Today* London: Bookmarks.

HARRIS, Nigel (1987) *The End of the Third World: Newly Industrializing Countries and the Decline of an Ideology* Harmondsworth: Penguin.

HEYZER, N., LYCKLAMA, A., NIJEHOLT, G. and WEERAKOON, N. (1994) editors, *The Trade in Domestic Workers: Causes, Mechanisms and Consequences of International Migration* London: Zed Books.

HOLLIFIELD, J.F. (1994) 'Immigration and republicanism in France: the hidden consensus' in **W.A. Cornelius, P.L. Martin** and **J.F. Hollifield** editor, *Controlling Immigration: A Global Perspective* Stanford, Calif.: Standford University Press.

HOLT, C. (1992) *The Problem of Freedom: Race, Labor and Politics in Jamaica and Britain, 1832–1938* Baltimore: Johns Hopkins University Press.

HONDAGNEU-SOTELO, Pierrette (1995) 'Women and children first: new directions in anti-immigrant politics', *Socialist Review* Vol. 25, No. 1: 169–90.

HOWE, Stephen (1991) 'Citizenship in the new Europe: a last chance for the enlightenment?' in **Andrews** (1991).

JACOBSEN, D. (1996) *Rights across Borders: Immigration and the Decline of Citizenship* Baltimore, Md: Johns Hopkins University Press.

JONAS, Susanne (1996) 'Rethinking immigration policy and citizenship in the Americas: a regional approach' *Social Justice* Vol. 23, No. 3: 68–85.

JOPPKE, C. (1997) Review of books by Thomas Faist, David Jacobsen and Marco Mariniello, *Contemporary Sociology* Vol. 26, No. 1: 65–8.

KYMLICKA, Will (1995) *Multicultural Citizenship: A Liberal Theory of Minority Rights* New York: Oxford University Press.

KYMLICKA, Will and NORMAN, Wayne (1994) 'Return of the citizen: a survey of recent work on citizenship theory', *Ethics* Vol. 104 (January): 352–81.

LAW UNION OF CANADA (1981) *The Immigrant's Handbook* Montreal: Black Rose.

LEVITT, Kari and McINTYRE, Alister (1967) *Canada-West Indies Relations* Montreal: The Canadian Trade Committee Private Planning Association of Canada and the Centre for Developing-Area Studies.

LIM, Lin Lean and OISHI, Nana (1996) 'International labor migration of Asian women: distinctive characteristics and policy concerns', *Asian and Pacific Migration Journal* Vol. 5, No. 1: 85–116.

McAFEE, Kathy (1991) *Storm Signals: Structural Adjustment and Development Alternatives in the Caribbean* Boston, Mass.: Zed Press and South End Press.

MANDEL, Michael (1994) *The Charter of Rights and the Legalization of Politics in Canada* Toronto: Thompson Educational Publishing.

MANOR, James (1991) editor, *Rethinking Third World Politics* New York: Longman.

MARSHALL, T.H. (1950) 'Citizenship and social class' in **Marshall** and **Bottomore** (1950).

MARSHALL, T.H. and BOTTOMORE, Tom (1950) *Citizenship and Social Class* London: Pluto Press, 1992.

MILIBAND, Ralph (1996) 'The new world order and the Left', *Social Justice* Vol. 23, Nos. 1–2: 15–20.

MILLER, David (1994) 'In defence of nationality' in **P. Gilbert** and **P. Gregory** editors, *Nations, Cultures and Markets* Aldershot: Avebury.

MILLER MATTEI, Linda (1996) 'Gender and international labor migration: a networks approach', *Social Justice* Vol. 23, No. 3: 38–54.

MODOOD, Tariq (1994) 'Establishment, multiculturalism and British citizenship', *The Political Quarterly* Vol. 65: 55–73.

MOMSEN, Janet H. (1993) editor, *Women and Change in the Caribbean* London: James Currey.

PAREKH, Bhiku (1991/2) 'Public morality for a plural world', *Jewish Quarterly* Vol. 144.

PATEMAN, Carole (1988) 'The patriarchal welfare state' in **Amy Gutmann** editor, *Democracy and the Welfare State* Princeton, NJ: Princeton University Press.

PHILLIPS, Anne (1991) 'Citizenship and feminist politics' in **Andrews** (1991).

RICHMOND, Anthony H. (1994) *Global Apartheid: Refugees, Racism, and the New World Order* Toronto: Oxford University Press.

RINGER, Benjamin B. (1983) *We the People and Others: Duality and America's Treatment of its Racial Minorities* New York and London: Routledge, 1992.

RODRIGUEZ, Nestor (1996) 'The battle for the border: notes on autonomous migration, transnational communities, and the state', *Social Justice* Vol. 23, No. 3: 22–37.

ROMERO, Mary (1992) *Maid in the USA* New York: Routledge.

ROSTOW, W.W. (1960) *The Stages of Economic Growth: A Non-Communist Manifesto* Cambridge: Cambridge University Press.

SOYSAL, Yasemin (1994) *Limits of Citizenship: Migrants and Postnational Membership in Europe* Chicago: University of Chicago Press.

STASIULIS, Daiva (1996a) 'Migration internationale et droits à la post-nationalité' (English version: 'International migration, rights, and the decline of "actually existing liberal democracy"') in **F. Gagnon, M. McAndrew** and **M. Page** editors, *Pluralisme, citoyenneté & education* Montreal: Harmatton, pp. 189–215.

—— (1996b) 'The regulation and empowerment strategies of migrant domestic workers', paper prepared for the Expert Group Meeting on Violence Against Women Migrant Workers, Manila, Philippines, 27–31 May.

—— (1996c) 'The political economy of race, ethnicity and migration' in **Wallace Clement** editor, *Understanding Canada: Building on the New Canadian Political Economy* Montreal: McGill Queen's University Press, pp. 141–71.

TAYLOR, Charles (1992) *Multiculturalism and the 'Politics of Recognition'* Princeton, NJ: Princeton University Press.

TENNYSON, Brian Douglas (1990) editor, *Canadian-Caribbean Relations: Aspects of a Relationship* Cape Breton: Centre for International Studies, University College of Cape Breton.

THOMPSON, E.P. (1963) *The Making of the English Working Class* New York: Vintage Books.

TURNER, Bryan (1990) 'Outline of a theory of citizenship', *Sociology* Vol. 24, No. 2: 189–217.

UNITED NATIONS (1995) *Proceedings of the United Nations Expert Group Meeting on International Migration Policies and the Status of Female Migrants*, Sanminiato, Italy, 28–31 March 1990.

—— (1996) *Report of the United Nations Expert Group Meeting on Violence Against Women Migrant Workers*, held in Manila, 27–31 May.

UNITED NATIONS DEVELOPMENT PROGRAMME (1995) *Human Development Report 1995* New York: Oxford University Press.

VELASCO, Pura (1997 forthcoming) ' "We can still fight back": organizing domestic workers in Toronto', in **Bakan** and **Stasiulis** (1997 forthcoming).

YOUNG, Iris Marion (1990) *Justice and the Politics of Difference* Princeton, NJ: Princeton University Press.

YUVAL-DAVIS, Nira (1996) 'Women, citizenship and difference', background paper for the Conference on Women, Citizenship and Difference, University of Greenwich, 16–18 July.

Women's Publics and the Search for New Democracies

Zillah Eisenstein

FEMINIST REVIEW NO 57, AUTUMN 1997, PP. 140–167

Abstract

The article examines the intersections between gender, racism, global capitalism and corporate multiculturalism. The notion of nation and nationalism for the twenty-first century is explored. Women's voices from Beijing provide a possible imaginary for transnation discourse.

Keywords

nation; globalism; corporatist multiculturalism; Western feminism for export; Beijing

I have some new queries for the twenty-first century that grow out of 'new-old' challenges to democracy from women and girls. My queries start midstream; after the gulfwar, rwanda, somalia, bosnia and O.J. Simpson and within the discourses of nationalism, globalism, multiculturalism and feminism.[1]

Some 800 million people are starving across the globe, while women represent about 60 per cent of the billion or so people earning $1.00 or less a day. Each day some 34,000 children die for want of food and medical care.[2] On the other side of the ledger, new excesses of wealth exist as never before. The very rich become billionaires, while everyone else loses ground. This vulnerability is new for professionals of the middle class(es).

Today, class exploitation is back with a vengeance, and the vengeance is written in racialized form, on women's bodies. Greed and excessive wealth exist alongside unbelievable poverty *within* the first world north and west with new veracity, among people who never expected it to be this way for them. Even white men are scared. There is a new arrogance by those who benefit from this exploitative abuse.

The 'new-old' globalism fuels a corporate hysteria that demands downsizing, massive firings and jobless recoveries. Corporate competitiveness is used to justify all forms of streamlining and workplace reorganization. Globalism becomes the new imaginary, like nation(alism) once was.

Of course, Lenin and Luxemburg called the global aspects of capital 'imperialism'. And, although much has changed here, especially since the fall of state socialism in 1989, much remains the same. This is truest in terms of the patriarchal transnational division of labour, which exists locally and globally, and is defined in and through racist structures with particular effect in the first world north and west. Although the new technologies make everything appear dispersed, seamless and worldly, some things, like the sexual division of labour(s) with their racialized meanings, are hardly new.

Where are we headed here? Globalism, as an economic imaginary, asks us to see the world as one village made of freely competing parts. Whereas eighteenth-century capitalism demanded 'the' fantasy nation, twenty-first-century capital demands the fantasmatic globe.

The former relations between politics/economics, state/economy, public/private, family/nation are utterly challenged. Global markets find political nations too constraining. They often find traditional patriarchal familial relations too constraining as well.

Enter the ugly politics of privatization. The neo-conservative agenda demands the elimination of public responsibility. Forget federal regulations on workplaces, or the environment; forget medicaid or medicare; forget vaccinations for poor children; forget the public/nation as an imaginary/reality. This privatization takes place on top of the existing patriarchal and racist inequities that structure the public/private divides.

The new greed is too greedy, and yet the voices of outrage have been muted. Nevertheless, there are the women and men in Chiapas, Mexico, demanding accountability from their own government and its connections with transnational capital. And there were the women meeting in beijing, at the UN Fourth World Conference on Women, who demanded an end to the massive poverty of the world's women and girls.

I shall use the Beijing 'Platform for Action' in order to imagine a different kind of globe – one that is not dominated by privatization of public responsibility. My exercise may be more fantasmatic than real, as I leave behind the constraints of the UN, the World Bank, the International Monetary Fund, etc. I shall focus on beijing's feminist voices heard across the globe, demanding government participation in the creation of sexual equality for women and girls. And this equality encompasses 'sexual rights', which requires a different kind of democracy than has ever been theorized or practised before (Eisenstein, 1994).

My querying is tentative and open. I theorize the radically democratic potential that exists within and between the conflicts of the transnational sexual division(s) of labour of the first world north and west and third world south and east, and the promissory of western feminism for export and the feminisms across the globe voiced at beijing. It is from these dialogues that a revised notion of a public sphere for the twenty-first century may be found.

What follows is an epistemological/political road map for revisioning publics/democracy, which remains partial and fragmentary. I intend to demonstrate how I have arrived at my queries more than I intend to answer them. The answers are yet to be articulated in the struggles of the twenty-first century.

On the north and west and its privatization

The US exports its version of culture around the world. Disney and CNN both control and disseminate versions of 'the' west for transnational consumption. Hollywood becomes the us (Wasser, 1995). New borders are constructed, while old ones are dumped or renegotiated. Culture gets globalized, and 'america' becomes a brand name like Calvin Klein (Yoshimoto, 1992: 194–5). The globe can watch Bill Clinton and Newt Gingrich spar as they both accede to the dismantling of government 'as we know it'.

The right-wing neo-conservative attack on government spending, which began in the early 1970s with Carter, took full bloom in the Reagan-Bush decade, and continues with Clinton. It has profoundly shifted the relationship between public and private domains. Public responsibility has diminished, while poor people are expected to take care of themselves.

We seem to be moving beyond the public/private divide, but in inconsistent and contradictory ways. The loss of public space sometimes parallels the loss of private space as well. As Jean Baudrillard states: 'The one is no longer a spectacle, the other no longer a secret.' The obscene is no longer hidden and forbidden, but rather, 'it is the obscenity of what no longer has any secret' (Baudrillard, 1983: 126, 131).

There are many private spheres – and many public ones. The publics of market, state and politics all seem to be in turmoil (Robbins, 1993). Newt's contract basically says we need to end public regardingness and let private people and private enterprise guide the country. Yet the selfishness has already begun to destroy us.

Because privacy always exists in relation to publicness, and because they shift and conflict with each other simultaneously, the privatization of the public realm has created a crisis for both realms. As more is made of the private – the importance of individual privacy and freedom of choice and markets – the public is crumbling. What can privacy mean when the public is gone? If a notion of public is gone, how does one live outside the self? Transnational capital needs privatization of multiple publics and democracy is revised for global marketing. As such, the revisions privilege the rights of the very rich. The rest of us get stomped on, while Disney fantasizes the process.

Full publicization of life leads to fascism, or statist communism. But what does full privatization lead to? It leads to the depiction of 'the' public as the enemy – as the arena of special/divisive interests that balkanize the country. The anti-tax, anti-government stance has displaced publicness and its notion of accountability.

Recognizing that enemies always have a colour and a sex is important. And this is because race is already sexualized, sexuality is already racialized and race is engendered while gender is racialized. Besides this, the sexual division of labour is racially encoded along class lines (see Eisenstein, 1994).

On a 'new-old' globalism

The global economy symbolizes a wholeness of a world without divisions, difference or conflict. Some have called it a borderless world (Kennedy, 1993: 151). But this reduces and simplifies borders to an economic reading. Instead, religious, familial, heterosexist and racial borders are called forth to renegotiate globalized spaces. Globalism, like nation, silences and covers over sex/gender hierarchies, while utilizing corporatist multicultural viewings of racial diversity.

'Capitalist universality' has triumphed to the point that it becomes invisible (Wood, 1995: 11). The mythic 'oneness' of the globe displaces the first/third world divide and the devastating inequalities of rich and poor.

*Trans*nationalism stands in for capital. Corporatist multiculturalism uses and absorbs cultural/ethnic/racial diversity to naturalize and depoliticize multiracialism's potentially disordering aspects (Elmer Griffin, 1995: 58). Or, as Terry Eagleton clearly states, 'Difference, hybridity, heterogeneity, restless mobility, are native to the capitalist mode of production, and thus by no means inherently radical phenomena' (1995: 64).

The problem with the prefixes of 'post'-times is that they misrepresent the newness of the twenty-first century. The new globalism and its multicultural agenda are 'new-old' developments with transnational origins. Corporate structures are identified by their economic trans-status (across and through and beyond) rather than their 1970s multi (many) national status. Trans cuts through and creates mobile borders. *Trans*-national imagines beyond known boundaries and allegiances.

The anti-statist-communist stance of eastern europe and western anti-government neo-conservatism leaves global capitalists with quite a free hand. Global capital operates in disguise with no acknowledged culprit. This disguise remains racialized and engendered: racism is still used to cover over the extreme poverty in africa, south america, asia, etc. (Appiah, 1995: 81). The opportunism of capital reconstitutes gender hierarchies while re-tracing first, second and third world divides.

Patriarchal familial and national allegiances are unsettled by global corporate searches for women's cheap labour second and in third world south and east countries. And new consumer markets in third world east countries redeploy sexuality through pornography and prostitution to undermine former communist statist notions of women's equality. Women, in these eastern european countries, are then, also, summarily displaced by these same markets and sent back to the home. These women view the new consumerism, but with no money to spend. In first world countries, women are used to symbolize the market's consumerist possibilities for women in third world countries.

Global capital sends Avon to brazil, fancy lingerie to argentina, prostitution and porn to eastern europe. There is little new here, but there are new ways of doing it. Transnational corporations defy economic borders while utilizing and adapting old formations and constructions of race and gender. The question is whether capital itself will erode the racialized/gendered borders that it depends on.

Transnational corporatism and eastern europe

Global capitalism has dominated eastern and central europe since the revolutions of 1989. The disintegration of the state socialist world allows for a mobility of capital which ignores cold-war boundaries. These corporations can now operate not 'merely without borders, but without responsibility' (Alterman, 1994: 60). As a result, eastern europe has been repositioned globally as a new third world.

The mobility of capital has been enhanced by the anti-communist rhetoric of eastern europe and the neo-conservative free-market model. The transition from communism to 'free-market democracies' has left the most vulnerable people in eastern and central europe – albania, bulgaria and former yugoslavia, slovakia, poland, russia, romania – poorer and less healthy. There has been a serious deterioration in people's living situations:

in russia, alcoholism has increased along with stress, infectious diseases and malnutrition (Crossette, 1994: 13). With the privatization of the market in hungary, the standard of living has been greatly lowered for most people. In poland, 38 per cent of the people live below the poverty line, with more than 15 per cent unemployed in 1994 (Singer, 1993: 765).

Global capital presents a conundrum: it is *dispersed* through the world, but is completely self-*centred*. With governments shrinking and transnational corporations growing, the relationship between public and private space collides. We can most clearly see this in arenas like public health, where the public cannot be wished away. As one russian health official, Mr Belyaev, states, 'These infections often come from beyond one's borders, but once they are here it is a problem for all of us' (Specter, 1994: 19).

Besides the problematic fallout for public life from privatized markets, the markets often do not work. General Electric bought the state-owned Tungsram in hungary (maker of lighting products), but has not been able to get it to turn a profit (Perlez, 1994: D1). In Russia, the market has been most successful for the criminal element. Seen from the eyes of a western businessman: 'Russia is not an "underdeveloped" or "developing" country. It's a misdeveloped country' (Schmemann, 1994: A14). Nevertheless, many young, new middle-class russians luxuriate in their new-found freedoms (Erlanger, 1995: A1).

The privatization of capital and the transnational corporate structure of the privatization denies public accountability. As a result, the process is highly undemocratic (Brecher and Costello, 1994a: 757). The transformations of state structures by global capital require downsizing, and the post-cold-war Pentagon becomes a little leaner and meaner (Panitch, 1994: 69). But no matter how much the us government shrinks, it still seems to operate as an imaginary enemy for neo-conservatives, displacing global capital (Nasar, 1995: E1).

As governments are redefined for the global economy, so are militaries. So the us sends troops across the globe, similarly to capital itself. And the post-cold war global economy speaks the hegemony of free-market ideology.

Transnational racialized/gender and the twenty-first century

Even the United Nations acknowledges that transnational corporations are the central organizers of the world economy and are fighting to establish themselves in each others' home markets. Each of them tries to build its own regionally integrated, independent network of overseas affiliates (UN

Center on Transnational Corporations, 1992: 1, 34). This requires build-ing international networks within culturally specific locales. The troubling relation between the universal and the particular, between sameness and difference, of transnational and national, meet in this globalizing corpo-ratism.

The global web is trans-state and multi-nation. Japanese corporate execs are controlling owners in CBS. Vast stretches of downtown los angeles are inhabited by internationally owned corporations. The 'fortunate fifth' (Reich, 1983, 1991: 250, 1994: 19) who succeed in this global web can succeed without the rest. The well-being of any nation as a whole is no longer necessary for capital's success. Neither is the social welfare state.

Corporate america has never been dependent on the success of the nation as a whole for its profits, but today it has greater options to leave the rest of the nation behind. So the rest of the nation must become competitive, with workers around the globe, or the us – as distinct from corporate america – will become a part of the new third world. The key is not 'which nation's investors own what part of them', but which work-force is most valuable to the economic web (Reich, 1991: 285).

Economic transnationalism stands in contrast to the political racial/ethic/sexual nationalisms of eastern and central europe or the complex racisms defining haiti, rwanda, south africa, etc. As economies diversify and inter-nationalize, they utilize and corporatize the racialized and gendered con-structions of otherness while also naturalizing the more traditional roles of race and sex/gender in bordering identities.

Transnational corporations do not promote a racism that is co-equal with the nation. Instead, corporate multiculturalism commodifies race for transnational capital, although there is no simple or complete absorption or adaptation here. So, nationalisms in the former yugoslavia, hungary and the soviet union are partial reactions to outsider economies symbolized by McDonald's in zagreb, Dairy Queen, Kentucky Fried Chicken and Dunkin' Donuts in budapest.[3]

The globalization of capital and its mobility have diversified and dispersed corporate interests in multiracial and multicultural ways. Although power remains concentrated in first world corporations, nations – as well as their first world status – are in turmoil. This stirs up fantasies of nation building which resonate with a fantasmatic of gender hierarchy. The gender aspect of nation – the presentation of woman as never the sister, and always the mother, and definer of border crossings – presses hard against the women of the third world factories of the twenty-first century, the rape victims of bosnia and haiti and feminists of the north and west, south and east.

As global capital spreads, women work harder – either in and from their homes and/or in specified third world markets. They become the third world of the third world, and the third world of the first world. They are the cheapest of the cheap workers. Reebok and Nike hire the women in indonesia for 16 cents an hour and the women in china for 10 to 14 cents an hour (Enloe, 1993, 1995: 12). These women build nations from their families and build the global market from their families, farms and factories (Ehrenreich and Fuentes, 1984). They supply the flexibility global capital needs. Two-thirds of all part-time workers and 60 per cent of all temporary workers are women (Brecher and Costello, 1994: 23). These women also supply enormous sustenance in the families they rear and meet private needs within this domestic sphere. Privatized markets un-employ women and dismantle state subsidies and access in eastern europe and super-exploit women in south-east asian factories.

The global marketplace is premised on a transnational sexual division of labour. Global capital displaces the economic nation, while relying on women in the family to nurture the globe. Women bear and rear children and they labour in the sexual ghettos of the global market. In asia, africa and the middle east, those women who labour outside the home work predominantly as agricultural labourers. In hong kong, china, south korea, vietnam, malaysia and singapore, growing numbers of women are employed in the factories. In first world countries, women disproportionately provide the low-paid service sector labour. This is also true in south america (Beneria, 1989).

The fantasmatic anglo-western woman is marketed in and by the global economy as symbolic of the market's freedom. This contrasts with the actual subordination of women in the global market. The contrast crisscrosses and unsettles the relations between family, nation and globe. This may just become a major stumbling block for global capital.

As global capital shrinks space and time, it allows for the subversive possibility of women seeing beyond the local to the global. This move puts male privilege clearly in view like never before.

On western feminism for export

Media advertising and romanticized displays fantasize the freedom of the 'west'. Beautiful, healthy, fashionable women image the promise of western democracy. Corporatist feminism of the west 'for export' assists in constructing the new-old gender borders of the global economy alongside and in dialogue with corporatist multiculturalism. This process uses multiracialism while establishing western cultural hegemony of the

147

market. Women's bodies, through advertising and pornography, are the sites for these renegotiations.

There are troublesome effects of this mass-marketing strategy for women of colour and poor women across colour divides inside the west, as well as outside. Western feminisms are themselves being privatized by the market and reduced to self-help strategies,[4] while women, especially poor women, are losing all forms of public help, as government programmes are dismantled. This mass marketing of depoliticized feminism is crucial to the downsizing and privatizing of the us government. The market advertises the successes of feminism as justificatory of the rollback of an affirmative-action state. The rearticulation of racialized/sex/gender borders for the twenty-first century are undermined by the global market, even as the boundaries of the fantasmatic 'east' and 'west' are re-encoded in the 'export' version of feminism.

Feminism of the 'west' for export is marketed as a caricature of sex equality and victimhood and becomes a fantasmatic nightmare, both locally and globally. Feminism operates discursively: man-hating, equal rights and victimization/protectionism stand in for each other and are positioned against one another. To complicate things further, feminism 'for export' creates its own allure.

This popularized/publicized feminism is marketed domestically, as well as offered as a part of colonialist and global politics.[5] Some variants of this popularized feminism hegemonize the 'west'; others assist the porn industry in eastern europe; others are used to mass-market products within our own borders. Some variants are used to demonize white women in women of colour communities; others are used to criticize women of colour for racial disloyalty. Others are used to normalize feminism and strip it of its militant voice.

Nation-building and Hillary

Much political talk about women today acts to neutralize once militant ideas. This happens more often as the borders between public and private become further skewed and the lines between politics and culture are mute. As the government gets more privatized, our president visits talk shows. As the nation is reconfigured for globalism, there is more need to co-opt political militancy into the privatized stances of the market.

This was before the multiply orchestrated Hillary transitions. Her shifting borders and ambiguity are much like the contours of gender today. She is used to symbolize and write the contradictory meanings of motherhood, wifehood and nation as they collide with feminism. Given one reading, she stands for the marketed/popularized version of feminism: she is white and professional and smart and determined, has a child, but does not spend much time raising her, appears aloof and focused on power, and cares about her maiden name.

But this is only one depiction. Hillary also changes her hair-dos and wonders why she is not liked more by the public. She carries a message to the nation in global times: as able as she is, she still is not president, but 'his' wife. It is her glass ceiling and she will live with it; but she tries to do it differently, more actively as a professional. She gets nailed at every turn. People keep asking, who elected her anyway?

Even though Hillary has never identified herself as a feminist activist, feminism has been attached to her: defame one and hurt the other. It is so much trickier than with Nancy Reagan or Barbara Bush. With no private identity allowed, Hillary becomes the scapegoat for men and women who fear feminism – whatever they think it is. She unsettles sex/gender borders because her presence collides with the symbolization of woman. She provokes hostility because she is a wife first, but not just a wife. She creates fear and hate because she is both stereotypic of feminism and not enough of a feminist.

So some hate her because she is too much like them and is supposed to be different. She stays with a man who has told us all, in so many words, that he has 'betrayed' her. Her marriage is supposed to sustain the nation, but it appears shaky. People do not want to be reminded that marriage is a sham. The nation does not need this right now.

The problem is that the Clintons are a bit too unsettling for unsettled times. Hillary represents the gender disorder that the nation needs to forget. This is all too much to handle. On the other hand, Bill's marital infidelities humanize Hillary as the suffering wife, even if they democratize her a bit too much for everyone's liking. The aggressive bitch is re-feminized, while Bill, the wimp, is re-masculinized.

Before becoming first lady, Hillary Rodham Clinton was a committed advocate for children's rights. There is little sign of this commitment while the attack against poor women and their children dominates the news. Such advocacy would position Hillary with a feminism that questions the privatizing of the state and the enforcement of traditional familial relations.

When Hillary presented the outlines of the health-care package on capitol hill, she did so always positioned *vis-à-vis* a male patriarch: as 'a wife, a mother, and a daughter'. 'She was proud to serve her country.' We are presented with yet another viewing here: a domesticated professional woman for the twenty-first century. She is wife and mother for the post-cold war nation.

This time Hillary speaks, subtextually, a 'power-feminism' *as* a devoted citizen with market appeal. She focuses on what women can do and not on how they are kept from doing. She shows 'no rage at men, no rhetoric about oppression or empowerment, not even a whisper of a Ms'. While on capitol hill, we are shown her competence, her intelligence, her fortitude. She is 'the feminist', recoded and neutralized as citizen-mother in a changing transnational and multicultural world.

Several months later, she looks different and talks differently, again. The health plan failed and Hillary, the professional, is disciplined; she is domesticated back to her family, once again. Gender is rewritten on her body: her hair, her clothes and her voice are re-scripted. She tells a group of women reporters that she does not know who the woman is that she reads about in the news. She says she is sorry for making a mess of health care and will take the blame. She says she must work harder at being good. The citizen-mother has been unfairly victimized, but she will do better. She is speaking the language of personalized co-dependency on a national level.

Hillary wants to rewrite her role as citizen-wife for post-cold-war times. As an active player/co-equal partner, she needs new rules – like global capital. But gender changes are even more unsettling than global ones. So her media experts nervously write old stories: on her headbands, pageboy hairdos, pink angora sweaters. The borders of feminism are left fluid and manipulable for the nation: popular culture vaporizes feminism while it privatizes it for the market and depoliticizes it for the state.

By March 1995, after the 1992 congressional election defeats, Hillary starts to stress women and children's issues as she travels abroad. It is interesting to see how her focus shifts once she leaves the country. Once outside us borders she speaks quite readily on behalf of poor women in india. From this space outside the us, Hillary criticized the 'rampant materialism and consumerism' of western countries.

However, Hillary Clinton reinscribes the east/west divide in her depiction of women's lives in south-east asia. She states: 'When I think about the women who've been imprisoned, tortured, discouraged, barred from involvement in education or professional opportunity – what any of us in america go through is minor in comparison.' According to this, america seems to have no great inequities. And the suffering elsewhere seems to be overwhelming. Women of the 'west' have little to complain about in comparison to women of the 'east'.

So Hillary leaves the country in order to speak as a feminist in other countries, and at United Nations conferences on women – most recently in beijing. She takes feminism, as an export, abroad. She defines the backwardness of india as the backdrop for her concern with 'girls and women', which becomes a 'human rights' issue. Strangely enough, because she is speaking about children, some in the media now call her a traditional first lady. Wrong again.

Hillary has been called just about everything because the nation does not know what she needs to be. Hillary merely em*bodies* the changing familial structures of the nation during globalization of the market, while the nation needs more fluid borders than the racialized/gender structure can easily deliver on.

The assaults on feminism issue forth from multiple cultural spaces. Much like liberalism, feminism is attacked for being too radical in all its guises: too committed to sexual equality, too committed to its victimhood, too committed to sexual freedom, to committed to women's difference, too committed to women's sameness. Forget that no one feminism is depicted fairly here. And forget that the earliest forms of western feminism were *radically* liberal in that they demanded women's inclusion into the bourgeois/liberal individualism of the day. Equal rights doctrine followed suit.

The backlash today is deep and profound: it is against individualism as it operates *radically* for women. The market has to transform the militancy of this feminist individualism into a privatized consumerism. It attempts to do this by focusing on freedom – which the mass market absorbs – instead of equality – which the market rejects. Feminism is redefined as an individualized consumer self-help market; and the politics surrounding the struggle for equality drops out of the bottom.

Mass-marketed pop feminism

Depictions of women's victimization and powerlessness blanket the media. Talk shows are filled with the concerns originally articulated by radical feminists: date rape, pornography, incest, sexual abuse, etc. But the media disconnect the original critique of patriarchal privilege from the sexual battery.[6] Whereas radical feminists connected the personal to the political, media depictions of sexual violence appear individualized and privatized. There is no politics to the personal because the personal is made private. 'Sexual politics' and the uncovering of power-defined private moments is mass-marketed.

Patriarchal privilege is depoliticized through a stunning array of individualized women's tragedies. Many of these moments are further appropriated by the fantasmania of TV news. O.J. Simpson declares that his marriage was abusive for both himself and Nicole and both become victim and victimizer. In this instance, the abuse is not merely neutralized, but concealed.

The consumer side of feminist discourse and its commercialization operate both to publicize feminist concerns and to disconnect these issues from their radical critique of male privilege. The popularization mainstreams their radically political content, although not completely. This process of depoliticization is similar to the corporatist use of multiculturalism; but, in this instance, the market focuses and isolates gender. Corporatist multiculturalism pluralizes ethnicity while privileging euro-american centrism. Feminism, in its mass-market guise, popularizes women's victimization, while leaving the phallus intact.

Interestingly, the racialized aspects of sexuality recombine in the market's attempt at neutralization. Anita Hill[7] and O.J. Simpson became household names in large part because of the popularization and mass-marketing of feminist concerns and the racialized content of their meaning. Both of these cases are instances, though quite differently, of the already popularized cultural discussions of sexual harassment and domestic violence and their interplay with race. Anita Hill's testimony about her sexual harassment mobilized women in extraordinary ways (Eisenstein, 1994: 79–85).

The collusion of the marketization of feminist concerns in the popular media criss-crosses the arenas of racial hate and sexual violence. It is why the Simpson trial was a media bonanza: domestic violence meets football star; interracial marriage meets racial hatred; racism meets sexism. Mix up the players on both sides of the courtroom by race and sex and one has a significant cultural event.

The process of popularization blurs the lines between using women as icons for the market and encoding feminist claims. These conflictual processes operate to create the fantasmatic of success. The mass-marketing absorbs, publicizes, normalizes and disciplines all at the same time. The marketing redefines the boundaries between privacy and publicness, inside and outside, mainstream politics and mass culture, feminist language and women's identities. Radical feminist politics drops out of the renegotiated boundaries, while woman's victim status becomes the new voyeurism.

Feminists are said to wallow in their victimhood, while this very status is used to underwrite a huge industry. TV news, talk shows, newspapers, self-help books, videos, movies, tabloids and MTV write their own text with the words and images from feminist discourse. So, even trials and politics have become a part of this massified culture market. Elections and courtrooms have none of the boundary markers they once had in this media-driven age. Politics enters our bedrooms on TV and collapses the public/private divide, but not entirely.

The language of sexual violence and battery is used to catch women's attention rather than change their lives. This mass-marketed feminism is a bit like fat-free food. Victimhood and sex sell. Liberal feminism's opportunity/equality focus is not sexy enough for the market these days. And, sadly, its demands have either become neutralized or (once again) become too radical for the neo-conservatives. Nevertheless, feminism of the west, as export, mixes the two. It advertises women in the us as sexy – 'free and equal' – to third world southern and eastern countries. The media moguls just forget to mention domestic battery and the glass ceiling and poverty rates among women here.

Responses vary. Some women in eastern europe react suspiciously to the equal rights stance of feminism which sounds too reminiscent of statist communism. Some muslim fundamentalists, as well as women in muslim countries, reject the pop/market version of 'man-hating' feminism as the worst of the excesses of western colonialism. These misreadings and misuses – with their transnational effect – construct anti-feminist stances both at home and abroad.

Today, although some aspects of liberal feminist equality discourse have been incorporated into everyday language, much remains unchanged. The mainstreaming of an idea is not equivalent to creating its reality. Saying women are to be treated equally is not the same as equal treatment. Expecting women on welfare to find jobs is not the same as enabling them to do so.

The limitations of political/legal talk are clearly in evidence if one is poor and needs an abortion. Even though one has the right to choose an abortion – as an idea – one may not be able to get an abortion – as the real.[8]

Some feminist successes act to conceal the continuation of patriarchal structures that radical feminists target for dismantling. I have long argued that feminism cannot be contained within the individualist model of opportunity. I believe that liberal feminism – with its individualism (liberal rights) and collectivism (recognition of women as a sexual class) – strains to radicalize beyond itself (Eisenstein, 1981); that the inclusion of women is never simple addition; a fundamental rearrangement of some kind is always necessitated. And, equality, even when it simply means sameness of treatment, is always destabilizing to racialized/patriarchal layerings.

Feminism always embodies a tension between individualism and collectivity, and it is a tension that cannot ever be fully resolved. It is this irresolution –

FEMINIST REVIEW NO 57, AUTUMN 1997

between the self and others – that contains utter uniqueness. Liberalism resolves the tension between self and others in favour of the individual, communism favours the collectivity, but feminism deploys the unanswerability of the tension in order to explore relationships between the private and public, familial and individual, and identities and communities.

Different historical moments trigger crises for feminism. As white, middle-class first world women were pulled into the labour-force through the 1970s, the conflicts between capitalism and patriarchy were exacerbated. Wage-earning women who traversed the worlds of market and home absorbed these conflicts within a double and triple day of work. These conflicts have more fully deepened as we enter the twenty-first century. In third world countries of the south and east, the excesses of transnational capital further heighten the exploitation of women factory workers in particular. They work endless hours for below poverty wages. And the women are often girls.

The radical recognition of women as distinct and discriminated against destabilizes the individualist stance of the new market economies, while calling attention to women's lack of individual rights. Individualism, and its corollary embrace of freedom, is completely seductive, as fantasy. It is what the revolutions of 1989 imaged for themselves.

Transnational markets are patriarchally individualist. Feminism(s) is egalitarian, collective and individualist simultaneously. The promissory lies within these conflicts. So today I say that the feminisms across the globe share the possibility of a radical future that develops out of the contradictory, promissory and punitive aspects of global capital.

Liberalism, as well as liberal feminism, has become way too radical for the new north american global state *at the same time* that it is marketed. Radical feminism has always been too radical. But the pop/mass/culture market has blended the two in brilliant fashion. The radical/structural critique of patriarchy has been reduced to a personal/individualized statement of victimhood. Therapy and recovery have become the solution. TV is very often its mode. The radical future of liberal feminism has been renegotiated to read as the privatized future of radical feminism.

'Feminism' is everywhere and nowhere. It operates in veiled references and orchestrated absences. It is disparaged at the same time that it is embraced. It becomes the perfect fictive symbol. Few ever quite know what it means, but it is the fantasy to fear.

The newly transnationalized economies are not fully able to absorb feminism, nor are third world countries of the south and east. But western feminism for export has been taken by feminists into dialogue with women of these countries. Even the Pope is worried about this talk. So he apologized, in his 1995 papal letter on women, for those in the church 'who have contributed to the oppression of women'. And he acknowledges the need to 'achieve real equality in every area: equal pay for equal work, protection for working mothers, fairness in career advancements, equality of spouses with regard to family rights' (*New York Times*, 1995: E7). He does all this *in order* to speak against abortion.

A transnational discussion among women is the most hopeful sign yet that it might be possible to think – together – through the nation, beyond transnational capital.

On feminisms of the global south and east

Feminism of the west, as export, operates colonially and imperialistically in third world countries of the south and east. And then it brings these women back to the west as foreigners. So women in these countries must find a way out of this dilemma on their own terms: requiring a noncolonialist feminism which challenges the patriarchalism of third world nationalisms.

There are many ways to think this dilemma through. Some women in iran who wear the veil support women's rights, others do not. Some women in algeria who identify as feminist mean that they support women's right to education, others mean the right to a good job. Others in egypt, slovakia and iran believe in these very issues, yet say they are not feminist. Others believe deeply in women's need to control their fertility, but silence their views within their islamic communities. Others in russia see abortion as a necessity and wish it were not.

Numbers of women in eastern europe, northern africa and islamic culture want a dialogue between north and west *and* south and east. The us itself is already home to many of these cultures. Women of poland, romania, the former soviet union, algeria, egypt, etc., have histories that women in the west can learn from. Women in these countries often already know the westernized feminism exported globally. But they also need to know the more dissident western feminisms, particularly that of western women of colour.

I am not arguing that there is one kind of feminism, or woman, or one kind of equality. But that the debate should focus on recognizing different feminisms rather than questioning their theoralizability. Let us use the dialogues between feminisms to build connections between these communi-ties of women.

Feminism recognizes and names women as a collectivity. It is, in part, fantasy and imaginary. It imagines beyond the differences between women to a comm*unity* that respects diversity and radical pluralism. This pluralism recognizes a sharedness among women that is not a given, but is rather a possibility. Sometimes the conflicts are too great – other allegiances overwhelm the possibility of feminist identities. By naming women *at the start*, so to speak, I mean to call attention to their absences and silences in the 'isms' of the twenty-first century.

Women in post-communist nationalisms

Whereas the revolutions of 1989 were depicted by the western media as a victory for capitalist democracy, exclusionary nationalisms now dominate the landscape. Women in eastern and central europe have had a troubled status in statist communism which makes them exceedingly important and, yet, particularly vulnerable to the process of nationalizing identity(ies). Gender boundaries are redefined for the privatized and global market, and this effects women's lives.

However punishing the new markets have been for women, women still hope for the freedoms that marketization promises. Nevertheless, there is no one scenario to uncover in women's lives in poland, russia, the czech republic and bosnia. The wide variety of circumstances, which vary from country to country, also tells a similar story. State services and supports for women have been cut everywhere. The privatized markets are with transnational gender effect (Rueschemeyer, 1994). And the bosnian war represents the ugliest side of the underbelly of post-communism. The new economies in eastern europe have displaced majorities of women in the labour force. These women have worked in the market for a long time and their forced unemployment is not welcomed. Many of these women's children, now also in the market, have been brought up in state day–care centres. They have had access – however humiliating the actual service rendered is – to abortion for several decades now. Women – their individual histories, their exhaustion, their desires, the assaults against them, the existence of dispersed and uncoordinated women's actions – are part of the feminist story starting to unfold. It is a story of new markets, new kinds of poverty, leftovers of statist communism, and nationalist wars.

Privatization and new markets are redefining the relationships between states and their economies, families and public/private life, and political and cultural life. Because these renegotiations retranslate masculinist privilege, women have a particular interest in affecting these changes. Agitation on the part of women in these post-communist societies is not new, and yet, it is also not simply like western feminism. After all, 'feminism has no particular ethnic identity' (Jayawardena, 1986: ix). So there are new possibilities for a crossover dialogue among women in the east, and between 'the' east and west given the transnational privatisation of the globe. Early on, the revolution of 1989 'imagined' religious freedom, political freedom, and sexual freedom. The hope was for a freedom for the 'private' self. Slavenka Drakulic, a feminist from zagreb, captures this sense of privacy when describing the lack of consumer goods under communism like toilet paper and tampons (Drakulic, 1991; Crnkovic, 1992). Many of her concerns with privacy are tied to bodily/sexual needs, which were much ignored under the old regime. At home, in Croatia, Drakulic is treated as a traitor to her country because of her feminism and her anti-nationalist views, which make her more popular outside her country than inside (Kinzer, 1993: A11).

Equality, and most particularly sexual equality, had a bad name with women living in statist communist regimes. Sexual equality was identified with forced work, low pay, abortion as *the* method of contraception, and days of triple labour (home, job and shopping). It was also associated with a series of expected entitlements like state day care, pregnancy leave, child subsidies, etc., which were sporadic and contradictory in their effect. Even though few women are happy about losing their jobs *and* their state entitlements to global capital, fewer yet, at least up to this point, would want to return to the old regimes.

Liberal democrats, as the philosophers of capitalism, and marxists, as the theorists of communism, totalize 'the' economy. Supposedly communism was to end class conflict and all other conflict with it. There is no theorisation of gender hierarchy within the economy. Gorbachev and Yeltsin, as well as Vaclav Havel, make the same mistake; women are not imaged in their nations as active citizens. Gorbachev even promised that perestroika would allow women to return to their homes and be feminine again (Gorbachev, 1987: 103; Eisenstein, 1993).

Women are *made* absent in discussions of the 1989 revolutions and their aftermath. Little is said about how many czech dissidents were women. Little is said about the way women kept civil society alive as a counter to the totalitarianism of the various regimes. Tatiana Bohm, of the GDR, says that the revolutionary changes in eastern and middle europe would never have been possible without the widespread participation of women (Bohm, 1993: 151).

One also hears very little of the women in ex-yugoslavia who fought against the war. Sonia Licht, of belgrade, tells of how women built a peace movement, helped organize the May 1992 demonstration of 100,000 people against the bombing of sarajevo, and maintained a candlelight vigil

FEMINIST REVIEW NO 57, AUTUMN 1997

for victims of the war from October 1991 to February 1992. She tells of the 'women in black', the Crisis Line, and Centres for Raped Women in belgrade – all of which are actions by women to stop the war (Licht, 1993). One hardly hears mention of *Viva Zena*, an anti-nationalist women's magazine published in sarajevo, or the women's therapy centre in multi-ethnic tuzla and medica, or the mixed ethnic women's therapy project in zenica. These women stand against masculinist nationalism and tell a different story (Coward, 1995: 11).

Post-communist/nationalist women's identities

The legacy of enforced collectivism and universalism encircles any and all possibilities for developing feminist politics in eastern europe (Funk and Mueller, 1993: 10). Many eastern european women remain highly critical and sceptical of the deformed gender similarity espoused in hypocritical ways by their former regimes. Communism's version of sexual equality meant standardization, weariness, sameness and dreariness. For these women, democracy represents the promise of a new freedom of individual expression: political, economic and sexual. In this scenario, equality and freedom are constructed as opposites.

Women, as a transnational category, with all their racial, ethnic, sexual, bodily and religious differences, can reveal the inadequacy of false homo-geneity as a standard, either in relation to themselves or to men. These differences necessitate a revisioning of equality discourse – both commu-nist and liberal democratic style. Like communist discourse, liberal demo-cratic notions of equality also assume likeness and similarity to a male standard. To be treated equal is to be treated *like* a man, but not exactly. Women are expected to have a job, but it will not be as well-paid. Preg-nancy is treated like a disability a man might have, even though it is com-pletely female. No wonder lots of russian women have been quite vocal in that they are not interested in being treated like men any longer. And they are not interested in western feminism if it is limited to this equality rhetoric. They are tired of their triple day of labour. They have yet to experience the enforced domesticity of the 1950s that white, western middle-class feminists critique Their wariness is quite similar to the posi-tion of women-of-colour feminists in the west during the 1970s. These women, already in the labour force and experiencing its racialized/gender ghettos, imagine beyond likeness to an equality rich in diversity.[9]

Alena Heitlinger interestingly argues that human rights discourse may hold more promise for eastern european women than western feminism simply because women's rights, as a politics, is overly identified with the former communist regimes. The Global Campaign for Women's Human Rights takes this tack. It uses the specific nationalism, the distortions of statist communism *and* 'free' market globalism.It is a feminism that recognizes individual diversity, freedom and equality, defined through and beyond north/west and south/east dialogues. It recognizes the necessity of entitlement and yet is cautious about statist interventionism, rejects privatisation by global capital and moves beyond masculinist nationalisms.

Such a feminism is poised between communism and capitalism; between collectivism and individuality; between publicness and privacy; between samenesses and differences; and between women's different imaginings. This demands feminisms beyond nationalism and global capitalism.

I began to believe such a feminism is possible in spite of the tremendous odds against it, on my visit to belgrade, May 1995 (Center of Women's Studies, 1994). Belgrade, as a part of the new serbia, is also home to feminists who daily reach out beyond the horrific borders of this new struggling nation. They shunned the safety of their birthing and instead spoke against the war, and for their sisters in sarajevo, sepa, bihac, and gorazde.

Women in belgrade and sarajevo

The nationalisms in bosnia speak the horrors of racialized/gender warfare. Serb nationalism uses and violates women as it nationalises identity along blood lines. In this scenario, motherhood has 'national' meaning and so does rape. Rape destroys 'others' and establishes serbia at the same time (Drakulic, 1993; Laber, 1993; Lewis, 1993: A1; Riding, 1993: A1; Pitter and Stiglmayer, 1993). In an interview with two bosnian muslim rape survivors, one a lawyer, the other a judge, they say that by killing/raping older women, history is erased; by killing/raping young women, the future is wiped away;[10] and a serb nation is built. Nevertheless, women in the refugee camps are 'resisting the temptation to hate' (Rosenberg, 1994: 15).

This was the backdrop for women's actions throughout the war-zone of bosnia. Everyone I met wanted the war to end. They identified more readily as yugoslav than as serb. They were desperate for an end to the slaughter in sarajevo, but saw no end in sight. Many of the women I spoke with said that they lived in an immoral situation in belgrade; that they were free of bombs, while friends and family were being killed elsewhere.

The war's madness seemed more real when I was closer to it. Not one woman I met would call herself a nationalist. Many identified as feminists and were desperately concerned for the fate of women, especially in sarajevo.

FEMINIST REVIEW NO 57, AUTUMN 1997

Many people tried to leave belgrade because they could not stand to live there while others died so close by. Others came to belgrade as refugees from sarajevo and mostar. It is a city steeped in loss and tension.

While there, I met with women who were both victims and survivors, who had no hope and still hoped; who searched for candles and cans of food to send to sarajevo; who were deeply torn between guilt about the war and activism against it. They wished the profiteers of the war would be stopped. They wished that they could get everyone out of sarajevo, especially the women and children.

Feminists in belgrade travelled to sarajevo whenever they could. After one visit, the feminists in belgrade wrote to the women in sarajevo:

'We are writing to you with the knowledge about the complexity of the fact of where each of us comes from. . . . We came back changed more than ever. We are full of traces of your testimonies and our deep feelings that life is far more difficult for you than you wanted to show us. We have seen your different women's groups. We have taken your papers, and statements to share with others. We will let others know what is happening to you. We are supporting you totally and ceaselessly. We will repeat ten thousand times how you are courageous. We will come to you again, as soon as possible. Drinking coffee with you in sarajevo touches our souls.'[11]

Lepa Mladjenovic, from Women in Black and the Autonomous Women's Centre in belgrade says that the women from belgrade and sarajevo are 'very different' and 'not so different.'[12] Jasna, a friend of Lepa's and a feminist from sarajevo, says that each one of them 'must be dignified for the position she occupies'. She says of the packages sent from belgrade, that they 'were equal to a dream. We would all sit around the table and open a box slowly and put each item out one by one and look, and not know whether to cry or feel joy; if we should just look at the food, or eat it.' Jasna argues that she could 'have never received these packages if the women in belgrade were not precisely in belgrade' to send them. And Lepa sadly acknowledges that 'we could only send packages and do nothing else from belgrade',[13] Women in Black demonstrated in belgrade for the world to hopefully hear and see that they 'are against the serbian regime, against militarism and war violence, against the raping of our sisters of all nationalities from all sides. . . . We are also against killing the treasures of differences that we have been living with for centuries, enjoying the differences, feeling more rich with them and really being rich from them.[14]

The warriors in croatia, serbia, and bosnia-herzegovina needed to listen to these women. And feminists across the globe must be witness to their ability to move through and beyond deadly difference.

Restructuring the public at beijing

Beijing happened after a quarter of a century of global capitalist market-ing of women's lives, while one to 1.2 billion women across the globe live below the poverty line. The transnationalizing of the sexual division of labour intensifies with the globalization of capital. Women of colour in first world countries, defined by their racial/ethnic status, occupy the margins of the labour-force. White women are increasingly finding them-selves in similar situations. In the third world, most women farm and/or work in industry for slave wages.

At the same time that the globe advertises western women as free and glamorous, the new markets in eastern europe displace their women and create new levels of poverty. Poverty and AIDS wreak havoc on women's lives throughout africa. New levels of exploitation define the women working in the factories in asia. Amid all this, and in part because of it, women from across the globe met in beijing to demand a better life for themselves, their children and, by default, their countries.

By the time women met in beijing they had already clarified, at previous meetings, that their goal was to eliminate all forms of discrimination against women. This stance against discrimination included 'the right to freely choose the number and spacing of their children' (Report of the Secretary-General, 1995: 243; Beijing Declaration and Platform for Action, 1995). This demand was connected to their overriding concern with women's poverty, which, they argued has a 'gender dimension'; 'poverty is becoming increasingly feminized' (Report of the Secretary-General, 1995: 33).

Although the women in beijing readily recognize their heterogeneity as a group, they also believe that 'the world's women share a common feature: discrimination' (Dept. of Public Information, 1995: 6). They also believe that they have a prominent role to play in the democratization of their societies. Their rights, as women, are seen as part of their human rights and, therefore, necessary to any conception of democracy.

Their vision of democracy necessitates women's equality as part of the development of a country as a whole. They envision a democracy which allows them reproductive rights as a necessary part of determining their own lives. This notion of sexual rights rewrites rights discourse. It redefines the relationship between public and private life because sexual rights break through the borders of patriarchal citizenry. Woman's control over her body becomes a fundamental human right. 'The human rights of women include their right to decide freely on "matters related to their sexuality," including sexual and reproductive health, free of coercion, discrimination and vio-lence' (Beijing Declaration and Platform for Action, 1995: 33).

FEMINIST REVIEW NO 57, AUTUMN 1997

Interestingly, the beijing initiative makes no mention of patriarchy or male privilege. The women ask for shared partnership – shared power and responsibility between men and women at home. The equality of women is seen as necessary for the public good of all countries, not as simply a specific need of women.

The Beijing Platform for Action also calls for active participation by governments to end discrimination. It demands that governments promote, increase, provide and ensure availability and access for women to move out of poverty; receive the health care they need; get the education that is required for literacy; end violence against women; and eliminate sexual harassment (ibid., 28, 30, 50, 65).

The beijing imaginary views the improvement of women's lives as benefiting the whole society. Feminism assumes a 'self' that is not simply self-contained. Instead, women are seen as fundamental to, and yet connected with, society as a whole. Improve women's lot and society as a whole will benefit. This is a version of feminist 'publicness' which attaches the importance of the individual to something other than the self, without denying the importance of the self. And the self, in this case, is a woman who must be freed of the constraints of poverty, illiteracy, violence, discrimination and, most important, reproductive vulnerability. Meet her needs and you move toward democracy.

This feminism imagines beyond the individual woman and beyond the communities of women to the public at large. Hillary Clinton, somewhat more paternalistically, makes a similar argument.

> If women are healthy and educated, their families will flourish. If women are free from violence, their families will flourish. If women have a chance to work and earn as full and equal partners in society, their families will flourish. And when families flourish, communities and nations will flourish.
>
> (Center for Research on Women, 1995: 5)

Beijing says less about family, and more about society

So beijing has given us much. An instance of incredibly different women coming together to try to inhabit the globe in better ways. An instance of imagining active governments creating access and limiting violation. A vision of sexual and racial equality. A notion of rights which starts from a recognition of women's bodily needs. And, finally, a notion of sexual rights which enables the public as a whole.

The promissory is also limited by the very conflicts that exist among women about the borders of sexuality and bodily autonomy. There is no declaration in the platform calling for the legalization of abortion. There is no discussion in the platform of 'sexualized female bodies claiming pleasures rather than fending off abuses' (Petchesky, 1995: 2). Issues of sexual freedom, as distinguished from sexual rights, have yet to be articulated.

Nevertheless, reproductive health for women requires a change in resources, both globally and locally. In a period when 'rights' discourse has been rejected in the us as overly egalitarian, and when western governments plead poverty rather than try to address poverty as a human crisis, beijing stands as a fantasmatic of what women across the globe can begin to imagine. It is an imagining of a globe, with governments willing and able to actively end discrimination against women, recognize their sexual rights, and embrace democracy for the 'rest of us'.

Notes

Zillah Eisenstein is Professor of Politics at Ithaca College. She is the author of multiple books, the most recent being *The Color of Gender* (University of California Press, 1994) and *HATREDS* (Routledge, 1996). She is presently working on a new book, *CyberFantasies, Modes of Information, and New Publics.*

1 Portions of this paper are excerpted from my book *Hatreds: Sexualized and Racialized Conflicts in the 21st Century* (Routledge, 1996). I do not capitalize nations, countries or racial identities to underscore their artificial borderlines.

2 From the address made by Gertrude Mongella, Secretary-General of the Fourth World Conference on Women, at the World Summit on Social Development, Copenhagen, Denmark, 6–12 March 1995 – available from UN publications. Also see a special report with Peter Menzel and Faith D'Aluisio (1995) 'In her hands' *Mother Jones*, Vol. 20, No. 5: 32–56.

3 I am indebted to Julie Mostov's discussion 'Do women have something to fear? Nationalism in Eastern Europe' presented at Cornell University, 14 November 1993, for eliciting the idea of an 'outsider' economy.

4 I identify western feminism as a mix of liberal and radical feminism; see Eisenstein (1981).

5 I do not hold to a neat division between popular (meaning of the people) and mass (meaning of the market) as the two realms of culture collide too often; see Ella Shohat and Robert Stam (1994) *Unthinking Eurocentrism* New York: Routledge, pp. 240–342, for clarification of the distinction.

6 See the original feminist writing of Ti Grace Atkinson (1974) *Amazon Odyssey* New York: Links; Shulamith Firestone (1970) *The Dialectic of Sex* New York: Bantam; Kate Millet (1970) *Sexual Politics* New York: Doubleday; Robin

FEMINIST REVIEW NO 57, AUTUMN 1997

Morgan (1975) editor, *Sisterhood is Powerful* New York: Vintage; Redstock-ings (1975) Feminist *Revolution* New York: Redstockings.

7 See David Brock (1993) *The Real Anita Hill* New York: The Free Press; Robert Chrisman and Robert Allen (1992) editors, *Court of Appeal* New York: Bal-lantine Books; Jill Abramson and Jane Mayer (1994) *Strange Justice: The Selling of Clarence Thomas* New York: Houghton Mifflin; Toni Morrison (1992) editor, *Race-ing Justice, En-gendering Power* New York: Pantheon; Kathleen Sullivan (1993) 'The Hill-Thomas mystery', *The New York Review of Books* Vol. 40, No. 14, 12 August: 12–16.

8 For a discussion of the complex relations of real/ideal and how these are embodied in liberal law, see Eisenstein (1988) *The Female Body and the Law* Berkeley: University of California Press, especially chapters 1 and 2.

9 For a sampling of this discussion, see bell hooks (1981) *Ain't I a Woman: Black Women and Feminism* Boston: South End Press; bell hooks (1984) *Feminist Theory from Margin to Center* Boston: South End Press; Gloria Joseph and Jill Lewis (1981) *Common Differences* Boston: South End Press; Barbara Smith (1983) editor, *Home Girls, A Black Feminist Anthology* New York: Kitchen Table Women of Color Press.

10 These statements were made in interviews in the film *War Crimes against Women* directed by Mandy Jacobson and produced by Bowery Productions, community television.

11 Cited in 'letter for women in sarajevo', from Women in Black, the Autonomous Women's Center, belgrade women's lobby, 20 April 1995.

12 Transcribed from personal meetings and interviews, May 1995.

13 From personal correspondence, 5 and 26 June 1995.

14 From a statement 'Who are women in black?' written by Sasa Kovacevic, December 1994, belgrade: 1, 2.

References

ALTERMAN, Eric (1994) 'Who speaks for me?', *Mother Jones* Vol. 19 No. 1.

APPIAH, K.A. (1995) 'The color of money', *Transition* Vol. 5, No. 6.

BAUDRILLARD, Jean (1983) 'The ecstasy of communication' in **Hal Foster** editor, *The Anti-Aesthetic, Essays on Postmodern Culture* Seattle: Bay Press.

BEIJING DECLARATION AND PLATFORM FOR ACTION (1995) *Report of the Fourth World Conference on Women* Beijing, 4–15 September: United Nations Publication.

BENERIA, Lourdes (1989) 'Gender and the global economy' in **Arthur MacEwan** and **William Tabbs** editors, *Instability and Change in the World Economy* New York Monthly Review Press, pp. 241–50.

BOHM, Tatiana (1993) 'The woman's question as a democratic question: in search of civil society' in **Funk** and **Mueller** (eds.)

BRECHER, Jeremy and COSTELLO, Tim (1994a) 'Taking on the multinationals', *The Nation* Vol. 259, No. 21.

—— and —— (1994b) *Global Village or Global Pillage* Boston, Mass.: South End Press.

BUCKLEY, Mary (1992) 'Political reform' in **Mary Buckley** editor, *Perestroika and Soviet Women* New York: Cambridge University Press, pp. 54–71.

BUNCH, Charlotte and CARRILLO, Roxanna (1991) *Gender Violence: A Development and Human Rights Issue* Rutgers Center for Women's Global Leadership.

BUSHEIKIN, Laura (1992) 'Is it possible to have feminism without man-hating?' *The Prague Post* 26 November–1 December.

CENTER FOR RESEARCH ON WOMEN (1995) 'First Lady Hillary Rodham Clinton's remarks to the Fourth World conference on Women', *Research Report* xv, No. 1: Wellesley College.

CENTER FOR WOMEN'S STUDIES (1994) *What can We Do for Ourselves?* East-European conference, Belgrade, June.

COWARD, Ros (1995) 'Women of peace against men of war' *Guardian* 24 July.

CRNKOVIC, Gordana (1992) 'Why should you write about Eastern Europe, or why should you write about "the other" ', *Feminist Issues* Vol. 12, No. 2: 21–42.

CROSSETTE, Barbara (1994) 'U.N. study finds a free Eastern Europe poorer and less healthy' *New York Times* 7 October.

DEPT. OF PUBLIC INFORMATION (1995) *Notes for Speakers, The Advancement of Women* United Nations.

DRAKULIC, Slavenka (1991) *How We Survived Communism and Even Laughed* New York: Norton.

—— (1993) 'Women hide behind a wall of silence', *The Nation* Vol. 256, No. 8: 253–72.

EAGLETON, Terry (1995) 'Where do postmodernists come from?', *Monthly Review* Vol. 47, No. 3.

EHRENREICH, Barbara and FUENTES, Annette (1984) *Women in the Global Factory* Boston, Mass.: South End Press Pamphlet.

EINHORN, Barbara (1993) *Cinderella Goes to Market* London: Verso.

EISENSTEIN, Zillah (1981) *The Radical Future of Liberal Feminism* Boston, Mass.: Northeastern University Press.

—— (1993) 'Eastern European male democracies: a problem of unequal equality' in **Funk** and **Mueller** (1993).

—— (1994) *The Color of Gender: Reimaging Democracy* Berkeley: University of California Press.

ELMER GRIFFIN, G.A. (1995) 'World bullets', *Transition* Vol. 5, No. 2.

ENLOE, Cynthia (1993) *The Morning After* Berkeley: University of California Press.

—— (1995) 'The globetrotting sneaker', *Ms* Vol. 5, No. 5: 10–15.

ERLANGER, Steven (1995) 'To be young, Russian and middle class' *New York Times* 23 July.

FABIAN, Katalin (1994) 'Overview of women's interest articulation in Central and Eastern Europe', unpublished paper, Collegium Budapest, Budapest, Hungary.

FUNK, Nancy and MUELLER, Magda (1993) editors, *Gender Politics and Post-Communism* New York: Routledge.

GORBACHEV, Mikhail (1987) *Perestroika: New Thinking for Our Country and the World* New York: Harper & Row.

HAMPELE, Anna (1993) 'The organized women's movement in the collapse of the G. D. R.' in **Funk** and **Mueller** (1993).

HAVEL, Vaclav (1986) *Living in Truth* Boston, Mass.: Faber.

HAVELKOVA, Hana (1993) 'A few prefeminist thoughts' in **Funk** and **Mueller** (1993).

HERBERT, Bob (1995) 'Children of the dark ages' *New York Times* 21 July.

JAYAWARDENA, Kumari (1986) *Feminism and Nationalism in the Third World* London: Zed Books.

KENNEDY, Paul (1993) *Preparing for the Twenty-First Century* New York: Random House.

KINZER, Stephen (1993) 'Feminist gadfly unappreciated in her own land' *New York Times* 11 December.

LABER, Jeri (1993) 'Bosnia: questions about rape', *The New York Review of Books* Vol. 40, No. 6: 3–6.

LEWIS, Paul (1993) 'Rape was weapon of Serbs, U.N. says' *New York Times* 20 October.

LICHT, Sonia (1993) Public policy forum 'Gender and nationalism: the impact of the post-communist transition' Network of East-West Women, Washington, DC, 26–7 October.

LILPOVSKAIA, Olga (1992) 'New women's organizations' in **Buckley** (1992).

NASAR, Sylvia (1995) 'The bureacracy: what's left to shrink?' *New York Times* 11 June.

NEW YORK TIMES (1995) 'The papal letter: to the women of the world, an affirmation of "feminine genius" ', 14 July.

O'SULLIVAN, Katherine and RACIOPPI, Linda (1995) 'Organizing women before and after the fall: women's politics in the Soviet Union and post-Soviet Russia', *Signs* Vol. 20, No. 4.

PANITCH, Leo (1994) 'Globalisation and the state' in **R. Miliband** and **L. Panitch** editors, *Between Globalism and Nationalism: Socialist Register* London: Merlin Press.

PERLEZ, Jane (1994) 'G. E. finds tough going in Hungary' *New York Times* 25 July.

PETCHESKY, Rosalind (1995) 'Reproductive and sexual rights in international perspective – a post assessment', talk presented at Rutgers University, Center for Critical Analysis of Contemporary Culture, 17 October.

PITTER, Laura and STIGLMAYER, Alexandr (1993) 'Will the world remember? Can the women forget', *Ms* Vol. 3, No. 5: 19–22.

REICH, Robert (1983) *The Next American Frontier* New York: Penguin.

—— (1991) *The Work of Nations* New York: Vintage.

—— (1994) 'The fracturing of the middle class' *New York Times* 13 August.

REPORT OF THE SECRETARY-GENERAL (1995) *From Nairobi to Beijing* New York: UN.

RIDING, Alan (1993) 'European inquiry says Serbs' forces have raped 20,000' *New York Times* 9 January.

ROBBINS, Bruce (1993) editor, *The Phantom Public* Minneapolis: University of Minnesota Press.

ROSENBERG, Karen (1994) 'A day in Croatia', *The Women's Review of Books* Vol. 11, No. 9.

RUESCHEMEYER, Marilyn (1994) editor, *Women in the Politics of Postcommunist Eastern Europe* New York: M. E. Sharpe.

SCHMEMANN, Serge (1994) 'Russia lurches into reform but old ways are tenacious' *New York Times* 20 February.

SINGER, Daniel (1993) 'Of lobsters and Poles', *The Nation* Vol. 257, No. 21.

SKVORECKY, Josef (1992) 'Can there be sex without rape?' *The Praque Post* 26 November–1 December.

UN CENTER ON TRANSNATIONAL CORPORATIONS (1992) *World Investment Report 1992: Transnational Corporations as Engines of Growth* New York: United Nations.

WASSER, Frederick (1995) 'Is Hollywood America? The trans-nationalization of the American film industry', *Critical Studies in Mass Communication* Vol. 12: 423–37.

WOOD, E.M. (1995) 'What is the "postmodern" agenda? An introduction', *Monthly Review* Vol. 47, No. 3.

YOSHIMOTO, Mitsuhiro (1992) 'Images of empire: Tokyo Disneyland and Japanese cultural imperialism' in **Eric Smoodin** editor, *Disney Discourse* New York: Routledge.

Reviews

FEMINIST REVIEW NO 57, AUTUMN 1997, PP. 168–178

Writing Women and Space: Colonial and Postcolonial Geographies

Edited by Alison Blunt and Gillian Rose
Guilford Press: London, 1994

House Garden Nation: Space, Gender and Ethnicity in Post-colonial Latin American Literature

Ileana Rodriguez
Duke University Press: Durham, NC, and London, 1994

The location of metaphors of space and position right at the centre of feminist and postcolonial discourses seems to have given geography a metaphoric shot in the arm, increasing its visibility and its significance to scholars in other disciplines. There is now a rapidly expanding set of books and papers by geographers dealing broadly with space as imaginary, or as textual, as well as 'real' in the sense of distances to be overcome and un-familiarities to be conquered. At the same time, literary theorists and others working in the humanities have become entranced by material spatial relations as well as by metaphors, as vast flows of people and capital across borders challenge the relationships between space, gender and identity and produce hybrid cultures and polities. These two books are recent examples of the exciting new work that is being done in these interfaces on women's relationships to place and nation in periods of tran-sition and transformation.

Writing Women is a collection of papers by, in the main, geographers, about the interconnections of gender and colonialism, revealing the complexities of the relations between power, class, race and gender, the expansion of empire and resistance to it. Its time frame is wide, from the mid-nineteenth century to the end of the millennium, as the terms 'colonial' and 'post-colonial' in the subtitle indicate, and spatially it includes travels in almost every continent, drawing in the main on travel writing and diaries, as well as analyses of the landscape. *House Garden Nation* is a single-authored text by a specialist in literatures written in Spanish and Portuguese. It is an analysis of post-colonial Caribbean Latin American novels by women, which deal directly or indirectly with political transitions in the region throughout the twentieth century. Both books share a location within poststructuralist and feminist theories of difference, discourse and deconstruction, aiming to add to the rewriting of colonial and post-colonial history which is such an exciting recent venture. While recognizing their debt to Said's work, feminist scholars are now correcting his silence about gender relations and uncovering their significance both in Western writing about imperial 'others' (*Writing Women*) and in the texts of 'others' (*House Garden Nation*).

Writing Women opens with a splendid introduction by the editors which sketches in the history of feminist approaches to geographical issues and their connection with postcolonial discourses. A clear critique of the assumption of transparent space and imperialist mapping strategies based upon it is presented, although the density of the writing just occasionally obscures the clarity of meaning and the chapter may be hard work for those relatively unfamiliar with poststructuralist literatures. The collection is divided into two parts. The first, 'Drawing the map', is based on a series of chapters examining white women's experiences of the 'other' places they travelled to because of colonization or war, alone or with a male partner. The focus is primarily historical, the view is from above, although the authors are concerned to establish the ambivalent location of white or colonizing women in the structures of imperial power/knowledge, which places their writing and acting both inside and outside colonial discourses. In the second part, 'Rethinking mapping', the perspective is from the postcolonial world, if not always from the point of view of postcolonial subjects, and focuses on strategies for disrupting the colonial mappings inherent in Part I. All the chapters draw on a fascinating range of sources, including letters, diaries and travel accounts, which bring the voices of these women alive for the contemporary reader.

The first four of the five chapters in Part I are united by their focus on nineteenth-century British imperial expansion, although the geographic areas considered include India, Africa and Australia. The odd chapter out here – in a geographic and a historical sense – is the fifth, which is about US women who joined the services in World War II and travelled to various 'fronts'. It is also distinct from the preceding chapters in that it is primarily an empirical analysis, not explicitly situated in the theoretical literatures drawing variously on Said, Foucault and Lacan as are the others.

I should have liked to have seen a greater emphasis on the location of the authors of these chapters in Part I and of us the readers. How does our

FEMINIST REVIEW NO 57, AUTUMN 1997

own positional knowledge add to the complex ambivalences of the interpretations presented here? In several places I was unhappy with what seemed to me unnecessarily facile or simple interpretations of the meaning and intentions of the writings being examined. This is a particular problem in the analysis of nineteenth-century texts as time, distance and feminist scholarship exclude us from the worlds of these intrepid women.

In Part II the four authors are themselves more centrally placed in their considerations of, variously, suburban Melbourne, environmental know-ledges in Australia (perhaps the best paper in the collection), the location of white women in the academy of the new South Africa and, to a lesser extent, the gendered landscape of Ireland. The dimensions of difference, the spatial distinctiveness of these geographies, fascinates the reader, as does the richness in the analyses by the contributors.

Turning to *House Garden Nation* I felt on less familiar territory. Ileana Rodriguez is a Mexican scholar teaching and writing at the University of Maryland, and clearly has a considerable personal experience of the dis-ruptions and translations that she writes about. In a moving excursus she locates herself and the origins of her book in her reactions to the Sandindista electoral in 1991. The aim of the book is to analyse the inter-sections of gender, ethnicity and nation as new nations and/or parties struggle to come into being. She chooses a range of different examples at particular historical moments to unpick the influence of modernity and political ideology, revealing masculine and feminine positions within each transition. The analysis is undertaken through the lens of a series of novels written between 1926 and 1990. They are *Ifigenia: Diario de una senorita que escribio proque se fastidia* (1926) by Teresa de la Parra, about Venezuela's political changes; the Cuban transition in Dulce Maria Loynaz' *Jardin* (1935); the Jamaican double transition in Jean Rhys' *Wide Sargasso Sea* (1966); the Guadaloupe novels by Simone Schwarz-Bart *Pluie et Vent sur Telumee miracle* (1972) and *Ti Jean L'Horizon* (1979) and the Nicaraguan transition in Gioconda Belli's *La mujer habitada* (1988) and *Sofia de los presagios* (1990). As a monoglot geographer I approached the book with trepidation, having previously read only Jean Rhys' wonderful challenge to the ethnocentrism of the Eng. Lit. I did years ago for A-level. I found this excursion into a strange land enchanting and enlightening.

At the end of a short review it is impossible to do justice to the subtlety of the arguments which link social science perspectives to literary analysis. Suffice to say that this book has a great deal of interest for all feminists, from whatever discipline or area-based perspective, interested in the links between modernization, the nation and gender. It also has the great attrac-tion for readers who are, like me, largely ignorant of the literature of

Caribbean Latin America of opening a treasure trove of unfamiliar narratives in which women appropriate the ever-widening spaces of 'house', 'garden' and 'nation' in struggles against colonial and masculine power.

Linda M. McDowell

Women and the Political Process in Twentieth-Century Iran

Parvin Paidar
Cambridge University Press: Cambridge, 1995, xvi + 363pp
£40.00 hbk ISBN 0 521 473403

Parvin Paidar's book is at the forefront of the current path-breaking approach to women and politics where labels such as 'Muslim' and 'Third World' women are being discarded in favour of detailed studies of the specificities of the experiences of particular women in particular countries at a particular time (Lazreg, 1994; Sayigh, 1981; Zubaida, 1989). The study is located firmly within the different construction of women by political discourses, of modernity, revolution and Islamization in Iran. In a thorough and wide-ranging analysis Paidar concludes that, far from being marginalized by the Islamic perspective, Iranian women have placed gender issues at the very heart of the political thought in contemporary Iran.

Paidar delves into the Iranian Shiia school of thought and the country's history to explode the myth of silent, subdued womanhood of Orientalists. Her work supports the view that it is not Islam, or even its early practices, but rather patriarchy that hinders women's participation in the public domain (Abbott, 1942; Ahmed 1992; Mernissi, 1993, among others). Across the centuries Iranian women have demanded the right to gain access to power (Mahmoudian, 1985; Mansur, 1984, among others) and have not shirked high-profile participation in revolutionary and resistance movements.

Eventually in the early twentieth century in Iran women gained recognition as citizens and by the mid-1960s became formal political participants. But, across the prevailing range of political discourses, they remained anchored within their roles as wives and mothers and 'transmitters of communal and national values to the next generation' (p. 357). Nevertheless, they forced the State to intervene, regulate and control polygamy, divorce and custody and to 'modernize' the prevailing patriarchal practices. By the mid-1970s the family was placed under the intervention of the State and its laws. This in turn led to the tension that women experience, throughout the development process, between the familial demands and their political and economic duties.

At the same time the religious establishment re-formulated its own position. Paidar's research on the 'modernization' of Shiism in the 1970s and 1980s demonstrates that women, as symbols of national identity, were placed at the centre of the new developing discourse (Omid, 1994). Religious leaders such as Ayatollah Morteza Mottahari defended the concept of complementarity between the sexes as being preferable to that of equality. At the same time, influential Shiia authors such as Ali Shariati offered a 'desexualized' woman (p. 181) as a role model, one which in every way echoed the silent hidden images that traditional Orientalists had imposed on 'Muslim women'. Shariati's exemplary woman, Fatemeh, the daughter of the Prophet of Islam, was applauded for being silent, self-sacrificing, simple, pure, shy, chaste and virtuous (Shariati, 1980). What these discourses had in common with the secular and Marxist revolutionary ones was their pursuit of the construction of a new national identity 'in relation to a redefinition of Iran's relationship with the "imperialist" powers. Cultural nationalism was the framework within which national identity and other features of the revolution were situated' (p. 220).

For the Islamist, women's identities were entwined with their domesticity. As a result, after the success of the Islamic revolution their legal recognition and constitutional rights were articulated largely in terms of the family and motherhood and their responsibility to defend and guarantee the survival of Islam and its laws in Iran:

> The Constitution of the Islamic Republic constructed a particular set of patri-archal gender relations which aimed to remove the historical tension between the family and the nation in relation to women. . . . The woman was constructed as a mother; the mother as creator of the Islamic family; the family as the foundation of the Islamic nation.
>
> (p. 262)

But, despite the continuous effort of the post-revolutionary state to impose its vision of domesticity on them, Iranian women have not succumbed.

Paidar is a scholarly and thorough academic whose research covers an extensive range of Iranian and Western sources up to the end of the twentieth century. Her views are presented succinctly and her arguments are consistent, well illustrated and firmly grounded in the history of the past century of Iranian women's political participation. Written in a clear, concise and readable style, Paidar's conclusions are convincing and well supported. They shed light on the complexities that historical and ideological juxtapositions of politics, economics and social ideals and relations place on women at particular times in particular places. In terms of Iranian, Islamic and Middle Eastern studies, Paidar's work contributes to the current scholarship of many feminists who are exploding the myth of the uniformity of submission and silence placed on 'Muslim women' by academics during much of the nineteenth and twentieth centuries.

This is a most welcome addition to the feminist historical literature. It is a book that would prove invaluable for all students of politics who are interested in understanding the complexities of discourses on women. It also presents a wide perspective on the variety of ways in which Iranian women have shaped and reshaped the political arena to overcome the prescribed roles attributed to them by their patriarchal state and its ideologues.

Haleh Afshar

References

ABBOTT, Nadia (1942) *Aishah The Beloved of Mohamad* Chicago: University of Chicago Press.

AHMED, Leila (1992) *Women and Gender in Islam* New Haven and London: Yale University Press.

LAZREG, Marnia (1994) *The Eloquence of Silence: Algerian Women in Question* New York and London: Routledge.

MAHMOUDIAN, Hoda (1985) 'Tahira: an early feminist' in **A. Fathi** editor, *Women and Family in Iran* Leiden: E.J. Brill.

MANSUR, Roshanak (1984) 'Chereye zan dar jaraid mashrutiati' (Women as reflected by the constitutional literature) *Nimeyeh Digar* Vol. 1, No. 1.

MERNISSI, Fatima (1993) *The Forgotten Queens of Islam* Minneapolis: University of Minnesota Press.

OMID, H. (1994) *Islam and the Post Revolutionary State in Iran* Basingstoke: Macmillan.

SAYIGH, Rosemary (1981) 'Orientalism and Arab women' *Arab Studies Quarterly*, Vol. 3, No. 3.

SHARIATI, Ali (1980) *Fatima is Fatima* translated by Laleh Bakhtiar, Tehran Hamdami Foundation.

ZUBAIDA, Sami (1989) *Islam, the People and the State: Essays on Political Ideas and Movements in the Middle East* London: Routledge.

FEMINIST REVIEW NO 57, AUTUMN 1997

Homeworking Women: Gender, Racism and Class at Work

Annie Phizaclea and Carol Wolkowitz

Sage: London, 1995

ISBN 0 8039 8874 5 £10.50 Pbk ISBN 0 8039 8873 7, £30 Hbk

This book makes a timely, and unapologetically feminist, intervention in current debates and myths around homeworking in Britain. Post-industrial apologists have conjured up images of new ruralists surrounded by computer equipment in their thatched cottages, self-determining their own work and communicating with clients or employers through cyberspace. Government-sponsored research also suggests that the traditional picture of home-workers as women toiling long hours for low pay by sewing garments or assembling light bulbs is out of date, replaced by that of a new kind of entre-preneur, working from home across a wide range of occupations and income levels. Moreover, the sweated homeworkers who still exist are argued to have chosen this form of work because of the advantages it offers. Phizaclea and Wolkowitz offer a less sanguine assessment of recent develop-ments. Their book will be of value to campaigners from and on behalf of homeworkers' groups, and should be taken seriously by those in a position to influence social policy, legislation and media discussion.

According to Phizaclea and Wolkowitz, gender remains central to home-based work, despite the variety of forms it now takes. Whether they are systems analysts, clerks or sewing machinists, homeworkers are still over-whelmingly female. And working at home represents their solution to the con-tinuing problem of combining their gendered responsibility for childcare with wage earning. Professional women, already well qualified and paid, may see homeworking as a way of avoiding a career break, and they may be able to translate their relatively privileged labour market position into their con-ditions of working at home. By contrast, women at the other end of the occu-pational scale exercise no such option: domestic and employment circumstances constrain them to take on homework even when many would prefer to 'go out' to work. Thus, inequalities of 'race' and class which differ-entiate women workers in general also characterize homeworking women, resulting in a minutely segmented labour-force with divisions between manual and non-manual, clerical and service workers, white and non-white. One of the great strengths of this book is to demonstrate, among those interviewed, the processes underlying the racialized divisions in homework and their effects for the (mainly) Asian women who endure the worst conditions.

The well-known difficulties of researching homeworking make it virtually impossible to achieve any reliable overview. Many who work at home are invisible in official statistics and inaccessible by standard survey techniques. Phizaclea and Wolkowitz adopted a combination of research methods so as to locate different groupings of women working at home. Meaningful assessment of persistence and change, of the variety of homeworking situations, of divisions and commonalities between homeworkers could be achieved only on the basis of imaginative qualitative research such as this. A questionnaire placed in *Prima*, Britain's best-selling women's monthly magazine, yielded over 400 responses, biased (inevitably, because of the readership) towards higher socio-economic groups and all English speaking. Their jobs spanned the whole range of occupations, divided almost equally (contra government surveys) between manual and non-manual work, and, notably, the vast majority were clearly defined as 'women's work'. The *Prima* respondents also provided little evidence of a burgeoning 'enterprise culture'. Some did run small businesses but others sold their services as childminders; some were directly employed by a firm, others were self-employed, some were disguised wage workers, and many did not fall neatly into any conventional category of employment status.

The other main research tool was a case study of Coventry, where forty-nine women were eventually interviewed. Of these thirty were white and English speaking, nineteen Asian. All of the nine clerical workers were white and their key technology was the telephone rather than the computer. Most were young mothers who worked less than seventeen hours a week. The majority of the Coventry sample, however, were manual workers, concentrated in clothing production. Phizaclea and Wolkowitz's detailed analysis of the differences between white and Asian manual homeworkers was for me a key point of the book. They dissect so clearly the processes involved in ethnicization of different sectors even of the manual homeworking labour market. White women manual homeworkers were spread across a larger range of occupations, including all the more highly skilled and better-paid jobs such as machine-knitting and bow-making. The Asian women worked an average of forty-eight hours (compared with twenty-six for the white women), and emphasized the pressures of homeworking rather than its advantages. Half would have preferred not to work at home. Not only did white and Asian women have different profiles as workers, but homework also assumed a different significance in their household economies and work histories. My only reservation about Phizaclea and Wolkowitz's interpretation of the inequalities they highlight so clearly is to suggest that what goes on in homeworking is itself *constitutive* of the differences of ethnicity, gender and economic circumstance that distinguish different groupings of women. Homeworking does not merely replicate and reproduce already existing, externally formed, class, 'race' and gender inequalities. Similarly, on the authors' own evidence, a

more nuanced analysis could be developed of the gendering and ethnicization of different kinds of homework since there is not just one kind of
gendering, and because differences of ethnicity and gender combine and
interact in numerous distinctive ways.

Since different methodologies located diverse kinds of homeworker Phizaclea and Wolkowitz provide several snapshots of the contemporary homeworking labour force. Indeed, this was partly the intention of their
all-inclusive definition of homeworking which encompasses all home-
based work, regardless of employment status. While this approach provides a wealth of qualitative material it also raises conceptual questions.
We would not dream of treating everyone who works in a designated
'workplace' as one undifferentiated economic category. The same should
hold for those who work 'at home'. But, while being aware of the danger
of treating the home as a 'natural category' (p. 14), Phizaclea and
Wolkowitz's inclusive approach leads them to underplay – at an analytical
and theoretical level – crucial differences in employment relations between
homeworking women. If we are to comprehend what is going on in homeworking today we need to be able to distinguish between different and
maybe new relations of employment. The authors provide just the rich
kind of evidence essential for such a project. For example, the conventional
distinction between employed/self-employed evidently cannot do justice to
the variety of homeworking employment relations they describe. Are there
new forms of subcontracting, franchising, quality control? How does
globalization impinge on homeworking? Some of the new modes of
remote, satellite and information and communication technology homeworking make nonsense of the traditional dichotomy of work versus
home. Women are at the forefront of many of the new developments and
it is important that feminist theory also leads in their analysis.

Miriam Glucksmann

Hidden in the Home: The Role of Waged Homework in the Modern World Economy

Jamie Faricellia Dangler
State University of New York Press, 1994
ISBN 0-7914-2129-5, $49.50 Hbk ISBN 0-7914-2130-9, $16.95 Pbk

Jamie Dangler's book is one of the finest works that the world system
approach has produced. It is an approach that primarily encourages us to
appraise the significance of micro-experiences in the wide context of

interactions between labour and capital in the world economy. The approach, likewise, guides us to evaluate the role of the state as a mediator between labour and capital, in the process of global and national economic restructuring. Much as I admire such an approach, I also believe, at times, a rigid systemic model tends to undermine the role of human agency in a historical process. Dangler's work admirably overcomes the basis of such an apprehension.

An inflexible approach, I must admit, would have been particularly unfortunate in the analysis of industrial homework: the subject of her book. It is indeed a form of wage employment that encapsulates women's predicament in the world of work that is solely geared to the life-cycle of men. In the midst of a juggling act, in trying to combine family health and career, women often opt for home-based work. Given the social norms and economic constraints, women do make a choice. They are not just passive recipients of capital's decision to decentralize work in order to reduce overhead costs. As Dangler recounts:

> 'What's wrong with working?' asked a woman I interviewed in 1986 as she sat at her kitchen table winding thin, colored wires through a small core to make transformers for a central New York electronics firm. Her question arose in the context of our discussion of the State Labor Department's depiction of her job as exploitative, substandard work. . . . In fact, I was becoming more confused about this question as I talked to homeworkers who emphasized the benefits working at home brought them and their disdain for those who sought to protect them from exploitation: 'People's impression of homeworkers is that we're all dummies because we're exploited. . . . If you're saying a person is exploited, you're saying they're dumb'.
>
> (p. 1)

While portraying the role of women's agency, the author also highlights, with a methodologically sound qualitative analysis, the subordinate position that the gender role assigns to women in their choice of career. An understanding of the complex interrelation between social norms and economic forces is important, as Dangler points out, in formulating policies that can root out the exploitative aspect of this form of work:

> Homework derives from the influence of women's contradictory role as laborers in the sphere of paid production and unpaid workers in the sphere of reproduction. Any attempt to eliminate exploitative homework must focus equal attention on transforming women's position in both spheres. It must bring together struggles in the home with struggles in the workplace. Concretely, women homeworkers must be able to pursue an alternative model for combining family and work responsibilities – one that would be free of the power inequalities that currently characterize their home and work lives. Such a model

FEMINIST REVIEW NO 57, AUTUMN 1997

might very well include home-based work, but under a fundamentally new set of social and economic conditions.

(p. 5)

Set in the context of industrial homework in Central New York, the book gives a clear picture of the way home-based work, as an emergent form of work organization, fits in with the latest phase of international capitalist restructuring, with its reliance on a flexible work-force. The book draws our attention also to the limitations of traditional labour process theory, associated with Braverman and Marglin, that in the 1970s predicted the inevitability of centralized factory-based production in a capitalist economy. The book postulates a new role for state regulatory measures in allowing women, or men, a real choice in the location and timing of work.

The centrality of gender in the formulation of homework legislation is important in the United States as elsewhere. This, as the author argues, is vital as the legislation could have little effect unless we improve the position of women in the home and in the labour market by adequate provision of childcare and eldercare. As Dangler points out:

> In short, we are still left with a large gap between the ideal of transforming the relation between waged and nonwaged work and a concrete agenda for implementing steps to realize that goal. Because homework is a particularly acute expression of this dilemma, its study offers much to the quest for a turly liberating organization of work.

(p. 167)

My only complaint is that the literature cited in the book is somehow old. So many quoted authors, including myself, have written extensively on homework even in the 1990s. They are included neither in the text nor in the bibliography, which mentions little after 1987.

Swasti Mitter

Noticeboard

Call for papers

Revealing Male Bodies, Edited by Nancy Tuana, William Cowling, Maurice Hamington, Greg Johnson and Terrance MacMullan. Submissions are invited for an anthology to be published by Indiana University Press exploring the experiences of male embodiment. *Revealing Male Bodies* will examine how men's bodies are physically and experientially constituted by the economic, theoretical and social practices in which men are immersed. Articles addressing, but not limited to, the following topics are sought: Intersections of Race and Maleness; Phenomenologies of Male Embodiment; The Social Construction of Male Bodies and Male Lived Experience; Relations Between Male Bodies and Power; The Epistemological Significance of Male Bodies; The Male Body as a Site of Resistance; Relations Between Cultural Imagery of Maleness and Lived Male Experience; The Impact of Male Lived Experience on Cognitive or Creative Activities. In addition to the above topics, the editors are interested in articles that address the intersections of phenomenological and social constructivist methodologies, as well as pieces that provide avenues for dealing with male bodies and male embodiment in ways that avoid or transform traditional understandings of essentialism. We encourage works that reflect diverse approaches, methodologies, and styles. Given the anthology's multi-disciplinary character, we invite papers which balance rigorous scholarship and general accessibility. There will be a two-step review process. If you are interested in writing for this anthology please submit an abstract of no more than 500 words and a vita by January 15, 1998. Based upon a review of the abstracts, potential contributors will be notified to submit a completed paper for consideration. The deadline for submission of the final article is July 1, 1998. Send two copies of abstracts and vitae to: Nancy Tuana, Department of Philosophy, University of Oregon, Eugene, OR 97403-1295, USA.

FEMINIST REVIEW NO 57, AUTUMN 1997, PP. 179–180

FEMINIST REVIEW NO 57, AUTUMN 1997

Gender, Sexuality, and Law Conference

Reflections: New Directions; 19–21 June 1998

The Keele University Research Investment Scheme has announced funding for a major international, interdisciplinary conference to be held at Keele from 19–21 June 1998. Confirmed plenary speakers are Jacqueline Alexander; Susan Boyd; Angela Harris; Ratna Kapur; Ruthann Robson; Carol Smart; and Jeffrey Weeks. Among the themes to be addressed and developed are: globalization and the postcolonial condition; citizenship and rights discourse; medicalization of the legal subject; revisiting consent; AIDS/HIV; the body and the sexual subject of law; bridging the theory/activist divide; law, literature and film; femininities/masculinities; transgendered subjectivities; legal education and the 'straight' subjects; connections between legal discourse and identity politics; international law; right wing movements; children and sexuality; race, religion and ethnicity; violence; law and psychoanalysis; and poverty and capitalism. Theoretically informed papers are welcome on any related topic. Offers of papers (one page abstracts) should be received by the Gender, Sexuality, and Law Research Group (GSL) (organizers of the conference) by 31 December 1997. Further information and registration forms are available from: GSL Conference, Department of Law, Keele University, Staffordshire, ST5 5BG, United Kingdom. Tel: 01782-583218; Fax: 01782-583228; Email: <GSL98@keele.ac.uk>; Web Page:<www.keele.ac.uk/depts/la/GSL98.htm>. The members of the GSL are: Doris Buss, Kathy de Gama; Didi Herman; Daniel Monk; Sally Sheldon; Carl Stychin; Michael Thomson; and Noel Whitty.

FEMINIST REVIEW NO 57, AUTUMN 1997, PP 181–190

1 Women and Revolution in South Yemen, **Molyneux**. Feminist Art Practice, **Davis & Goodal**. Equal Pay and Sex Discrimination, **Snell**. Female Sexuality in Fascist Ideology, **Macciocchi**. Charlotte Brontë's *Shirley*, **Taylor**. Christine Delphy, **Barrett & McIntosh**. OUT OF PRINT.

2 Summer Reading, **O'Rourke**. Disaggregation, **Campaign for Legal & Financial Independence** and **Rights of Women**. The Hayward Annual 1978, **Pollock**. Women and the Cuban Revolution, **Murray**. Matriarchy Study Group Papers, **Lee**. Nurseries in the Second World War, **Riley**.

3 English as a Second Language, **Naish**. Women as a Reserve Army of Labour, **Bruegel**. Chantal Akerman's films, **Martin**. Femininity in the 1950s, **Birmingham Feminist History Group**. On Patriarchy, **Beechey**. Board School Reading Books, **Davin**.

4 Protective Legislation, **Coyle**. Legislation in Israel, **Yuval-Davis**. On 'Beyond the Fragments', **Wilson**. Queen Elizabeth I, **Heisch**. Abortion Politics: **a dossier**. Materialist Feminism, **Delphy**.

5 Feminist Sexual Politics, **Campbell**. Iranian Women, **Tabari**. Women and Power, **Stacey & Price**. Women's Novels, **Coward**. Abortion, **Himmelweit**. Gender and Education, **Nava**. Sybilla Aleramo, **Caesar**. On 'Beyond the Fragments', **Margolis**.

6 'The Tidy House', **Steedman**. Writings on Housework, **Kaluzynska**. The Family Wage, **Land**. Sex and Skill, **Phillips & Taylor**. Fresh Horizons, **Lovell**. Cartoons, **Hay**.

7 Protective Legislation, **Humphries**. Feminists Must Face the Future, **Coultas**. Abortion in Italy, **Caldwell**. Women's Trade Union Conferences, **Breitenbach**. Women's Employment in the Third World, **Elson & Pearson**.

8 Socialist Societies Old and New, **Molyneux**. Feminism and the Italian Trade Unions, **Froggett & Torchi**. Feminist Approach to Housing in Britain, **Austerberry & Watson**. Psychoanalysis, **Wilson**. Women in the Soviet Union, **Buckley**. The Struggle within the Struggle, **Kimble**.

FEMINIST REVIEW NO 57, AUTUMN 1997

9 Position of Women in Family Law, **Brophy & Smart**. Slags or Drags, **Cowie & Lees**. The Ripper and Male Sexuality, **Hollway**. The Material of Male Power, **Cockburn**. Freud's *Dora*, **Moi**. Women in an Iranian Village, **Afshar**. New Office Technology and Women, **Morgall**.

10 Towards a Wages Strategy for Women, **Weir & McIntosh**. Irish Suffrage Movement, **Ward**. A Girls' Project and Some Responses to Lesbianism, **Nava**. The Case for Women's Studies, **Evans**. Equal Pay and Sex Discrimination, **Gregory**. Psychoanalysis and Personal Politics, **Sayers**.

11 **Sexuality issue**
Sexual Violence and Sexuality, **Coward**. Interview with Andrea Dworkin, **Wilson**. The Dyke, the Feminist and the Devil, **Clark**. Talking Sex, **English, Hollibaugh & Rubin**. Jealousy and Sexual Difference, **Moi**. Ideological Politics 1969–72, **O'Sullivan**. Womanslaughter in the Criminal Law, **Radford**. OUT OF PRINT.

12 ANC Women's Struggles, **Kimble & Unterhalter**. Women's Strike in Holland 1981, **de Bruijn & Henkes**. Politics of Feminist Research, **McRobbie**. Khomeini's Teachings on Women, **Afshar**. Women in the Labour Party 1906–1920, **Rowan**. Documents from the Indian Women's Movement, **Gothoskar & Patel**.

13 Feminist Perspectives on Sport, **Graydon**. Patriarchal Criticism and Henry James, **Kappeler**. The Barnard Conference on Sexuality, **Wilson**. Danger and Pleasure in Nineteenth Century Feminist Sexual Thought, **Gordon & Du Bois**. Anti-Porn: Soft Issue, Hard World, **Rich**. Feminist Identity and Poetic Tradition, **Montefiore**.

14 Femininity and its Discontents, **Rose**. Inside and Outside Marriage, **Gittins**. The Pro-family Left in the United States, **Epstein & Ellis**. Women's Language and Literature, **McKluskie**. The Inevitability of Theory, **Fildes**. The 150 Hours in Italy, **Caldwell**. Teaching Film, **Clayton**.

15 Women's Employment, **Beechey**. Women and Trade Unions, **Charles**. Lesbianism and Women's Studies, **Adamson**. Teaching Women's Studies at Secondary School, **Kirton**. Gender, Ethnic and Class Divisions, **Anthias & Yuval-Davis**. Women Studying or Studying Women, **Kelly & Pearson**. Girls, Jobs and Glamour, **Sherratt**. Contradictions in Teaching Women's Studies, **Phillips & Hurst-field**.

16 Romance Fiction, Female Sexuality and Class, **Light**. The White Brothel, **Kappeler**. Sadomasochism and Feminism, **France**. Trade Unions and Socialist Feminism, **Cockburn**. Women's Movement and the Labour Party, **Interview with Labour Party Feminists**. Feminism and 'The Family', **Caldwell**.

17 **Many voices, one chant: black feminist perspectives**
Challenging Imperial Feminism, **Amos** & **Parmar**. Black Women, the Economic Crisis and the British State, **Mama**. Asian Women in the Making of History, **Trivedi**. Black Lesbian Discussions, **Carmen, Gail, Shaila** & **Pratibha**. Poetry. Black women Organizing Autonomously: a collection.

18 **Cultural politics**
Writing with Women. A Metaphorical Journey, **Lomax**. Karen Alexander: Video Worker, **Nava**. Poetry, **Riley, Whiteson** and **Davies**. Women's Films, **Montgomery**. 'Correct Distance' a photo-text, **Tabrizian**. Julia Kristeva on Femininity, **Jones**. Feminism and the Theatre, **Wandor**. Alexis Hunter, **Osborne**. Format Photographers, Dear Linda, **Kuhn**.

19 The Female Nude in the work of Suzanne Valadon, **Betterton**. Refuges for Battered Women, **Pahl**. Thin is the Feminist Issue, **Diamond**. New Portraits for Old, **Martin** & **Spence**.

20 Prisonhouses, **Steedman**. Ethnocentrism and Socialist Feminism, **Barrett** & **McIntosh**. What Do Women Want? **Rowbotham**. Women's Equality and the European Community, **Hoskyns**. Feminism and the Popular Novel of the 1890s, **Clarke**.

21 Going Private: The Implications of Privatization for Women's Work, **Coyle**. A Girl Needs to Get Street-wise: Magazines for the 1980s, **Winship**. Family Reform in Socialist States: The Hidden Agenda, **Molyneux**. Sexual Segregation in the Pottery Industry, **Sarsby**.

22 Interior Portraits: Women, Physiology and the Male Artist, **Pointon**. The Control of Women's Labour: The Case of Homeworking, **Allen** & **Wolkowitz**. Homeworking: Time for Change, **Cockpit Gallery** & **Londonwide Homeworking Group**. Feminism and Ideology: The Terms of Women's Stereotypes, **Seiter**. Feedback: Feminism and Racism, **Ramazanoglu, Kazi, Lees, Safia Mirza**.

23 **Socialist-feminism: out of the blue**
Feminism and Class Politics: A Round-Table Discussion, **Barrett, Campbell, Philips, Weir** & **Wilson**. Upsetting an Applecart: Difference, Desire and Lesbian Sadomasochism, **Ardill** & **O'Sullivan**. Armagh and Feminist Strategy, **Loughran**. Transforming Socialist-Feminism: The Challenge of Racism, **Bhavnani** & **Coulson**. Socialist-Feminists and Greenham, **Finch** & **Hackney Greenham Groups**. Socialist-Feminism and the Labour Party: Some Experiences from Leeds, **Perrigo**. Some Political Implications of Women's Involvement in the Miners' Strike 1984–85, **Rowbotham** & **McCrindle**. Sisterhood: Political Solidarity Between Women, **Hooks**. European Forum of Socialist-Feminists, **Lees** & **McIntosh**. Report from Nairobi, **Hendessi**.

24 Women Workers in New Industries in Britain, **Glucksmann**. The Relationship of Women to Pornography, **Bower**. The Sex Discrimination Act 1975, **Atkins**. The Star Persona of Katharine Hepburn, **Thumim**.

25 Difference: A Special Third World Women Issue, **Minh-ha**. Melanie Klein, Psychoanalysis and Feminism, **Sayers**. Rethinking Feminist Attitudes Towards Mothering, **Gieve**. EEOC v. Sears, Roebuck and Company: A Personal Account, **Kessler-Harris**. Poems, **Wood**. Academic Feminism and the Process of De-radicalization, **Currie & Kazi**. A Lover's Distance: A Photoessay, **Boffin**.

26 Resisting Amnesia: Feminism, Painting and Post-Modernism, **Lee**. The Concept of Difference, **Barrett**. The Weary Sons of Freud, **Clément**. Short Story, **Cole**. Taking the Lid Off: Socialist Feminism in Oxford, **Collette**. For and Against the European Left: Socialist Feminists Get Organized, **Benn**. Women and the State: A Conference of Feminist Activists, **Weir**.

27 Women, feminism and the third term
Women and Income Maintenance, **Lister**. Women in the Public Sector, **Phillips**. Can Feminism Survive a Third Term?, **Loach**. Sex in Schools, **Wolpe**. Carers and the Careless, **Doyal**. Interview with Diane Abbott, **Segal**. The Problem With No Name: Re-reading Friedan, **Bowlby**. Second Thoughts on the Second Wave, **Rosenfelt & Stacey**. Nazi Feminists?, **Gordon**.

28 Family secrets: child sexual abuse
Introduction to an Issue: Family Secrets as Public Drama, **McIntosh**. Challenging the Orthodoxy: Towards a Feminist Theory and Practice, **MacLeod & Saraga**. The Politics of Child Sexual Abuse: Notes from American History, **Gordon**. What's in a Name?: Defining Child Sexual Abuse, **Kelly**. A Case, **Anon**. Defending Innocence: Ideologies of Childhood, **Kitzinger**. Feminism and the Seductiveness of the 'Real Event', **Scott**. Cleveland and the Press: Outrage and Anxiety in the Reporting of Child Sexual Abuse, **Nava**. Child Sexual Abuse and the Law, **Woodcraft**. Poem, **Betcher**. Brixton Black Women's Centre: Organizing on Child Sexual Abuse, **Bogle**. Bridging the Gap: Glasgow Women's Support Project, **Bell & Macleod**. Claiming Our Status as Experts: Community Organizing, **Norwich Consultants on Sexual Violence**. Islington Social Services: Developing a Policy on Child Sexual Abuse, **Boushel & Noakes**. Developing a Feminist School Policy on Child Sexual Abuse, **O'Hara**. 'Putting Ideas into their Heads': Advising the Young, **Mills**. Child Sexual Abuse Crisis Lines: Advice for Our British Readers.

29 Abortion: the international agenda
Whatever Happened to 'A Woman's Right to Choose'?, **Berer**. More than 'A Woman's Right to Choose'?, **Himmelweit**. Abortion in the Republic of Ireland, **Barry**. Across the Water, **Irish Women's Abortion Support Group**. Spanish Women and the Alton Bill, **Spanish Women's Abortion Support Group**. The Politics of Abortion in Australia: Freedom, Church and State, **Coleman**. Abortion in Hungary, **Szalai**. Women and Population Control in China: Issues of Sexuality, Power and Control, **Hillier**. The Politics of Abortion in Nicaragua: Revolutionary Pragmatism – or Feminism in the Realm of Necessity?, **Molyneux**. Who Will Sing for Theresa?, **Bernstein**. She's Gotta Have It: The Representation of Black Female Sexuality on Film, **Simmonds**. Poems, **Gallagher**. Dyketactics for Difficult Times: A Review of the 'Homosexuality, Which Homosexuality?' Conference, **Franklin & Stacey**.

30 Capital, gender and skill

Women Homeworkers in Rural Spain, **Lever**. Fact and Fiction: George Egerton and Nellie Shaw, **Butler**. Feminist Political Organization in Iceland: Some Reflections on the Experience of Kwenna Frambothid, **Dominelli & Jonsdottir**. Under Western Eyes: Feminist Scholarship and Colonial Discourses, **Talpade Mohanty**. Bedroom Horror: The Fatal Attraction of *Intercourse*, **Merck**. AIDS: Lessons from the Gay Community, **Patton**. Poems, **Agbabi**.

31 The past before us: 20 years of feminism

Slow Change or No Change?: Feminism, Socialism and the Problem of Men, **Segal**. There's No Place Like Home: On the Place of Identity in Feminist Politics, **Adams**. New Alliances: Socialist-Feminism in the Eighties, **Harriss**. Other Kinds of Dreams, **Parmar**. Complexity, Activism, Optimism: Interview with **Angela Y. Davis**. To Be or Not To Be: The Dilemmas of Mothering, **Rowbotham**. Seizing Time and Making New: Feminist Criticism, Politics and Contemporary Feminist Fiction, **Lauret**. Lessons from the Women's Movement in Europe, **Haug**. Women in Management, **Coyle**. Sex in the Summer of '88, **Ardill & O'Sullivan**. Younger Women and Feminism, **Hobsbawm & Macpherson**. Older Women and Feminism, **Stacey; Curtis; Summerskill**.

32

'Those Who Die for Life Cannot Be Called Dead': Women and Human Rights Protest in Latin America, **Schirmer**. Violence Against Black Women: Gender, Race and State Responses, **Mama**. Sex and Race in the Labour Market, **Breugel**. The 'Dark Continent': Africa as Female Body in Haggard's Adventure Fiction, **Stott**. Gender, Class and the Welfare State: The Case of Income Security in Australia, **Shaver**. Ethnic Feminism: Beyond the Pseudo-Pluralists, **Gorelick**.

33

Restructuring the Woman Question: *Perestroika* and Prostitution, **Waters**. Contemporary Indian Feminism, **Kumar**. 'A Bit On the Side'?: Gender Struggles in South Africa, **Beall, Hassim and Todes**. 'Young Bess': Historical Novels and Growing Up, **Light**. Madeline Pelletier (1874–1939): The Politics of Sexual Oppression, **Mitchell**.

34 Perverse politics: lesbian issues

Pat Parker: A tribute, **Brimstone**. International Lesbianism: Letter from São Paulo, **Rodrigues**; Israel, **Pittsburgh**, Italy, **Fiocchetto**. The De-eroticization of Women's Liberation: Social Purity Movements and the Revolutionary Feminism of Sheila Jeffreys, **Hunt**. Talking About It: Homophobia in the Black Community, **Gomez & Smith**. Lesbianism and the Labour Party, **Tobin**. Skirting the Issue: Lesbian Fashion for the 1990s, **Blackman & Perry**. Butch/Femme Obsessions, **Ardill & O'Sullivan**. Archives: The Will to Remember, **Nestle**; International Archives, **Read**. Audre Lorde: Vignettes and Mental Conversations, **Lewis**. Lesbian Tradition, **Field**. Mapping: Lesbians, AIDS and Sexuality: An interview with Cindy Patton, **O'Sullivan**. Significant Others: Lesbians and Psychoanalytic Theory, **Hamer**. The Pleasure Threshold: Looking at Lesbian Pornography on Film, **Smyth**. Cartoon, **Charlesworth**. Voyages of the Valkyries: Recent Lesbian Pornographic Writing, **Dunn**.

35 Campaign Against Pornography, **Norden**. The Mothers' Manifesto and Disputes over 'Mutterlichkeit', **Chamberlayne**. Multiple Mediations: Feminist Scholarship in the Age of Multi-National Reception, **Mani**. Cagney and Lacey Revisited, **Alcock & Robson**. Cutting a Dash: The Dress of Radclyffe Hall and Una Troubridge, **Rolley**. Deviant Dress, **Wilson**. The House that Jill Built: Lesbian Feminist Organizing in Toronto, 1976–1980, **Ross**. Women in Professional Engineering: the Interaction of Gendered Structures and Values, **Carter & Kirkup**. Identity Politics and the Hierarchy of Oppression, **Briskin**. Poetry: **Bufkin, Zumwalt**.

36 'The Trouble Is It's Ahistorical': The Problem of the Unconscious in Modern Feminist Theory, **Minsky**. Feminism and Pornography, **Ellis, O'Dair Tallmer**. Who Watches the Watchwomen? Feminists Against Censorship, **Rodgerson & Semple**. Pornography and Violence: What the 'Experts' Really Say, **Segal**. The Woman In My Life: Photography of Women, **Nava**. Splintered Sisterhood: Antiracism in a Young Women's Project, **Connolly**. Woman, Native, Other, **Parmar** interviews **Trinh T. Minh-ha**. Out But Not Down: Lesbians' Experience of Housing, **Edgerton**. Poems: **Evans Davies, Toth, Weinbaum**. Oxford Twenty Years On: Where Are We Now?, **Gamman & O'Neill**. The Embodiment of Ugliness and the Logic of Love: The Danish Redstockings Movement, **Walter**.

37 Theme issue: Women, religion and dissent
Black Women, Sexism and Racism: Black or Antiracist Feminism?, **Tang Nain**. Nursing Histories: Reviving Life in Abandoned Selves, **McMahon**. The Quest for National Identity: Women, Islam and the State in Bangladesh, **Kabeer**. Born Again Moon: Fundamentalism in Christianity and the Feminist Spirituality Movement, **McCrickard**. Washing our Linen: One Year of Women Against Fundamentalism, **Connolly**. **Siddiqui** on *Letter to Christendom*, **Bard** on *Generations of Memories*, **Patel** on *Women Living Under Muslim Laws Dossiers 1–6*, Poem, **Kay**. More Cagney and Lacey, **Gamman**.

38 The Modernist Style of Susan Sontag, **McRobbie**. Tantalizing Glimpses of Stolen Glances: Lesbians Take Photographs, **Fraser and Boffin**. Reflections on the Women's Movement in Trinidad, **Mohammed**. Fashion, Representation and Femininity, **Evans & Thornton**. The European Women's Lobby, **Hoskyns**. Hendessi on *Law of Desire: Temporary Marriage in Iran*, **Kaveney** on *Mercy*.

39 Shifting territories: feminism & Europe
Between Hope and Helplessness: Women in the GDR, **Dölling**. Where Have All the Women Gone? Women and the Women's Movement in East Central Europe, **Einhorn**. The End of Socialism in Europe – A New Challenge For Socialist Feminism? **Haug**. The Second 'No': Women in Hungary, **Kiss**. The Citizenship Debate: Women, the State and Ethnic Processes, **Yuval-Davis**. Fortress Europe and Migrant Women, **Morokvasíc**. Racial Equality and 1992, **Dummett**. Questioning *Perestroika*: A Socialist Feminist Interrogation, **Pearson**. Postmodernism and its Discontents, **Soper**. Feminists and Socialism: After the Cold War, **Kaldor**. Socialism Out of the Common Pots, **Mitter**. 1989 and All That, **Campbell**. In Listening

Mode, **Cockburn. Women in Action: Country by Country:** The Soviet Union; Yugoslavia; Czechoslovakia; Hungary; Poland. **Reports:** International Gay and Lesbian Association: Black Women and Europe 1992.

40 Fleurs du Mal or Second-Hand Roses?: Nathalie Barney, Romaine Brooks, and the 'Originality of the Avant-Garde', **Elliott & Wallace**. Poem, **Tyler-Bennett**. Feminism and Motherhood: An American 'Reading' **Snitow**. Qualitative Research, Appropriation of the 'Other' and Empowerment, **Opie**. Disabled Women and the Feminist Agenda, **Begum**. Postcard From the Edge: Thoughts on the 'Feminist Theory: An International Debate' Conference at Glasgow University, July 1991, **Radstone**. Review Essay, **Munt**.

41 Editorial. The Selling of HRT: Playing on the Fear Factor, **Worcester & Whatley**. The Cancer Drawings of Catherine Arthur, **Sebastyen**. Ten years of Women's Health 1982–92, **James**. AIDS Activism: Women and AIDS activism in Victoria, Australia, **Mitchell**. A Woman's Subject, **Friedli**. HIV and the Invisibility of Women: Is there a Need to Redefine AIDS?, **Scharf & Toole**. Lesbians Evolving Health Care: Cancer and AIDS, **Winnow**. Now is the Time for Feminist Criticism: A Review of *Asinimali!*, **Steinberg**. Ibu or the Beast?: Gender Interests in Two Indonesian Women's Organizations, **Wieringa**. Reports on Motherlands: Symposium on African, Carribean and Asian Women's Writing, **Smart**. The European Forum of Socialist Feminists, **Bruegel**. Review Essay, **Gamman**.

42 Feminist fictions
Editorial. Angela Carter's *The Bloody Chamber* and the Decolonization of Feminine Sexuality, **Makinen**. Feminist Writing: Working with Women's Experience, **Haug**. Three Aspects of Sex in Marge Piercy's *Fly Away Home*, **Hauser**. Are They Reading Us? Feminist Teenage Fiction, **Bard**. Sexuality in Lesbian Romance Fiction, **Hermes**. A Psychoanalytic Account for Lesbianism, **Castendyk**. Mary Wollstonecraft and the Problematic of Slavery, **Ferguson**. Reviews.

43 Issues for feminism
Family, Motherhood and Zulu Nationalism: The Politics of the Inkatha Women's Brigade, **Hassim**. Postcolonial Feminism and the Veil: Thinking the Difference, **Abu Odeh**. Feminism, the Menopause and Hormone Replacement Therapy, **Lewis**. Feminism and Disability, **Morris**. 'What is Pornography?': An Analysis of the Policy Statement of the Campaign Against Pornography and Censorship, **Smith**. Reviews.

44 Nationalisms and national identities
Women, Nationalism and Islam in Contemporary Political Discourse in Iran, **Yeganeh**. Feminism, Citizenship and National Identity, **Curthoys**. Remapping and Renaming: New Cartographies of Identity, Gender and Landscape in Ireland, **Nash**. Rap Poem: Easter 1991, **Medbh**. Family Feuds: Gender, Nationalism and the Family, **McClintock**. Women as Activists; Women as Symbols: A Study of the Indian Nationalist Movement, **Thapar**. Gender, Nationalisms and National Identities: Bellagio Symposium Report, **Hall**. Culture or Citizenship? Notes from the Gender and Colonialism Conference, Galway, Ireland, May 1992, **Connolly**. Reviews.

FEMINIST REVIEW NO 57, AUTUMN 1997

FEMINIST REVIEW NO 57, AUTUMN 1997

56 **Debating discourses, practising feminisms**
Who Needs (Sex) When You Can Have (Gender)? **Baden & Goetz**. To Whom Does Amina Belong? **Mankekar**. Pat Cadigan's *Synners*: Refiguring Nature, Science and Technology, **Cherniak**. 'I Teach Therefore I Am': Lesbian Studies in the Liberal Academy, **Munt**. American Eve (poem), **Burnett**.